THE WORKING MEN'S COLLEGE

AUSPICIUM MELIORIS

ÆVI· MDCCCLIV·

Purchased

R.E.Tyler Del.ᵗ 1913. C.H.Perry Sc.

THE PREFECTS

RUPERT WILKINSON

The Prefects

BRITISH LEADERSHIP AND THE
PUBLIC SCHOOL TRADITION

*A Comparative Study in the
making of Rulers*

London
OXFORD UNIVERSITY PRESS
NEW YORK   TORONTO
1964

Oxford University Press, Amen House, London E.C.4

GLASGOW NEW YORK TORONTO MELBOURNE WELLINGTON
BOMBAY CALCUTTA MADRAS KARACHI LAHORE DACCA
CAPE TOWN SALISBURY NAIROBI IBADAN ACCRA
KUALA LUMPUR HONG KONG

*Printed in Great Britain by
The Camelot Press Ltd.
London and Southampton*

To
My Father

Introduction

How did the Victorian public school produce rulers, and what sort of rulers did they turn out to be? That is the basic theme of this book. It is a theme with myriad implications—for the sociologist, the educationist, and the historian, as well as the student of political power.

If I state the topic somewhat baldly, I do so in the hope that it may add a slightly different note to a controversy that has been raging for a good hundred years. In the torrents of literature that the public schools debate has inspired, there has been little real dialogue between eulogists and critics. Each side has used arguments which, in the main, can only appeal to their own supporters. The fault, perhaps, has been mostly that of the critics, whose attack on the public schools has so often been confined to an *ethical* attack—an assault on values that the public schools purportedly stand for. With brilliant exceptions—Rudyard Kipling was one—the critics have failed to question in any depth the public schools' *efficiency* at reaching their own educational goals.

Take, for example, those familiar arguments accusing the public schools of defending social inequality and curbing the expression of individual feeling. As long as the critics assume that social inequality and the inhibition of feeling are self-evident evils, their complaints will not make much headway against the public schools' champions. To convince the latter, the critics must show that public school life produces effects which are hostile to the system's own ends, to the schools' self-declared responsibility for producing national leaders.

Even when the critics do this, even when they attack public school efficiency rather than public school ethics, their attack has generally been one-sided and unfair. It is all very well, for instance, to castigate 'amateurism' in high government circles and to trace its links with a public school-gentlemanly tradition. But the attack would be all the more convincing if it first acknowledged the *contributions* of the amateur ideal to effective leadership— versatility, public responsibility, and so forth.

From the foregoing the purpose of this book will become plain. It is to describe the main goals of the late Victorian public schools, and then to discuss the schools' efficiency in meeting these goals.

In the society of late Victorian and Edwardian England—so I am going to argue—the role of the public schools was predominantly political. Behind the aim of 'character-building' lay a political bent that was inseparable from the traditions of the English gentry. Whether he intended it or not, Thomas Arnold's formula for creating 'the Christian gentleman' became an educational device for maintaining a public servant *élite*.

Because this book treats the public school system as a political device, three notes of warning should be sounded. First, the book is basically amoral. It judges the Victorian public schools by asking whether, and in what sense, they produced effective governors. Inevitably, of course, one must be arbitrary in deciding what constitutes *effective* government. For our purpose here, I define it as a government which maintains its own vigour, power, and security, which obtains peace and order throughout its domain, and which performs its tasks with minimum wasted effort.

Various democratic ideals—the satisfaction of popular wants, equality of social opportunity, and so on—may be compatible with this concept of effective government, but here I shall only consider them in Machiavellian terms. That is to say, I shall value them merely to the extent that they render government more effective. All governments, of course, especially elected ones, must pay some attention to the material wants of their people if they wish to survive. Whether equality of opportunity and respect for individual freedoms also produce more effective government—for example, by culling forth intelligent leaders—is an open question. It will be a vital question in our assessment of the public school system.

This brings us to the second warning that the reader should be given. In our discussion of the public schools, there is to be an underlying assumption that a social institution can perform roles that no individual ever consciously intended. For this reason, the book should not be read by those who seek history in the decisions and designs of strong men. It is unlikely that any Victorian headmaster, even in his most imperial moments, could have plotted the extraordinary strategy by which the public school system 'captured' middle-class talent in its promotion of gentry-class power. (Most Victorian headmasters, it seems, were of middle-class origins themselves anyway.) Social institutions and classes, so one might claim, can readily be viewed as creatures, each with a will, a survival-impulse of its own. In the case of the Victorian public schools, this will was the sum of unconscious motivations as much as the sum of explicit designs.

However tacitly the public schools performed their political function, their relationship with government becomes clearer when we look at another, remarkably similar education system whose political ties were highly *explicit*. The comparison between Confucian education and the Victorian public schools is both so intriguing and, I think, instructive that I have devoted a chapter to it in the last part of the book. The chapter describes the social role of Confucian education as it developed over four dynasties: the Tang, the Sung, the Ming, and the Ching, and it closes on a speculative note—with an attempt to find the curious combination of factors (social, political, economic, and geographic) that gave the public schoolboy and the Mandarin so similar an experience.

Since our comparisons in education will not be limited to Confucian China, I should state more generally why I value the comparative approach. There are two main reasons for its usefulness to this study. First, the mechanism of the English public school, both as an education system and as a self-contained political community, throws a light on human society that can be extended to many different cultures. We will later argue, for example, that a political system which maintains order by ethical restraints rather than by law has certain tendencies—though by no means inevitable tendencies—to become totalitarian. However far-fetched it may seem, the anthropology of the public school community, and its pressures on the individual, provides a perspective on the educational techniques of Communism.

If the history of the Victorian public schools sheds light on other systems, the reverse is also true. Here lies our second reason for using a comparative approach to education. When we come to assess the public schools' efficiency at turning out effective leaders, it will not be very convincing if we evaluate the system *in vacuo*, or in comparison with some untried blueprint like Plato's educational dream. As we are going to suggest in Chapter I, all systems of moral education, and especially political education, face immense dilemmas in the tasks they have to perform. If we expose the failings of the Victorian public schools, we should also ask in what sense other systems with the same approximate ends were, or are, able to do better.

The third warning about this book concerns the tortuous problem of historical cause. It may appear that I claim for the public schools an exaggerated causal role in moulding political leadership and affecting political processes. No such claim is in fact intended. One purpose of my story is to describe the marked parallel between the values and mechanism of public school society and those of British government. This does not imply that one begot the other, but rather that both were equal reflections of British social character. An education system, like a governing system, will inevitably reflect values of a whole society, however much it appears to be the preserve of one class.

It would be wrong, on the other hand, to absolve the public schools of all political responsibility. An institution like the public schools does not simply transmit values; it selects them and reinforces them. Every sophisticated society evolves contradictory beliefs; and an education system cannot help but emphasize some beliefs to the virtual exclusion of others. Thus, the public schools lauded public loyalty and limited individual privacy; they cultivated the 'thick skin' and usually ignored the tender heart. Yet all four values, privacy just as much as patriotism, humane feeling as much as hardy reserve, were a part of England and western Liberalism. Over other values, too, the public schools faced a choice. The 'nation of shopkeepers' and the newly won status of the engineer were both prime phenomena of Victorian England, but neither trade nor technology became serious concerns of the public school.

To the extent, therefore, that education chooses the values shared by political leaders, it can be viewed as an independent influence on government. The most valuable education system will indeed perform what David Riesman calls the 'counter-cyclical' function.[1] In other words, it will offset changing tendencies in social—and for our purposes, political—life that may sap the society's vigour if carried too far. It is easily forgotten, however, that even the countervailing values which a school instils must have deep roots in the society. Once these roots have withered, the education system cannot counter for long the society's central tendencies. Recent English history provides a good demonstration of this fact.

Until the Second World War, the public schools helped Britain to fulfil one of Joseph Schumpeter's prerequisites for effective political democracy—namely, the creation of a 'social stratum, itself the product of a severely selective process that takes to politics as a matter of course', one that is 'neither too exclusive nor too easily accessible for the outsider. . .'[2] This prerequisite had to resist two tendencies in democracy: first, the tendency of democratic politics, with their vulgarity and emotionalism, to discourage able men from entering government, and, secondly, the democratic tendency towards social equality. On a later page Schumpeter's prerequisites for democracy will be dealt with more fully; what concerns us here is that the democratic tendency towards equality finally diminished the political usefulness of the 'social stratum' by weakening its spirit of public service. The Welfare State replaced *noblesse oblige*; steeply progressive income taxes—supplemented, ironically, by high public school fees—discouraged wearers of the Old School Tie from taking relatively

[1] David Riesman, *Constraint and Variety in American Education*. Riesman applies the concept of 'counter-cyclical' education mainly to a society's treatment of academic freedom, but it might just as well be applied to other values and attitudes as well.
[2] Joseph Schumpeter, *Capitalism, Socialism, and Democracy*, 290–1.

low-paid government jobs.[1] In other words, a central tendency of democracy succeeded in uprooting a countervailing value, the idea of a 'social stratum' that prided itself on discharging public duties.

The public schools, of course, had different effects on different people; and at times this book may seem to exaggerate the singleness of the public school system as a social force. Critics may suggest that phrases like 'Public School outlook' and 'Public School opinion' have little value, that in effect there were many public school outlooks and many public school opinions. My answer to this argument is that, for all the variations and exceptions, the education system did produce a strong prevailing ethos. One way to identify this ethos is to examine the public school as a political constitution. For every constitution, however cleverly it is engineered, depends for success on certain qualities of mind and character. It is these assumptions about human nature that we seek to identify when we look at the public school system.

[1] Roy Lewis and A. Maude, *The English Middle Classes*, 273. Peregrine Worsthorne, 'British Class and Diplomacy', *Foreign Affairs*, April 1959.

Acknowledgements

This book is the development of an undergraduate Honours thesis presented to the Government Department, Harvard University, in the spring of 1961. Parts of the thesis were subsequently published in the *British Journal of Sociology* and the *Teachers College Record*, Columbia University. My first expression of thanks, therefore, should go to Harvard for providing an *émigré* Englishman with an entirely happy milieu, and to the Government Department for encouraging further work on the thesis by awarding it the Philo Sherman Bennett Prize.

Inspiration for the thesis came from a sudden realization that public school education displayed amazing similarities with Imperial China's Confucian system. The first men I asked about this idea were Tatsuo Arima (who became my tutor) and David Riesman. To my relief neither laughed at the notion; both went out of their way to encourage me. I am particularly grateful to David Riesman who had already influenced and stimulated my thoughts about education and has continued to do so.

I also owe a debt to several people who read the completed thesis. Suzanne Rudolph of Harvard, George Lanyi of Oberlin College, and his son Tony, all made constructive criticisms which I have tried to meet in the book; and I am likewise grateful to Stephen Graubard, editor of *Daedalus*, and John Conway, Master of Leverett House, Harvard, for encouraging me to pursue the study further.

In England Mrs. Jean Floud, formerly of the London University Institute of Education, gave me kind advice and support, as did George Baron of the same Institute. Joseph Lauwerys of the Institute supplied me with invaluable material on Japanese education, and I am grateful to Ronald Dore of the L.S.E. for lending me his then-unpublished paper, 'Education and Politics in Japan, 1870–1960'.

All of these people made me aware of a teaching function quite different from that of formal instruction or even tutoring: the function of the intellectual broker who, frequently at little advantage to himself, introduces the student to books and to other teachers, and who sets off a whole train of thought by a deft word of encouragement. A prime example of such teaching was given me by Paul Sigmund, Senior Tutor of Quincy House, Harvard, who in a chance, five-minute conversation suggested some reading in Jesuit education as a comparative perspective on the public schools. The fruits of his suggestion are to be found in the last chapter.

It must be clearly stated, however, that I alone can take responsibility for the content of this book. If my kind teachers agree with everything I have said in it, I will be surprised. This applies particularly to the last two chapters, which nearly entirely represent work done after I left Harvard.

For advice on the book's presentation, my thanks are due to Charles Drage and his son, Charles; and I am particularly grateful to William Hardy of the Atomic Weapons Research Establishment, and his wife Paddy, for long thought-forming talks about the public schools over a span of several years. Not least there is the Christiansen family of Atherton, California, and my own family of Kingsclere, England, who afforded me both encouragement and privacy during unrelenting week-ends of writing—and my brother-in-law, Philip Pettyfer, who regularly drove thirty miles to perform summer chores which otherwise would have delayed the writing intolerably. Of such curious stuff, even mown grass, are authors' debts made.

The extracts from *Thought Reform and the Psychology of Totalism* by Robert Jay Lifton which appear on pp. 186 and 190 are reprinted by permission of the publisher, W. W. Norton & Company, Inc., New York. And finally, it must be confessed that the best phrase in the book is pilfered, quite unattributed, from my Harvard contemporary and first editor, Craig Comstock.

RUPERT WILKINSON

Stanford, California
May, 1963

Contents

Part One

THE NOURISHMENT OF POWER

Chapter 1

The Dilemmas of Education

During the late Victorian era, the public schools developed many of the features that made them a controversial topic today. And it was during nearly the same period, from about 1870 to the First World War, that the schools enjoyed their greatest *political* importance. The products of the Victorian-Edwardian public schools dominated public affairs right up to the Second World War; for better or for worse, their abilities and prejudices have left a powerful legacy to the social climate of modern Britain. This book is an attempt to view that legacy, to assess the public school impact on the national leadership. More precisely, it is a study of British political character as it was reflected and transmitted by the education system of the ruling class.

The statistical link between Government and public school is well known. 'I remember how in previous governments there had been four, perhaps five Harrovians,' Stanley Baldwin once told the Harrow Association, 'and I determined to have six . . . I managed to make my six by keeping the post of Chancellor of the Exchequer for myself.'[1] Random figures from random years tell the same story of public school predominance. In 1928, 152 out of 225 senior Civil Servants came from public schools; between 1931 and 1936, Eton alone supplied 27 per cent. of Foreign Office recruits.[2] Less than half the 1934 House of Commons were public schoolboys, but the latter made up in concentration what they lacked in quantity: most of them were to be found in the

[1] Stanley Baldwin, *On England* (and other addresses), Speech to the Harrow Association, 1923.
[2] R. H. Tawney, *Equality*, 78. J. D. Kingsley, *Representative Bureaucracy*, 127 *et seq*. The 152 Civil Servants mentioned above were the majority of those senior men who answered the poll and who were earning over £1,000 per annum.

3

Conservative majority, and 89—over a sixth of the House—were Old Etonians.[1]

Behind the statistics lay the public schools' function as a political device. It was a many-sided function: there was more to it than simply inspiring boys to become Justices of the Peace and Indian administrators. The recruiting needs of a new, expanding bureaucracy demanded middle-class participation in government. The public schools met this need by opening their gates to the commercial and professional classes. They took the fees of the textile magnate and the lawyer, and in return they exposed their sons to the full public service traditions of the aristocrat and the country squire. In this way, the schools really served as an instrument of class power.[2] They perpetuated the political supremacy of the landed classes by 'capturing' talent from the rising bourgeoisie and moulding that talent into 'synthetic' gentlemen.[3] As we shall see, the public school bias that preferred government service to private profit-making was all part and parcel of a gentleman ideal.

Not that the ideal was peculiar to England. In a culture as far removed as that of Imperial China, the same pattern emerged.[4] The comparison is instructive because the Chinese educators formalized their political bent, in writing, to an extent that the public school authorities never did. Like the public schools, Confucian education made public servants by making gentlemen (*juin-tze*): it defended privilege as a symbol of duty; it taught contempt for Trade; it spun a web of ritual and etiquette that exalted communal loyalties; it tailored a classical curriculum to the standards of civil service examinations. The remarkable likeness between Confucian education and the Victorian public schools suggests that there is an intrinsic link between landed traditions, the gentleman ideal, and a certain political bias in education.

Covert as the public schools' political function was, the working

[1] H. M. Stout (ed.), *Public Service in Great Britain*, 61.
[2] This is not to deny middle-class influence in public school life, nor the middle-class origins of many headmasters. The gentry conceded much to its servants. (See Chapter 2.)
[3] cf. E. Wingfield-Stratford, *The Squire and his Relations*, 335.
[4] The comparison is particularly striking for the four dynasties reviewed in Chapter 12: the *Tang*, the *Sung*, the *Ming*, and the *Ching*.

of most school communities mirrored the English Constitution in a very pronounced fashion. Take, for example, the constitutional reliance on ethical restraints, the assumption that executive power will let itself be bound by unwritten etiquette as much as by formal law. Or consider the Constitution's use of ceremony to bolster authority by making it dignified. Or the emphasis in British politics on party discipline. All these facets of parliamentary government had, and still have, their counterparts in public school life. And similar likenesses can be found between public school values and the spirit and working of the British Civil Service. It is this parallelism that makes the public schools so useful a 'window' through which to view political, and bureaucratic, character.

At the same time, the community of the Victorian public school makes a fascinating study in its own right. The paradox is that the school communities which helped support liberal institutions of government were in themselves essentially totalitarian. This is not to say that they were highly coercive: prefectorial bullying was on the wane, and the formal rules that bound the schoolboy were seldom as restrictive as a Rudyard Kipling would have us believe.[1] The pressures that public school society placed on the individual were more akin to the educational techniques of advertising and brainwashing. That is to say, they operated almost subliminally, moulding the individual's very desires. In the case of the public schools, aesthetic appeals to 'good form' and tradition usually made the individual *want* to identify himself strongly with his group—*want* to show 'House spirit'.

To an extent, of course, every society invades its members' privacy with totalitarian pressures of this sort. But the development of mass propaganda has posed the manipulation of desire as a steadily increasing threat to free choice and free thought. The public school experience, therefore, provides a perspective on the perpetual conflict between Authority and Individual Freedom in a society which needs both.

On the strictly educational plane, this philosophical dilemma becomes the problem of academic freedom. As such it confronts

[1] cf. Rudyard Kipling, *Stalky & Co.*

every college and school which feels a direct commitment to serving social authority—a responsibility for teaching morals and inspiring public loyalties. But the problem is especially pronounced in a political education system like the Victorian public schools. Such a system must teach both faith and doubt, both moral commitment and rational questioning. To produce responsible public servants, it must instil loyalty; to produce decisive leaders, it must induce self-assurance. On the other hand, the requirements of intelligent leadership demand that political education inspires a critical spirit of inquiry; and here lies the conflict. For loyalty and self-assurance are ultimately rooted not in reason but in the emotions—in emotional beliefs which the free play of reason may shake.

An essay by the American sociologist, Thorstein Veblen, illustrates this potential conflict well. In *The Intellectual Pre-eminence of Jews*, Veblen noted that the great Jewish contributions to scholarship were frequently made under conditions of social uneasiness. The leading Jewish thinkers, he observed, were often men living outside their own racial communities, who none the less resisted absorption by their Gentile environment. Veblen's conclusion was that their position as social outsiders made them sceptics, and that scepticism was handmaiden to a true spirit of inquiry.[1]

How did the public school community—a ghetto, in its monasticism and close-knit living—meet the faith-doubt dilemma as Veblen portrayed it? That the public school instilled loyalty, integrity, and moral assurance is widely assumed. But what sort of loyalty, what sort of moral assurance? Did these qualities permit intelligence, and if so, what kind of intelligence? The kind that understands political change . . . technological change? These are some of the questions that this book seeks to answer. Here again, we can seek perspective in comparisons. The national school in pre-war Japan, for example, was strongly committed to moral training and loyalty-indoctrination. Yet the Japanese system was also committed to producing nation-builders, imaginative leaders who could recognize and exploit the vast changes befalling their

[1] Thorstein Veblen, 'The Intellectual Pre-eminence of Jews' in *The Portable Veblen*.

country. The same dual commitment dominates the Russian and Chinese schools today, and it has really been a major characteristic of the Jesuit educational tradition. (For all their attention to faith and dogma, the Jesuit schools had to produce mission leaders who could think for themselves in novel situations far from home authority.) Each of these education systems, then, has faced to an unusual degree the problem of loyalty and intelligence. And like the case history of the public schools, the experience of each system offers its own possible solution.

But this is not the only dilemma confronting political education. Another liability is that the system may starve key nongovernmental professions, in industry, for example, or the arts. On one hand, it may divert able men away from these occupations; on the other, it can quite easily develop unsuitable aptitudes in those who do enter them. As John Stuart Mill put it,

the absorption of all the principal ability of the country into the governing body is fatal, sooner or later, to the mental activity and progressiveness of the body itself.[1]

Political education, in other words, can become the victim of its very success. If it tries to serve one master, if it fails to reward private professions that nourish the nation both materially and intellectually, political education may sow weakness where it sought to sow strength. In the last analysis, the public schools' effectiveness must be rated by their ability to pursue contradictory goals—to support public service and private practice, to instil loyalty and imagination, and to adapt traditional ideals to the requirements of change.

[1] J. S. Mill, *Essay on Liberty*, Chapter V, quoted by Roy Lewis and Angus Maude, *The English Middle Classes*, 333.

Chapter 2

The Setting: Victorian England and
the Gentleman Ideal

As a sheer spectacle of power, the political fortunes of Britain's landed families in the nineteenth century provide unusual drama. For against them during this period a formidable combination of forces was arrayed. Politically, there was the advent of democracy, the gradual extension of the vote to the entire male population. Economically, there was the Industrial Revolution and the repeal of the Corn Laws; the rise of an aggressive, entrepreneur group; and the increased financial dependence on that group of the old landlord-squirearchy.[1]

Despite these forces, the landed families retained a grip on the country's government out of all proportion to their numbers or even their wealth. In 1866, fifty-four years after the Reform Act enfranchised the middle class, half the places in the Cabinet were still being filled by titled aristocracy. Right up to the First World War, peers comprised over a third of each Cabinet. And even the House of Commons, as one sociologist has pointed out, continued to represent the aristocracy and 'lesser county families . . . to an excessive degree'.[2]

The political power of the landed classes rested, among other things, on the English public schools. By the latter I refer to the group of private secondary schools, mainly boarding, which together came to form the Headmasters' Conference after that body was born in 1869. But I refer particularly to the most influential of these schools, the long-established and famous 'Seven',[3]

[1] E. Wingfield-Stratford, *The Squire and His Relations*, 390-1.
[2] W. L. Guttsman, 'The Aristocracy and the Middle Class in the British Political Elite, 1886-1916', *British Journal of Sociology*, March 1954.
[3] Charterhouse, Eton, Harrow, Rugby, Shrewsbury, Westminster, and Winchester.

plus a handful of newer schools which sprang to fame during the nineteenth century.

Somewhat naturally, the Victorian public-schoolboy himself tended to define 'public school' according to his own school's place on a rigorous social hierarchy. At the top of the ladder the definition became comically exclusive. In 1866 Westminster refused to play Shrewsbury on the grounds that it was not officially listed as a public school; and a few years later Mill Hill, which had requested a match with Harrow, got this reply back—on a postcard: 'Eton we know, and Rugby we know, but who are ye?'[1] For our own purposes, however, the 'Headmasters' Conference' will provide the most unprovocative definition.

Behind the social influence of the public schools lay two factors which only came fully into play during the nineteenth century. First, there was the development of road and rail transport, encouraging parents who could afford it to send their sons away to boarding school. Not only was there a rapid multiplication of Anglican boarding schools after 1850, but the student population of already well-established schools became increasingly cross-regional.[2] A national public school accent emerged, linking social prestige with the hallmark of a good education.[3] Both in speech and outlook, the public schools exerted a unifying influence on the country's leadership.

What the system had in fact created was a central pool of ruler-trainees. This pool the public schools expanded—and here lay the second factor in their power—by opening their gates to middle-class individuals. It was a process that only became apparent after Thomas Arnold's reign at Rugby, from 1827 to 1842. For all his unworldly interests, one historian observed, Arnold

had a flair for a new market. He surveyed the social scene and he knew that a class of prosperous people was pressing forward to power and that their sons needed educating.[4]

Tenuous as this commercial interpretation of the Doctor may

[1] Vivian Ogilvie, *The English Public School*, 168
[2] T. W. Bamford, 'Public Schools and Social Class, 1801–1850', *British Journal of Sociology*, September 1961.
[3] Lewis and Maude, *The English Middle Classes*, 15
[4] Ogilvie, op. cit., 144.

be, the Arnoldian ideal—the 'Christian gentleman'—did provide a convenient formula for a fusion of classes. On one hand, the public schools' exaltation of Chapel suited the 'Philistine respectability' of the devout bourgeois: 'character-building' became an obsession that pervaded everything from playing games to the mental rigours of learning Latin. On the other hand, the schools' claim to inculcate gentlemanly manners met the landed classes' aesthetic requirements and, at the same time, attracted the ambitious *nouveau riche*. As the phrase 'Christian gentleman' almost implies, the concept of 'character' wedded middle-class morality to gentry-class style. The requirements of character-building upheld Samuel Smiles' gospel of hard work, but the Victorian public schoolboy learned early to leaven moral earnestness with gentility, a manner of casual assurance and leisurely grace.

But moral concern was not the only mark that the middle-class influx left on the public schools. A new spirit of efficiency was abroad—in government as well as in education. The emergence of an industrial State, not to speak of Imperial responsibilities, demanded the creation of bureaucracy. Bureaucracy, in turn, depended for members on middle-class participation, and for efficiency on merit standards in recruitment. During the eighteen-fifties and eighteen-sixties, entrance requirements for the Civil Service and the Army altered radically. In the place of the old patronage system came, first, limited competition—examination for the select few whom the authorities had personally nominated—and then, in 1870, open competition.

Significantly, the decade 1861–70 which saw bureaucratic reform was also the great period of public school reform. In 1864 the Clarendon Commission investigated nine schools—the illustrious 'Seven' and two major day schools, Merchant Taylors' and St. Paul's. Much of its report was favourable; but it made a loud plea for a wider curriculum. The subsequent Public Schools Act established State interest in what were, by tradition, private institutions. Not only did the Act require government approval of each public school's controlling body, but it strengthened each headmaster's power to appoint staff. This was a strong blow on behalf of the forces of internal school reform. At Uppingham, Edward Thring represented a new era of headmaster reformers who widened and intensified the curriculum, adding languages and, before the century was out, sciences. Despite these changes, however, classics remained the most venerated subject both in the public school classroom and, to a lesser extent, in Civil Service examinations.[1] As long, anyway, as Oxford and Cambridge continued their traditional emphasis on classical studies, the public schools felt obliged to follow suit, for winning scholarships to the two universities provided a major source of prestige.

How closely was the pattern of public school reform connected with that of government reform? In what sense could the public school system be called a pre-eminently political system, organized for supplying the State with leadership material? As early as 1821, Samuel Butler, one-time Headmaster of Shrewsbury, had described the public school as a place where 'boys are educated in the higher departments of literature, with a view to their entrance into public life'.[2] This is one scrap of evidence to support the argument that the public school authorities pursued a consciously political role. Other evidence might be sought in the case of Haileybury. When the East India Company pioneered competitive recruitment for civil service in 1833, it was in a position to do so because Haileybury, the company's training college, could easily be geared to an open examination system. Haileybury, at this time, was already run on public school discipline and a prefectorial system; although it catered to a university age-group until its second founding as a regular public school.

Despite these straws in the wind, the way in which the public schools served government remained tacit and unofficial. Admittedly, curricular reforms in the schools added to their new emphasis on moral education and leadership training, enabled them to stake out special claims on the bureaucracy. To the men who interviewed candidates for executive government posts, a public school accent and public school mannerisms spelt 'quality'

[1] Herman Finer, reporting on the Civil Service Administrative Class in the 1930's, writes that more senior officials had studied classics at university than any other subject—Finer, *The British Civil Service.*

[2] Samuel Butler, *Open Letter to Brougham.*

—predictable quality. In 1937 a retired Colonial Office administrator could write, of the attributes needed for his Service:

Such qualities are not the monopoly of the products of the Public Schools and Oxford and Cambridge. But recruits drawn from these sources are more certain to possess them than are candidates of different antecedents. . . .[1]

In no sense, however, could the State be said to have deliberately moulded public school education to its own requirements. The links between public school and public careers were more subtle than this. What the school system basically did was to encourage attitudes that saw greatest prestige and pleasure in public service. These attitudes reflected the historic connexion between the landed classes and political power; and the landed classes, it must be remembered, were the public schools' traditional clientele. Until 1850 at least, the sons of 'gentry' at the old-established Seven Schools by far outnumbered those from 'professional' and business families.[2]

The remarkable thing about the public-school-gentry ethos of public service was the way that it survived the school system's absorption of new blood from the rising capitalist group. 'Look at the bottle-merchant's son and the Plantagenet being brought up side by side,' wrote Matthew Arnold. '. . . Very likely young Bottles will end up by being a lord himself.'[3] At least Bottles would end by being a country gentleman—and an unpaid Justice of the Peace to boot. Trade, the source of his fortune, he might respect as a necessity, but public position would seem infinitely more noble. Bottles' public school, in other words, would have made another capture for the gentry. Rule England he might, but as a gentleman, not as a bourgeois.

'The bourgeoisie', noted Joseph Schumpeter in *Capitalism, Socialism and Democracy*,

[1] Robson (ed.), *The British Civil Servant*, 245–6, quoting Leonard Barnes.
[2] T. W. Bamford, op. cit.: The proportion of gentry, too, represented in the public schools was larger than the proportion of business and private professional families. This report, however, is slightly exaggerated by the fact that where a family was both gentry and professional or business, Bamford classed it as gentry.
[3] Matthew Arnold, *Friendship's Garland*, quoted by Asa Briggs in *Victorian People*, 145.

produced individuals who made a success at political leadership upon entering a political class of non-bourgeois origin, but it did not produce a successful political stratum of its own although, so one should think, the third generation of the industrial families had all the opportunity to form one.[1]

True to Schumpeter's thesis, the public schoolboy's political bent was inseparable from a gentleman ideal which the schools promoted. There were three components to the gentleman ideal, and the first of these was the attainment of 'magic'. By magic, I refer to that mysterious aura of different-ness which distinguishes certain leaders and makes them respected for what they are rather than what they do. The property of magic, so Schumpeter argued, was more vital to political leadership than to industrial leadership, and it was more easily attained by the medieval lord than it was by the businessman.

The stock exchange is a poor substitute for the Holy Grail. . . . The industrialist and merchant, as far as they are entrepreneurs, also fill a function of leadership. But economic leadership of this type does not readily expand, like the medieval lord's military leadership, into the leadership of nations.[2]

Schumpeter maintains that the bourgeois, 'rationalist and unheroic', lacks 'the mystical glamour and the lordly attitude' which makes the feudal lord respected as a ruler of men. Realizing his limitations, the bourgeois often 'wants to be left alone and to leave politics alone'.[3]

How far did the case of public school England bear out the Schumpeter theory of magic? Certainly Walter Bagehot, the Victorian commentator on the British Constitution, agreed with Schumpeter that governments have a special need to inspire men by magical display as well as persuade them by reason and efficiency.[4] It is also true that a prime characteristic of the public school gentleman ideal was to attach great importance to a dignified

[1] Joseph Schumpeter, *Capitalism, Socialism and Democracy*, 298.
[2] Ibid., 137–8.
[3] Ibid.
[4] A major theme in Walter Bagehot's book, *The English Constitution*, is his distinction between the 'dignified' (or magical) role of government and its 'efficient' (or utilitarian and rational) role.

bearing and an aura of command. Such leadership qualities were readily identified with character—a confusion of manners with the morals they were meant to symbolize.

What Schumpeter does not fully say is that the gentleman's predilection for magic and the aesthetic produced political motivation as well as political aptitude. In other words, it wasn't simply that the gentleman felt best equipped for a public career; he generally preferred such a career, however low its material rewards. And it was here that public school education played its part. 'Manners makyth man', said William of Wykeham, the fourteenth-century founder of Winchester; and with the passage of years 'manners' came to denote a network of school etiquette— a host of rules backed by the aesthetic sanction of 'good form'— which moulded the public schoolboy into a keen public servant. In later chapters, we shall examine the mechanism of public school etiquette, and the political loyalties it helped to implant.

According to Schumpeter, it will be remembered, political magic was closely associated with military leadership. Certainly the military commander, with his need to exact instinctive obedience under conditions of great stress, had call to acquire every attribute that would enhance his authority. Yet when we come to study Confucian China, we will find a gentlemanly concept of leadership that placed great reliance on dignified style, but attached little prestige to soldiering. In fact, the history of both societies suggests that the gentleman's concern with magic stemmed basically from a landed way of life. In Britain as in China, a *rentier* group enjoyed leisure in which to perfect elegant manners and style. Sheltered, moreover, by geographical isolation, both societies found stability enough to develop the political uses of etiquette—rules of social behaviour backed by custom and 'good taste' as much as by legal force.

This brings us to the second component of the gentleman ideal, the great importance attached to leisure. In the world of the landed gentry leisure was a status-symbol, signifying that a man could take up pursuits for their own sake rather than toil for bread alone. It followed from this that the gentleman's premium on leisure was closely bound up with the amateur tradition, so faithfully perpetuated by the public schools. Pursuits that were unremunerative—classical study, voluntary service as a magistrate —conferred prestige by the very token that they *were* unremunerative. Extended to the realm of national politics, the amateur outlook represented a powerful factor in luring men to parliamentary office. In order to become an M.P., a lawyer or landlord did not have to feel he should sacrifice his non-political activities. Financially as well as intellectually, this increased the appeal of political life.

So far we have mentioned two components of the gentleman ideal—the property of magic, and the status-symbol of leisure. The third component lay in the gentleman's attitude towards privilege and duty. In the little world of the public school, as in the adult world of the English gentry, social status and community service were intimately linked. When the games hero won his 'colours'—that dazzling train of special caps, blazers, scarves, sweaters, and garters in which public school athleticism revelled —he was being honoured not only for individual prowess but for bringing glory on 'House and School'. This, indeed, may have been one factor in the public school cult of the playing field. The quieter achievements of the scholar and poet were not so obviously a community service.

The relation between privilege and duty was, in part, that of a *quid pro quo*. At most public schools, the prefect or monitor could feel that, years before he came to power, he had earned his privileges by first performing menial household chores as a 'fag'. Not that his duties ceased with 'fagging'. Prefectorial position itself involved considerable administrative work.

But there was more to privilege and duty than a *quid pro quo* relationship. The essence of the gentleman ideal was that it identified social status with moral superiority. As Reinhold Niebuhr points out, the very word 'gentleman', like 'nobility', denotes superior virtue,[1] and the same is true not only in other European tongues but in Chinese. (*Juin-tze*, the nearest Chinese equivalent to gentleman, literally means 'superior man'.) We have already noted that the gentleman tended to identify aesthetic

[1] Reinhold Niebuhr, *Moral Man and Immoral Society*, 126.

manners with moral virtue; and, ideally, the possession of leisure was supposed to enable the gentleman to work dutifully for others.

It follows, then, that the gentleman idea did not rely solely on altruism to produce a spirit of public service. Altruism there certainly was: no one can deny the sincere humanitarian impulse which created, for example, public school missions to slum areas. But *within* the appeal to altruism, the gentleman ideal, lurked hidden appeals to egoism—the egoism of the patron. It posed public service as a moral status-symbol, the credential of membership in a select social club, enjoying moral prestige as well as political power.

We must realize, however, that the gentleman's outlook on privilege and duty could only obtain in a certain social climate. It was a climate that strongly characterized late Victorian England. Here, amid the subsiding influence of Evangelicalism, appropriate assumptions persisted about goodness and political leadership. Goodness meant Good Works; virtue was largely seen as civic virtue. Political leadership was inseparable from moral leadership —as the scandal of Charles Dilke testified—and the men who ruled England ruled as a moral elect. Assumptions such as these formed a bridge between the devout bourgeois and the country squire. Among the aristocracy and older gentry, political service remained a family tradition,[1] to be championed and perpetuated by the public schools.

Subsidiary to the gentleman ideal were other means by which the public schools produced public servants. Spartan hardships, for example, so proudly described by many an 'Old Boy', may well have played their part in acclimatizing young men to the material disadvantages of a government career. This would apply especially to the colonial service where physical discomforts and family sacrifice had their public school counterparts in unheated dormitories, cold baths, and monastic isolation. As John Patrick Pringle suggested in his article, 'The British Commune', boarding school society really posed family life and the distractions of women as potential threats to public service.[2] If homosexuality

---

[1] W. L. Guttsman, op. cit., 14 and 17.
[2] John Patrick Pringle, *Encounter*, February 1961.

and sexual inhibition were the price, it was a price basically accepted—however much the school authorities might rant when they discovered 'immorality'.[1]

Even more akin to public school life than the colonial service were conditions in the Army. The military characteristics of the Victorian public school are too striking to be overlooked. Not only did the school Rifle Corps offer the one exception to the rule prescribing a 'non-vocational' general education, but the schools previewed regimental life itself. When one thinks of public school monasticism, hierarchy, and hardship, of barrackroom living and discipline, of teamwork rewarded by decoration, of the reverence paid to community tradition—when one parades these factors together, it is not difficult to understand why public school gentlemen became military officers.

The same facets of public school life which gave it such a marked military overtone made it basically hostile to Trade. In this the public schools were simply transmitting certain prejudices that the landed classes felt about the merchant. If the schools were ready to take the businessman's fees, they were not ready to take all that he stood for. Ideally, the gentleman viewed money as a mere *provider*, guarantee of leisure, culture and 'the good life'. He could not view money as a *score*, the proud measure of industrial creativity, for he was brought up to seek honour in community leadership rather than in private enterprise-building. On those occasions when the public schoolboy did become an unabashed merchant adventurer, it was in spite of his schooldays and not because of them.[2] For where the public school reverenced tradition, the businessman courted innovation. Where one stressed magic, etiquette, and ceremony, the other worshipped efficiency and utility. In the dynamic conditions of nineteenth-century capitalism, before the rise of the 'organization man' and the bureaucratic corporation, the archetype industrialist was the

[1] G. G. T. Heywood, 'Boys at Public Schools', in E. H. Pitcairn (ed.), *Unwritten Laws and Ideals*.
[2] One exception to the generally low status of 'Trade' was merchant banking, whose dominant families were involved with more than one national government and displayed a cosmopolitan aura. Brewing, as an occupation linked with land, was perhaps another exception, *viz* the Guinnesses of Ireland. It has been suggested, though not thoroughly substantiated, that by and large 'middlemen'—brokers, distributors, etc.—were less highly considered than producers.

risk-taking *entrepreneur*. Individualist, grasping, and eminently rational, the entrepreneur was diametrically opposed to the public school ethos, which subordinated the individual to the group. It was not surprising, therefore, that long after the public schools admitted the middle classes, Trade was still considered unfashionable, a vulgar and slightly selfish pursuit.[1]

Even when the businessman married into a family of public servants, Trade still retained its stigma. Frederick Lugard, the great colonial administrator, portrayed this phenomenon in a letter he wrote from his public school, Rossall, in 1875. The son of a poor clergyman with a large family, young Lugard had been offered a job in the business of his elder half-sister's husband. Lugard seriously considered leaving school early to take the job, but he realized that if he did so he would forgo any chance of sitting the Indian Civil Service examination. He wrote about his quandary to his younger half-sister and confidante, Emma; his letter reflects not only the gentleman's outlook on careers but a strong sense of family tradition:

... If I go in for this [the business job] I have to throw overboard the I.C.S. which if I passed it would be an infinitely better thing besides being a thoroughly gentlemanly occupation, and look at it how I may, I can't bring myself to think that an Assistant in a Sugar Factor is such. Of course 'a gentleman is a gentleman wherever he is', but still the Lugards have been in the Army and in the Church, good servants of *God* or the *Queen*, but few if any have been tradesmen.[2]

In the end, Lugard plumped for the I.C.S.; he failed the examination and went into the Army instead.

On the hierarchy of careers, between Trade and government service, a middle ground of prestige seems to have been occupied by the private 'professions'.[3] There is some evidence, however inconclusive, to suggest that the most famous public schools admitted with complete readiness the sons of professional men at

---

[1] cf. Lewis and Maude, op. cit., 44–45, 65–66. The princely, cosmopolitan merchant banker an exception—52–53. *cf.* T. C. Worsley, *Barbarians and Philistines*, 99–100.

[2] Margery Perham, *Lugard*, Vol. I, *The Years of Adventure*, 35.

[3] Lord Salter, *Memoirs of a Public Servant*, 32, 35. Salter tells how at Oxford around 1900 nearly all his contemporaries preferred the government and private professions to business. The Oxford undergraduates of that time, we should remember, were very largely public school.

an earlier date than they did the sons of businessmen.[1] More than one public school, in fact, possessed special ties with a profession. Written into the charter of such institutions were to be found provisions that the school train boys for the profession or that it take sons of men already in it. In this way Marlborough maintained close connexions with the Church, Epsom with Medicine, and Wellington with the Army.

The place held by the professions in Victorian society provides further evidence that the public school ethos was politically oriented and basically opposed to commercial profit-making. A marked feature of most professions has been an outward contempt for aggressive salesmanship. As T. H. Pear suggests in *English Social Differences*, a private profession has clients, whereas a trade has customers. What is healthy competition to the second is client-stealing for the first.[2] In other words, a profession—like a public school—possesses a group spirit which mutes any competitive individualism that occurs within it.

This anti-commercial trait of the professions was especially pronounced before the First World War. The nearer a profession was to flagrant 'money-grubbing' the less prestige it accrued. According to T. H. Escott, the Victorian commentator, G.P.s, and solicitors had lower occupational status than had barristers and clergy, partly because the former had to undergo the 'vulgar' commercial process of receiving money direct from their clients.[3] Hypothetical as this argument is, the fact that a distinguished Victorian could write it is significant in itself.

We have already suggested that, in contrast to most commercial occupations, the Victorian professions portrayed a marked group spirit. In this respect they were fairly similar to branches of the government. Like a bureaucratic civil service, a profession derives some of its most *élite esprit de corps* from formal methods of recruitment. These, in fact, form an integral part of what constitutes a profession. Thus, the professions have been defined as

---

[1] cf. T. C. Worsley, op. cit., 97–98. cf. T. W. Bamford, op. cit.
[2] T. H. Pear, *English Social Differences*, 22.
[3] T. H. Escott, *England: Her People, Polity and Pursuits* (1885), 355–6.

those vocations which rest upon a systematic body of knowledge of substantial intellectual content and which are entered by advanced degrees, i.e. examinations demonstrating minimum standards of education and competence.[1]

The professional examination, like its civil service counterpart, invests a group with a mystique. By confronting new members with a traditional body of knowledge to be rigorously learned, the profession acquires the aura of historic continuity: it appears as an entity which is more than the sum of present members. Recruitment by formal examination, moreover, gives the profession the image of a community not lightly entered nor easily understood by the outsider. On a later page, it will be seen how this professional mystique bore certain similarities to the public school's own cult of the community.

Admittedly, to the extent that the professional examination stressed specialized and theoretical expertise it was opposed to the amateur concept of the generally educated man—a concept which dominated public school education and the British Government alike. At this point it is interesting to recall another observation of T. H. Escott's. The barrister and the bishop, he said, held high occupational status because their doings made a *general* impact on the *public* mind.[2] More narrowly technical professions seemed to have inferior prestige.

All in all, the comparative prestige of the professions supports our argument that the public schools were geared mainly to producing public servants. In no case was this more true than in that of the Church. The Church was, in a sense, the most political of the private professions, and it had prestige second to none. Its special ties with the State were matched only by its close connexions with the public schools. In 1928, reports R. H. Tawney, fifty-two bishops out of fifty-six were old public schoolboys[3]—a situation hardly surprising when, twenty-nine years before, an ex-Harrow headmaster, turned Bishop of Calcutta, could write, 'An unwritten law seems to have decreed that headmasters at

[1] John Davies, editor of the *Princeton Alumni Bulletin*, writing in the *Harvard Alumni Bulletin*, 17 March 1962.
[2] T. H. Escott, op. cit., 355–7.
[3] R. H. Tawney, *Equality*, 300–1.

public schools shall be clergymen'.[1] Certainly there were head-masters who were not clergymen. But true it is that churchmen were represented among public school dons and headmasters out of all proportion to their numbers. Not until after the First World War did their personal involvement in public school life start to decline.

As a social institution, what services did the public schools help perform for the emerging industrial democracy that was Victorian England? Above all, they provided an anchor in the midst of turbulence, a force for cohesion offsetting centrifugal tendencies in the environment. Against the rising affluence of the British nation, the public schools maintained an outpost of monastic asceticism. Against the competitive individualism of the Industrial Revolution, they kept alive the traditional gentleman's assumption that private privilege meant public duty. And amid the intellectual furore, the doubts and cross-questioning that characterized the England of Darwin and Huxley, the schools defended a mainstream of moral faith, a 'gentilized' version of Evangelicalism. They took the Protestant ethic of the capitalist—the creed which sanctioned a fierce individualist striving—and they helped make it a group ethic. The spirit of competition remained, but it became a team spirit rather than the spirit of a lone individual. On the football field and on the river, the public school taught its boys to compete, not so much in personal contests, as in struggles between groups—between teams, houses, and schools. In this way, the public schools 'socialized' their middle-class recruits. They preserved middle-class morality and energy, but they adapted these to the needs of the public servant. A balance was struck between competition and social co-operation.

It would be wrong, of course, to claim for education a powerful causal role in shaping societies and their government. In the next chapter we will ask to what extent the public schools did in fact *create* social patterns, rather than merely reflect them. All that can be said here is that the public schools did help to support a stable political structure. This structure endured despite the

[1] E. H. Pitcairn, op. cit., 271, quoting the Rt. Rev. J. E. C. Welldon.

momentous social and economic changes of the nineteenth century.

In several senses, the Victorian public schools provided a hinge between traditionalism and a new rationalism. They were traditionalist in the way they kept alive the historic public loyalties of the landed gentry. They were also traditionalist to the extent that they instilled love of custom. In the economist's sense, the organizational sense, however, the reformed public schools could be called rationalist. They provided certain professions with a predictable calibre of material, and they were able to do this, largely because they had standardized and formalized their institutions. Gone were those schooldays of virtual anarchy, the days that Stalky & Co. longed for, when boys could choose bird-nesting over football. During the eighteen-fifties, eighteen-sixties, and eighteen-seventies, the schools tightened discipline, acquired uniforms and old school ties, and elaborated their customs into a detailed and restrictive etiquette. The founding in 1869 of the Headmasters' Conference only hastened the process of standardization.

True, there were many differences between individual schools, which indeed survived. Not all schools gave complete power to their prefects and monitors, nor was every establishment subdivided into semi-autonomous Houses. Some variation in the social class composition of schools always existed, and the personality of a strong headmaster or teacher inevitably left its distinctive imprint.

Despite these and other variations, they were dwarfed by a fundamental uniformity between the schools.[1] This was partly due to the increased cross-regional composition of the public school's clientele. But, it was also because the schools had girded themselves, however unofficially, to meet the new merit standards in recruitment that the government professions were setting. Even here, however, over the question of social opportunity, the public schools merely effected a balance between rationalized organization and traditional power. In fact, the balance represented a compromise—between the reward of intellectual merit, on the

[1] E. Wingfield-Stratford, *The Squire and His Relations*, 396–7.

one hand, and the reward of hereditary privilege, on the other.

The new government examinations, Gladstone predicted happily in 1854, would confer 'an immense superiority [upon] all those who may be called gentlemen by birth and training'.[1] His prediction was fulfilled. Long after Civil Service examinations became 'open competition', the public schoolboy continued to receive preferred treatment at the examinations' oral interviews. The public schools, for their part, excluded the working-class boy of no means, whatever his promise. Even where scholarship programmes existed, entrance tests attached great importance to Latin, a subject which private education virtually monopolized. In any case, public school headmasters tended to resist lower-class admission as a threat to their schools' traditional character.[2]

The extent to which hereditary privilege actually prevailed in high office seems to have varied between different branches of government. By all accounts, it applied less to the Home Civil Service than it did to the Foreign Office (and to Conservative Cabinets). H. E. Dale, in his analysis of eighty Home officials who entered the Administrative Class between 1899 and 1908, reckoned that only a very bare majority were born into the upper and upper-middle classes; 18 per cent. had gone through the 'greater boarding schools' as opposed to 25 per cent. from the 'greater day schools'—St. Paul's, Merchant Taylors', Dulwich, King Edward's (Birmingham), and so on.[3] It should be said, however, that many of the 'greater day schools' boasted public school institutions and customs. In any event, a large section of Home Civil Servants came from 'minor' boarding schools.

Turning to the Foreign Office and Diplomatic Service, we find a somewhat different social picture. Walter Bagehot's contention that 'an ambassador is not simply an agent; he is also a spectacle' and that aristocrats are specially 'trained for the theatrical side of life' appears to have been a basic principle in Foreign Office recruitment.[4] As late as 1918, entrants to the Diplomatic Service had to guarantee a private income of at least £400 per annum

[1] Letter to Lord John Russell, quoted by Kingsley in *Representative Bureaucracy*.
[2] T.W. Bamford, op. cit.
[3] H. E. Dale, *The Higher Civil Service*, 49–54.
[4] Walter Bagehot, *The English Constitution*, 106–7.

for their first two years in office. In addition to this qualification, they had to be known personally to the Secretary of State or else recommended to him by 'men of standing and position on whose judgment he could rely'.[1] Not surprisingly, 67 per cent. of all attaché-ships given between 1908 and 1913 went to Old Etonians. The Foreign Office was indeed the magic sanctuary of gentlemanly power.

When we view Victorian society as a whole, it becomes quite apparent that the public school concession to social mobility did nothing to weaken class distinction. By indoctrinating the *nouveau riche* as a gentleman, the public schools really acted as an escape-valve in the social system. They helped avert a class conflict which might have ended the reign of the landed gentry. Curiously, the same interplay between social mobility and class distinction occurred at approximately the same time in Japan: Ruth Benedict's description of this phenomenon could virtually be taken for a description of Victorian England.

Money-lenders settled on the land and collected rents, and such 'ownership' of land gave prestige as well as profit in Japan. Their children married samurai (hereditary knights). They became gentry. . . . It is easy to point out that the common cause made by these two classes was mutually advantageous in Japan, but it would have been mutually advantageous in France too. It was advantageous in those individual instances where it occurred. But class rigidity was strong in Europe and the conflicts of classes led in France to the expropriation of the aristocracy. In Japan they drew closer together. . . . The modern era in Japan preserved the aristocratic system. It could hardly have happened without Japan's sanctioned techniques for class mobility.[2]

Thus abetted by social mobility, landed power could continue, and with it a general acceptance of class inequality. The period in which middle-class boys first entered Harrow and Winchester saw just as much snobbery as any other; it probably saw more.[3] At least one public school history tells the story of the Clifton

[1] Kingsley, *Representative Bureaucracy*, 127.
[2] Ruth Benedict, *The Chrysanthemum and the Sword*, 72–73.
[3] Edward Mack, *The Public Schools and British Opinion*, 248–50. T. C. Worsley, op. cit., 92–98.

boy who felt unable to talk freely to his brother on the street simply because the latter attended the nearby—and socially inferior—Bristol Grammar School.

> The rich man in his castle,
> The poor man at his gate,
> God made them, high or lowly,
> And ordered their estate.[1]

So wrote Mrs. Alexander, that most prolific of Victorian hymn-writers, and it is significant that the verse just quoted comes in a much-loved children's hymn praising the divine beauties of nature. (Equally significantly, the verse has now been dropped from most hymn-books.) If the public school system indulged the ambitions of the rising bourgeois, it must be remembered that it did nothing to bridge the social divide between the 'leadership classes' and the manual worker. On the contrary, the isolation and exclusiveness of boarding school life increased the distance between ruler and ruled. What efforts had to be made by Egremont, the noble-born hero of Disraeli's *Sybil*, in order to find out how the nation's other half lived.

The pattern was set. Democracy—political democracy—had arrived, but gentlemanly power had won a reprieve. For decades to come Britain would be governed not by sundry individuals but by a class, selected at an early age, and indoctrinated together with certain concepts of leadership. It is our task now to examine the type of leadership that the political class gave.

[1] 'All Things Bright and Beautiful', *Hymns Ancient and Modern*, 573.

Part Two

CHARACTER AND THE CONSTITUTION

Chapter 3

Unwritten Restraint

As the spirit of Thomas Arnold eddied out through the public schools, the latter came to see their role first and foremost in terms of 'building Character'—a phrase more often used than closely analysed. Educational critics like John Ruskin and Matthew Arnold endorsed this priority by arguing that a school should train emotions and will before attending to the brain.[1] Within the system itself even great renovators—Warre of Eton, Sanderson of Oundle—saw public school education as a process primarily ethical rather than intellectual.[2] Many schools built large and awe-inspiring chapels, and used them frequently.

There were always those, of course, who spoke out against too exclusive an obsession with character. At Uppingham, Edward Thring wrote and worked for a better balance between moral training and scholarship. Without just that balance, feared Thring, the schools would produce either 'big-headed dwarfs', mere academic 'prize-winners', or else 'headless animals'.[3] Thring's very words, however, reflected a prevailing public school assumption about character-building. In the tension between body and mind—and it was so often thought of as a tension—character was on the side of body, the headless animal. As David Newsome writes in *Godliness and Good Learning*, 'Thring was clearly of the muscular school', identifying character with athletic ideals of manliness.[4]

If 'muscular Christianity' characterized Thring, even more so did it mark the whole system. Physical hardship—cold baths,

[1] Edward Mack, *Public Schools and British Opinion Since 1860*, 67. Asa Briggs, *Victorian People*, 143.
[2] Edward Mack, op. cit., 95, 260-1.
[3] Edward Thring, *The Theory and Practice of Teaching*, 9.
[4] David Newsome, *Godliness and Good Learning*, 220.

unheated dormitories, outdoor lavatories, and cross-country runs—was deemed a vital part of the character-building process. Built-in adversity, felt the system's proponents, would not only elicit courage, endurance, and industry, but the external discipline it imposed would somehow enter the individual and become *self-discipline*, an internalized force. As such it would create men who controlled short-run and selfish desires, who would always work for their group as they once played for the team.

Not surprisingly, public school character-building became practically inseparable from the moral glorification of Games. The brute schoolboy energies which, before Arnold's time, had made Rugby a place of anarchy were now channelled into institutional wars on the playing field. This led to a striking effect. The alliance between character-building and games promoted self-restraint and co-operation without wholly destroying a competitive sense of struggle. In this regard the group ethic of the public school differed from the group ethic of *The Organization Man*, William Whyte's portrait of the contemporary industrial bureaucrat. Where the latter is purported to have replaced competitive ideals with a premium on stability and co-operation,[1] the Victorian public school sought to combine both.

But more about *The Organization Man* later. What concerns us here is the way in which the public school inculcated self-restraint. Another ingredient in the process, besides games, was the prefectorial system. By 1880, the prefects in most schools had acquired immense power. Frederick Malim tells the story of a Marlborough housemaster, the immensely bearded W. E. Mullins, who delegated authority so much that when his head prefect reported a fire, he was said to have roared, 'That part of the House is your department, not mine'.[2] Prefects ran house activities and helped legislate rules; they kept order, judged offences and often did the punishing themselves. They were, in short, an administration, a judiciary, and part of the legislature rolled into one. (The political analogy was particularly apt at Eton where 'Pop', the senior boys'

[1] *The Organization Man*, *The Affluent Society* by J. K. Galbraith, and *The Lonely Crowd* by David Riesman *et al.* are the well-known trio supporting this thesis.
[2] Frederick Malim, *Almae Matres*, 21.

most exclusive club, was also known as a debating society.[1])
Nominated by housemaster, headmaster, or their own number,
prefects enjoyed a tenure of office that was virtually unshakeable.

Despite the lack of formal checks on their power, prefects
generally acted with self-restraint. Certainly they did so by comparison with their opportunities to oppress. True, one didn't have
to go far to find abuses: until the First World War and after,
there were cases of favouritism and excessive beating.[2] But these
incidents were much less than the bullying which had gone on in
the *early* Victorian public school. However imperfect, Arnold's
plan of putting senior boys on their honour, of making the potential bully an official disciplinarian, did work.[3] T. H. Escott, in
fact, goes so far as to suggest that the worst abuses occurred where
official prefectorial power was severely limited.[4]

It was a phenomenon that we have already observed. Like the
institution of Games, the prefectorial system channelled rather
than suppressed aggressive impulses. The senior boy, accorded
official status by the community, put his energies into tasks of
social leadership; he didn't have to prove his authority by bullying, fighting, or other forms of anti-social behaviour. At Westminster, an ex-Captain of the School reported that serious fighting had become a 'rare occurrence'. When it did occur, it was
conducted with all the formality and reserve of a duel. At dawn
or dusk, the contestants, their principals, and a few friends would
gather in Westminster's 'little cloisters' and there settle the dis-
pute, well away from the public gaze.[5]

The same social attitudes which turned schoolboy fights into
gentlemanly duels tempered the prefect's self-reliance with a new
tradition of responsibility. This tradition, acting as an internalized
check on the ruler, had two aspects. First, the community conferred high office only as a *quid pro quo*, offering prefectorial
privileges—special living comforts, freedom from certain rules,
and so on—in return for duty. Memory assisted the *quid pro quo*

[1] C. E. Pascoe (ed.), *Everyday Life in Our Public Schools*, 23–24.
[2] G. F. Lamb, *The Happiest Days*, 182, 187. Cyril Connolly, *Enemies of Promise*, 179–80.
[3] cf. C. E. Pascoe, op. cit., 23, 29. Eton and Winchester had praeposters before Arnold's
day, but these were not given powers of punishment till later—cf., Lamb, op. cit., 181.
[4] T. H. Escott, *England: Its People, Polity, and Pursuits*, 296.
[5] Pascoe, op. cit., 127. Chapter on Westminster by W. A. Peck.

obligation, since each prefect could remember what it was like to be on the receiving end of prefectorial commands before he came to office.

Secondly, the school could maintain the tradition of responsibility by inserting it into an unquestioned body etiquette that regulated most aspects of behaviour. Rule by custom was nothing new to the public school. 'There are no such bigoted holders by established forms and customs', wrote Thomas Hughes in *Tom Brown's Schooldays*, 'be they never so foolish or meaningless, as English schoolboys.' But even 'established forms and customs' were susceptible to a certain amount of change. Among other things, they were coming to prescribe the 'light touch' in command, the order given as a suggestion and accompanied by a jest. The gentlemanly leader was the man who secured *instinctive* obedience by virtue of his social—here, prefectorial—rank. He was most likely to win consent if he wore the mantle of authority lightly and pursued a policy of minimum government.

Despotic prefects continued to flourish, but more and more public schoolboys seemed to realize that lightly held power was the most effective power. Certainly this was true at Eton, where, despite arbitrary acts of oppression, there was some concern with popularity and what Cyril Connolly called 'prettyness'—a mixture of 'talent' and graceful behaviour.[1] Public school etiquette also limited prefectorial power by supporting an ascending scale of freedoms and immunities according to seniority. Thus, between fags and prefects, there existed a privileged 'middle class', subject to standing rules and customs, but relatively free from arbitrary interference by authority.

On a more general plane, public school etiquette worked in diverse ways to produce self-restraint. Conceit above one's station seems to have been counted a prime offence at many public schools. At Harrow, for instance, a junior boy who had the temerity to roll up his umbrella out of doors—very much a senior privilege—was called 'swagger'. And at Haileybury, a junior who let hair show under his cap might be told by prefects

[1] Cyril Connolly, op. cit., 174, 214. Pascoe, op. cit., page 23, reports that at Eton in the 1880's occasional revolts occurred against prefectorial tyrants, and that most prefects had learned the advantages of the 'light touch'.

or others to 'take side off'. Note that words like 'swagger' and 'side' carry slightly unpleasant overtones of aggressive, individualist behaviour. The public schoolboy learnt early that 'keeping in one's place' was a prime value of the community.

On the playing-field, etiquette again made for self-restraint by promoting the chivalrous ethic of 'fair play' and 'the good loser'. In the eighteen-eighties an Eton Oppidan wrote of the sportsmanlike courtesies that the great Eton-Winchester match entailed: how, for all the 'play up the School' patriotisms, spectators frequently applauded outstanding performances by the opposing side. He tells, too, how the home team's school detailed boys to show each visitor from the other side around the school—'sometimes independently of his own wishes'![1] The games player tempered the determination to win demanded by 'house spirit' with the amateur's enjoyment of sport for its own sake. (Remember that, since the gentlemanly figure was supposed to afford and enjoy leisure pursuits, the gentleman ideal and the amateur were closely linked images.)

A prime thesis of this book is that various facets of the Victorian public school ethos closely resembled political assumptions underlying the British Constitution. In this the ethic of self-restraint was no exception. The discussion that follows applies mainly to the working of the Constitution up until the Second World War: from that time on, men who had been at school after the 1870–1914 era were beginning to dominate the highest rings of power. I do not mean to imply that men who went to school after the First World War showed dramatic differences from those who were at school before 1914. But it is best to limit our study to a finite period of history.

Like public school authority, British Cabinet government has depended for responsibility on human character rather than on written laws. By contrast with the United States Presidency, the British executive has been free of such institutional curbs as a fully written constitution and a formal separation of powers. No 'Founding Fathers' have been at work in England, ingeniously

[1] Pascoe, op. cit., 60.

devizing an American-style system of 'checks and balances'. The British executive sits right in the legislature; it controls its business and the order of that business. By dominating the majority party, it dominates Parliament, and—in theory at least—Parliament can change any law. There is no Supreme Court to rule a legal change unconstitutional.

Yet, in spite of his great powers, the Prime Minister does not become a dictator, or even an oligarch. The House of Commons may *deliberate* rather than, of its own initiative, *legislate*; but it still cannot be called a mere rubber stamp on Government policy. (Certainly it could not be called so during the modern period up until 1939.) It is partly due to the self-restraint decreed by custom and etiquette that the executive has refrained from riding roughshod over Parliament and party, especially when the next election is some years off.

Most of this is well known. Nevertheless, we easily forget the extent to which the British Constitution depends on ethical restraint, on internalized, psychological checks, to circumscribe authority. We easily forget, because in Britain custom and tradition provide a common base for both internal, ethical checks on the ruler and external, legal checks. The distinction between the two sorts of restraint is consequently blurred. British legal institutions have emerged not from dramatic constitution-building, nor from a total, Napoleonic re-codification of law, but from steady development over time. Thus, the attention to traditional precedent which supports formal law and legal institutions reinforces rather than weakens the unwritten restraints on government; for the latter restraints also depend on an appeal to precedent.

What is it that gives custom its special binding force in England? Perhaps one factor lies in geography. Like the monastic public school community, Britain has been relatively insulated from the outside world and the disruptive effect of alien ideas. Foreign influences have been absorbed gradually and in security. Both communities, therefore, have been able to develop their own strong customs for the purpose of regulating social relations: tradition, revered as a source of stability and a nationalist reminder of a 'glorious past', came to be worshipped simply for its own

34

sake. Under these conditions, characterizing the public school as much as the nation, it is not surprising that the British Constitution made full use of customary usage and etiquette, nor that the British Civil Service based its high standards of dedication and integrity, at least to some extent, on unwritten codes.

If custom has created forces of self-restraint within the ruler, it has also lent a quality of mutual trust to the process of government by making the range of political behaviour predictable. To an extent, it is because the legislature *knows* that the Cabinet will treat it with some consideration that it will accept a considerable measure of executive initiative. Likewise, the backbencher is additionally encouraged to show strong party loyalty when he knows that his party leader will listen thoughtfully to his individual complaints.

The device of restraint by custom, furthermore, speeds up the whole process of decision-making. At Cabinet or party meetings, the Prime Minister may show sensitivity to a general consensus of opinion, but he usually feels no need to take a vote by a formal and lengthy process.[1] The same applies to the Speaker's conduct of debates in the House of Commons. The custom of giving the floor to whomsoever 'catches the Speaker's eye' lends a spontaneous and flexible quality to Parliamentary discussion—or tends to. It also reflects a certain trust that the Speaker will be responsible and fair.

Like the etiquette that binds the public schoolboy, Parliamentary usage extends to some detail. Some of it becomes written law; some remains unwritten; some passes into oblivion— e.g. the rule setting a one-shilling fine for anyone who disturbed the House with loud chatter.[2] But much of Parliamentary usage acquires the personal nature of manners, with all the aesthetic sanction that manners entail. To breach it is not only incorrect but in bad taste. When Hugh Dalton, as Chancellor of the Exchequer (to take an example after our period), publicized parts of his Budget Speech before making it to the House, he was forced to resign. Apart from any economic embarrassment he might

[1] Lord Morrison of Lambeth, *Government and Parliament*, 5–6.
[2] E. H. Pitcairn (ed.), *Unwritten Laws and Ideals*: 'The House of Commons' by Sir Reginald Palgrave.

have caused the Government, he had shown bad manners in breaching a rule of the Parliamentary club.

Parliamentary usage and etiquette, therefore, like the manners of private life, derive force from the very implicitness of their authority, from a silent and unquestionable appeal to good taste rather than any explicit rationale. The rationale does exist, however. The purpose of manners is to subordinate selfish impulses and to standardize outward behaviour, with the accent on moderation and courtesy. Political manners create a common ground of communication between different interest groups and tend to make compromise a good in itself. A disadvantage of setting great store by political manners is that it may encourage hypocrisy, concealing conflict from the public eye by wrapping it in the mists of official harmony. Issues which ought to be aired are relegated to committee politics. On the other hand, political manners do make for smooth transition between elected Governments and relatively smooth changes of party leadership—again, the ethic of 'fair play' and 'the good loser'.

To conclude: the ethic of self-restraint strongly characterized both prefectorial government and British constitutional government. Self-restraint maintained its hold on the individual by its links with tradition and by the aesthetic appeal of a detailed etiquette, derived from the idea of government by gentlemen. Both systems displayed a certain optimism about human nature in their belief that indoctrination could, at least partly, replace external checks on the ruler. Consequently, both systems—prefectorial government and the British Constitution alike—made few formal provisions for curbing the power of a strong executive.

Because it channelled the leader's energies into group loyalty, the ethic of self-restraint was not merely negative. At the same time, however, it did counter totalitarian tendencies which the public school worship of the historic community might otherwise have fostered. The games player was required to display keen 'house spirit' but, as we have already seen, he was also obliged to show graceful sportsmanship to the other side. Implicitly, the public schools recognized that nearly any set of virtues will contradict itself if each virtue is pushed too far. The solution, as the public schools implied it, was to achieve a balance of values by making moderation and practicality virtues also. 'Above all, a sense of proportion'—this quality, described in *The Men Who Ruled India* as the District Officer's most valuable asset,[1] was a prime component of the gentleman ideal. 'Nothing in excess' was not only a value underlying political self-restraint; it supplied a moral rationale for the amateur all-rounder, the man who attained a happy *equilibrium* of talents and virtues. That, at any rate, was the ideal.

[1] Philip Woodruff, *The Men Who Ruled India*, Vol. II—*The Guardians*, 269.

Chapter 4

Loyalty, Co-operation, and the
Historic Community

One of the central arguments behind Rudyard Kipling's *Stalky &
Co.* was that the Victorian public school threatened the manly
self-reliance of a Tom Brown. Individualism was fast waning
under a flurry of rules and regulations; collective co-operation
had acquired precedence over the rigours of competition.
Although in fact the public schools continued to stress adversity
and struggle in the moral training they offered, Kipling saw
correctly that their new-found attachment to discipline and group
loyalties brooked ill for the schoolboy who might have wanted to
go his own way. I say 'might have wanted' because the public
schools made their members usually *want* to conform to the
pattern of life that the authorities prescribed.[1] By devious ways,
the education system taught the individual to identify his private
desires with a mystical fondness for the community and a deference to hierarchy. In the end, it taught them to enjoy co-operation
and loyalty for their own sakes, irrespective of their context.

Through its clearly defined ladder of ranks and privileges, the
public school could closely identify love of the community with
deference to senior office. The two, in fact, reinforced one another.
School tradition sanctioned the privileges of rank, while the
latter, for their part, conferred stability on the school and bolstered the prefects' authority. The allocation of privileges accustomed the public schoolboy to sharp differences of rank, in
things both great and small. At Rugby a boy had to have a year's
seniority before he could walk around outside with his hands in

[1] Pressure of opinion in schools—cf., Vivian Ogilvie, *The English Public School*,
183.

38

his pockets; at Harrow, only members of a certain form and above could walk more than two abreast out of doors.[1] At nearly all public schools senior boys, especially prefects, enjoyed privileges that ranged from an extra hour abed in the morning to the personal service of a fag.

The public schools' emphasis on rank differences encouraged the individual to equate private desires with public loyalties. School hierarchy might subordinate the younger boy, but it held out to him colourful prospects of future power and privilege within the school. Such prospects tempered natural rebelliousness. Through other devices, too, school life encouraged the individual to find pleasure in community activities. Games, for example, hitched a schoolboy love of sport on to 'team spirit', an amalgam that blended co-operation with decisiveness and vigour, and made group loyalty a prerequisite for the joy of winning. Monasticism also played its part, removing the 'subversive' influence of women who—to quote another public school commentator—'thank goodness are incapable of putting the interests of any outside body above the interests of those they love'.[2]

But the main device by which the community made the individual want to focus his energies on loyalty and co-operation was an *aesthetic* device. Only the most resilient individualist would willingly adopt an independent style of life when he knew that etiquette classed such behaviour as showing bad taste. At Winchester, walking to morning Chapel alone was frowned upon as 'sporting a loather' and the boy who made close friends in a house other than his own might be deemed guilty of infringing the 'notion' of 'house spirit'. Similarly, it was 'not done' for a junior boy at Harrow to enter other houses than his own uninvited.[3] Such rules tended to exalt collective action and the possessiveness of the individual's own community. As phrases like 'not done' and 'bad form' suggest, the sanction behind the rules was aesthetic, appealing to group standards of good taste. In fact, the appeal

[1] G. F. Lamb, *The Happiest Days*, 20. E. H. Pitcairn, *Unwritten Laws and Ideals of Active Careers* (pub. 1899), 289.
[2] John Pringle, 'The British Commune', *Encounter*, February 1961.
[3] E. H. Pitcairn, op. cit., 288.

was largely tacit, for aesthetic standards are difficult to articulate, to defend, or explain in rational terms.

Tacit acceptance of how to behave and how not to behave was, therefore, a strong public school code. It was a code well in keeping with the gentleman ideal. 'I myself am not a gentleman', writes Simon Raven in the Introduction to his book, *The English Gentleman*. 'If I were, I would almost certainly not be writing this book, for one of the marks of a gentleman is that he seldom mentions the question of gentility, whether in application to others or to himself.'[1] Arthur Balfour, the political gentleman *par excellence*, would have agreed: 'I am more or less happy when being praised, not very uncomfortable when being abused; but I have moments of uneasiness when being explained.'[2]

Certainly the principle of tacitness applied to public school loyalties. Writing in 1881 about the hardships of the Westminster dormitory, the public school commentator, C. E. Pascoe, suggested that for boys to complain about the cold and discomfort would have been 'rank sacrilege . . . destructive of the most cherished traditions of the place'.[3] Pascoe wrote with his tongue in his cheek, but he appears to have meant it none the less. Perhaps one reason why Victorian public schoolboys so readily accepted freezing dormitories and primitive food was that these conditions gave greater proof of their House-and-School loyalty.

Closely connected with the device of tacitly accepted etiquette was a process which economists of the American automobile industry today call 'marginal product differentiation'. Although the Victorian period saw a basic standardization of public school institutions, it was also a time when each school strove to make itself a unique object of loyalty by elaborating its own language, folklore, and customs, and—for such schools as Eton and Winchester—making compulsory its own special variants of football. At several schools the 'new boy' had to take an examination testing his knowledge of the school and its unique-seeming traditions.[4] The effect of this exam was to crown the newcomer's

---

[1] Simon Raven, *The English Gentleman*, 9.
[2] Quoted by Andre Maurois, *King Edward and His Times*, 92.
[3] C. E. Pascoe, *Everyday Life in Our Public Schools* (1881), 108.
[4] Vivian Ogilvie, op. cit., 181.

period of orientation with an initiation rite; it presented the school as an awe-inspiring and complex institution whose details had to be learned rigorously by rote if the individual wished to fit in. The public schoolboy quickly learned to treat the pettiest custom, the quaintest Latin rhyme out of the traditional lore, as beautiful accoutrements in his worship of the school community.

There were other kinds of initiation rite, too. Many of these seemed to be designed to humble the individual, especially the newcomer, before the community. At Rugby, in the eighteen-eighties, a new boy had to stand on an old bedstead and sing before his assembled house. A fairly similar ritual occurred at Shrewsbury, where it was liable to be repeated throughout the new boy's first year. Among Eton Collegers of the eighteen-seventies, the standard initiating ceremony was somewhat rougher: the 'candidate' was obliged to retrieve an object from a high ventilator, and as he climbed he was often attacked by the mob from behind.

Winchester was more elaborate in its treatment of the new-comer. In some houses—the custom was dying out by 1900—the new boy had to climb the neighbouring St. Catherine's Hill up to a chalk pit; he had to run round a maze of paths marked out on the hill, take a stone from the pit, kiss it, and place it on Domum Cross, an 'x' marked in the chalk below a small precipice.[1] (It was all a somewhat contradictory rite, since Domum Cross was meant to mark the spot where the Wykehamist who wrote the Latin words to the school song fell, when he committed suicide by jumping off the precipice. According to school lore, the un-fortunate boy had been kept in during the holidays, and as a result the school song, *Dulce Domum*, is all about home. But that was well before the days of Victorian school spirit.)

Besides loyalty-inculcation, there was another incentive for humbling the newcomer. Many new boys came fresh from preparatory schools where they had headed the student hierarchy. Initiation rites dramatized their need to adjust to their new, low status as fags and juniors. But the deeper function of public school initiation rites was to honour the idea of an historic community.

[1] For all these initiation rites, see G. F. Lamb, op. cit., 23–26.

Even the rite which was cunningly and arbitrarily thought up by a prefect quickly acquired the force of custom and appeared to stem from the society as a whole. In fact, many initiation rites were pre-Arnold in origin.

Like Edmund Burke, the public schools posed tradition and historic institutions as time-tested oracles of wisdom. Against these the individual cut a puny figure. Only in so far as he contributed to the community and deferred to tradition did his actions carry meaning. If he failed to contribute, if he failed to defer, he was liable to be scorned by his fellows and occasionally even punished by the prefects. At Eton, despite its reputation for accommodating eccentric minorities, the junior who showed a consistently disloyal attitude was considered to be committing an offence, the offence of 'generality'.[1] At many public schools it was enough to call an object quite simply a 'School institution' or part of 'The School Tradition' to give it the highest seal of approval.

The public schools, in short, fanned group loyalty by making the individual value himself only as part of the group and as part of an historical continuum. If the antiquity of many school institutions—e.g. the officer training corps—was really quite recent, this only went to prove Burke's point that the requirements of continuity can and must allow for change—as long as it is gradual change. In fact, public school opinion sometimes showed a readiness to forget that not all facets of the community stemmed from time immemorial. A colourful portrait of this tendency occurs in a novel, *The Lanchester Tradition*, written by G. F. Bradby, son of the headmaster of Haileybury, and himself a housemaster at Rugby, just before the First World War. Bradby tells the story of a new headmaster's battle to institute much-needed reforms against the opposition of older housemasters and dons. As authority for maintaining things as they are, the conservative opposition constantly cites the Lanchester Tradition— the school Way personified by Dr. Lanchester, the school's revered second founder. To his amazement, a lone dissenter on the staff who respects the new headmaster unearths the

[1] Cyril Connolly, *Enemies of Promise*, 180.

completely forgotten fact that Lanchester, far from worshipping tradition, was a revolutionary who sacked one-third of the boys and two of the senior masters.

The belief that the historic community possessed a wisdom of its own amounted at times to a mystical animism. Sir James Barrie teased the public schools about just such a belief during a speech that he made in 1924. Apparently, he said, the schools owned a 'mysterious something [that] oozes out of the historic old walls'. In reply *The Times* claimed solemnly that the 'something' came from outside the individual; it was 'non-analysable' and non-intellectual, and it induced boys *to distrust their individual intellects and do an unselfish job* (italics mine). Shortly thereafter, Cyril Alington—headmaster of Shrewsbury 1908–16, of Eton 1916–33—wrote that this 'something', the public school spirit, came from 'clubable' living, and that it existed as early as 1870.[1] Decades before this exchange, Edward Thring of Uppingham had made his own tribute to the historic community. School spirit and observation of school tradition were, he said, an important factor in public school education, a force which 'enables the meanest to feel that they are part of a great living organism of life. . . '.[2]

Burke's concept of a community wisdom was reflected in the very name that Winchester gave to its body of custom and etiquette. The Wykehamist term 'Notions' included everything from details of school architecture and tradition covered by the new boy's 'Notions exam' to unwritten rules of behaviour. (Thus, for a junior to leave his coat button undone out of doors was a 'bad Notion'.) It is interesting that the word 'notion' usually denotes a thought, an intelligent idea. What is more, a notion *comes* to an individual: it wafts upon him as if from an external source.

Edmund Burke, however, is not the only political thinker that the public school community brings to mind. In many ways it reminds one of Jean-Jacques Rousseau and his preference for the small, simple society. A pungent—and here particularly relevant

---

[1] Edward Mack, *Public Schools and British Opinion Since 1860*, 401.
[2] Edward Thring, *The Theory and Practice of Teaching* (1883), 257–8.

—description of the Rousseauan ideal appears in *The Political Tradition of the West* by Frederick Watkins; it could very nearly pass muster as the portrait of a Victorian public school.

As Watkins puts it, Rousseau believed that

the problem of reconciling individual and group action had been solved in the life of earlier communities. Modern anthropologists know that the rigid training to which people are subjected in many primitive communities tends to produce a high degree of social integration. By favouring the development of socially acceptable personality traits, this training makes it possible for most individuals to accept their traditional roles with a minimum of personal conflict. . . . Educated from earliest youth in a framework of common traditional values, the citizens of these communities were able to work together for the attainment of common objectives *without feeling that their desires were being sacrificed in the process* (italics mine).

Rousseau's legislator could not hope to win the consent of ordinary men by a process of rational demonstration. His hold over society was based in part on the magnetic attraction of his own personality and in part on conscious fraud. . . . Respect for the law, moreover, should be perpetuated by a host of impressive ceremonies and customs which, however meaningless in themselves, would give the people an unquestioning devotion to the way of life laid down for them.[1]

The advantage that the *small* community enjoys in securing loyalty is its nearness to the individual, its ability to appear as a living thing rather than a remote and abstract one. It was the same advantage which Alexis de Tocqueville portrayed in the aristocratic class, *vis-à-vis* the whole nation.[2] In the small community, furthermore, it is difficult for the individual to seek freedom in anonymity and to defy the customs that the majority hold sacred. Every person counts for much relative to everyone else; the pettiest irregularity may be seen as subversive to social stability. Those public schools, therefore, which divided themselves into fairly autonomous houses, magnified group loyalties still further: first, loyalty was given a more vivid object, and secondly, the group's surveillance of the individual was intensified.

Similarly, public schools which severely limited individual

[1] Frederick Watkins, *The Political Tradition of the West*, 96, 110–11.
[2] Alexis de Tocqueville, *Democracy in America*, Vol. II, 105.

privacy were in a specially favourable position for inducing group loyalties and co-operation. About the effects of dormitory and study-hall living, Bernard Darwin speculates in *The English Public School*.

The more boys live in their own rooms, the more intimate, as one imagines, will be their talk. . . . On the other hand, the more they live in common rooms, the more they will be likely to restrict themselves to general topics, such as the obvious one of the doings of the house team, and by so doing incline to a more passionate local patriotism.[1]

The same observation was made recently to me by the Head-master of Marlborough, John Dancy. In one large study-hall for junior boys, reported Dancy, it had been noticed that newcomers rapidly lost any individual hobbies that they had when they first entered. Such, at any rate, was the tendency. It might also be claimed that the collective living conditions of the public school inhibited the expression of individual emotions which threatened to challenge or replace the group spirit. Even more than the British nation as a whole, the public schoolboy was both reserved and sentimental. Emotional expression he quietly reserved for the group; in other, more personal spheres he cultivated the 'thick skin'.

In the case of the public school, communal living proved a specially useful way for obtaining group loyalties, since the latter were instilled so largely by custom. Lack of privacy meant that the minority who might have resisted irrational appeals to tradition and good taste were confronted abruptly and constantly by the majority, those who are always content to follow convention. If the public school dwarfed the individual against the historic community and made the latter a value in itself, it only did so via public opinion. In this sense the system was totalitarian, playing almost subliminally on the individual's very desires.

What the public school inculcation of loyalty really amounted to was a sort of 'education by symbol'. The school community symbolized whatever group would claim the public schoolboy's

[1] Bernard Darwin, *The English Public School*, 88.

45

energies in later life. Once his capacity for loyalty had been developed by the school and its psychological devices, the individual was expected to transfer that loyalty to his adult group. To an extent the transfer probably worked for any group: a business man recently told me that in his experience—twenty-five years in the Far East—Englishmen were far more apt than Americans to stay with one company and regard it as 'The House'. But the public school community symbolized most aptly groups which boasted strong traditions and which somehow exuded a magical aura—the House of Commons, the military regiment, the nation itself.

In the process of transferring loyalty, however, two developments often occurred. First, the individual came to value loyalty for its own sake, forgetting to question the worth of its object. Secondly, the community, the group, or the political system hypnotized the public school graduate until he no longer viewed them as instruments serving the individual and/or spiritual ends. Survival of the institution itself became the ultimate goal.

Any totalitarian tendencies, however, that the public schools might have engendered accompanied counter-tendencies also fostered by the schools. It has already been noted that the ethic of self-restraint ameliorated the worship of the community. But the notion of loyalty itself seemed, at least, to require individual freedom. For one thing, the custom and etiquette that instilled group loyalties were carried by public opinion. However tyrannical the latter may sometimes have been, the public school graduate did take away with him the belief that loyalty and co-operation should be voluntary. As often as not he proved the sincerity of this belief by unpaid service as Justice of the Peace or chairman of the village council, thereby supporting the principle of local self-government.

In the second place, public school loyalty entailed moral obligation to inferior social ranks as well as deference to those in senior office and co-operation with colleagues. If the rough-and-tumble monasticism of boarding school life bred neither sympathy for fine shades of feeling nor great understanding of other social classes, the public school experience did pose responsibility and fairness as the hallmarks of a ruling class. When the First World War came along, public school graduates surprised some of their critics by their capacity as officers to get along well with their men.[1]

Admittedly, however, public school values stressed individual values less than the nation as a whole did. The same might be true of many school systems for, as Emile Durkheim suggests, one function of education is to socialize the individual, to temper his egoist drives with the discipline that social harmony demands.[2] If Englishmen accepted an education system that paid less attention to freedom than most systems did, it may have been because they felt they could afford it: the security of the seas had given them a chance to evolve a stable society which saw little incompatibility between deference to social rank, and respect for individual freedom and its legal safeguards.

Both in structure and behaviour, British government placed— as it still does—a special premium on deference to official rank and on loyalty. The fact that Cabinet members held parliamentary seats and included among their number the Leader of the House imposed considerable discipline on backbenchers of the party in office. Parliamentary procedure as well as the ultimate power of dissolution strengthened the Executive hand: Government legislation took precedence over 'Private Members' Bills, and in Question Periods the rules forbade cross-examination of ministers.

Faced with a government party that voted virtually as one man on all major issues, Her Majesty's Loyal Opposition could not afford to show much less unity in its own ranks. Here again, the salaried status of the Leader of the Opposition and the less formal entity of a Shadow Cabinet proclaimed the importance of hierarchy and attention to party unity. In both parties, the rank-and-file M.P. usually knew that his constituents would only vote for him if they wanted his leaders to form a government; and this realization encouraged him to support his side's official programme.

In all parties, too, as in the public school, topography played

[1] Edward Mack, op. cit., 307.   [2] Emile Durkheim, *Education and Sociology*, 71.

47

its part in compelling discipline. As Christopher Hollis, the Conservative M.P., has pointed out, the Member of Parliament 'has to sit in proximity to the members of [his] own party. Nothing is more unpleasant than to sit side by side day after day with people who think that you are behaving like a traitor.' Hollis goes so far as to say that 'this motive more than any other' binds political loyalties.[1] Party discipline, in other words, rests at least partly on the subtle pressures of group opinion. To the extent that this is so, the M.P. may think that his loyalties are completely *voluntary* more often than is the case.

Although hierarchy and discipline characterize all parties, it is generally recognized that Labour has been less successful than the Conservatives at maintaining the unity required for electoral success. 'At no period in the [Labour] party's history has internal strife not thriven', wrote Bernard Crick in 1960.[2] He went on to attribute the troubles of Labour not to doctrinal conflict so much as to the clash of different interests within the party structure. One might also cite the fact that the Labour parliamentary leader lacks the authority over his national party enjoyed by the Conservative leader.[3]

But this is not the whole story. The parliamentary Conservative party has also come to represent different interest-groups, farmers as well as manufacturers, small professional men with fixed salaries, stockbrokers, shopkeepers, and elderly widows. From an economic viewpoint particularly, such groups obviously do not always want the same things. Yet the fact remains that a common school background—public school, Oxford and Cambridge—has helped facilitate communication and understanding between Conservative M.P.s representing these groups. In his memoirs, L. S. Amery spoke of the relief he felt when a Conservative Cabinet replaced coalition government in 1922. One-party government meant that the Cabinet again shared 'a common tradition and instinctive way of looking at things'.[4] In the

---

[1] Christopher Hollis, 'Parliament and the Establishment' in *The Establishment*, ed. by Hugh Thomas, 176.
[2] Bernard Crick, letter to *The Reporter*, Washington, 10 November 1960.
[3] Carter, *The Office of Prime Minister*, 135.
[4] L. S. Amery, *My Political Life*, II, 241.

same context Amery reported that the new Cabinet contained five Old Harrovians—a footnote reminiscent of Sir Edward Grey who once wished aloud that all foreign statesmen could have gone to public schools and there learned a common set of ground-rules.[1]

By contrast with the Tories, the parliamentary Labour Party has had to face not only the potential clash of different interests but the predominance of attitudes that make such conflict real and exacerbate it. These attitudes are somewhat different from the public school order of values, generally preferred by the Conservatives. To quote Christopher Hollis again—'the Labour Party thinks of itself as a party of a creed and therefore, even when it has not got a creed, it likes to behave like one. . . . The Conservative Party, on the other hand, thinks of itself rather as a regiment than as a Church.'[2] The Tories, in other words, lay greater stress than do the Socialists on discipline and loyalty, while the Socialists have tended to overlay even interest-disputes with the bitterness of moral conflict.

To generalize still further, it is safe to say that many Conservatives have been inclined, within moral limits, to view politics as a game to be won—and won by team-spirit.[3] There was much in the background of Conservative M.P.s, especially those M.P.s who came from public schools, to justify enjoyment of the political system for its own sake. The party, hardly less than the public school, was an historic community exacting deference from the individual; victory for the community became a good in itself. At the same time, the concept of politics as a game, however serious a game, relieved any fanaticism that a strong group spirit might have encouraged. Sir Edward Grey, awaiting the Turks' reply to an ultimatum and impatient because he wanted to get away to his Fallodon estate, provides a very caricature of the gentlemanly amateur in politics.[4]

His opponents would have called it cynicism. But in a democracy the enjoyment of the political system for its own sake was

[1] Andre Maurois, op. cit., 107.
[2] Christopher Hollis, op. cit., 179–80.
[3] cf. J. M. Keynes, *Essays on Biography*—essay on Bonar Law.
[4] Andre Maurois, op. cit., 107.

not incompatible with a nineteenth-century tradition of Tory philanthropy and *noblesse oblige*. For the Conservative, the requirements of electoral victory happily coincided with public school respect for public opinion as the carrier of custom and voice of the historic community.

Within the party caucus, too, parliamentary leaders usually did something to match rank-and-file loyalty by displaying sensitivity to the general consensus. The idea of the consensus, as an informal influence on policy, is particularly vital to the whole British parliamentary system. Since discipline deprives the non-ministerial M.P. of a formally legislative function, he can only affect government policy by contributing to the deliberative function of the whole House. And this deliberative function, for its part, only influences policy when ministers show 'prefectorial' responsiveness to the consensus of their followers.[1] This is not to say that Cabinets always obey the 'feeling of the House' nor that a predominant consensus is always identifiable: far from it. But the very fact that ministers must spend hours sitting in Parliament exposes them constantly to backbencher points of view. It is the minister's recognized job, moreover, to tell his Civil Service department what measures public opinion—as reflected by Parliament—will not stand.

The consensus principle also crops up in the British Cabinet system. Unlike the United States President who may sometimes ignore or repudiate his department heads, the Prime Minister must show some respect to the collective opinion of his Cabinet, whose leading men are successful vote-getters with assured seats in Parliament. Again, however, note the voluntary element. With voluntary co-operation made an ideal, the Prime Minister seldom takes a formal Cabinet vote, thereby hardening the lines of disagreement.[2] Instead, he can show flexibility in following the consensus: where two opinions claim fairly equal support numerically, he may select the one that will arouse less intransigent opposition.[3] At other times he may go against the Cabinet majority, feeling that in the long run his solution will prove acceptable.

[1] Ivor Jennings, *Cabinet Government*, 443, 445.
[2] Ibid., 258.
[3] Carter, op. cit., 207–9. Morrison, *Government and Parliament*, 5–6.

The pursuit of voluntary co-operation for its own sake appears at its most vivid, perhaps, in the memoirs of L. S. Amery, a man who was able to frame his Conservatism in unusually theoretical terms. As Colonial Secretary from 1924 to 1929, Amery believed that public opinion at home and abroad could respond to 'the idea of Empire production and purchase; of the Empire as a co-operative venture. Above all as a co-operative venture . . . of vivid human interest as well as of practical promise.'[1] During the days of coalition government, Amery saw the Imperial idea as a way to 'kindle the imagination of working men', a better road to national unity than the 'narrow insular anti-socialism' of the Unionist leaders.[2]

The co-operative ideal, of course, has not always inspired enlightened practices. Amery himself claimed that by 1922 the wartime coalition government had forgotten constructive economic planks in order to preserve the agreement needed for its own survival.[3] And the political system was always liable to produce men like Stanley Baldwin whose concern with national and party unity deterred them from forging constructive policies that might have divided the nation. As Robert Blake argued in his essay, 'Baldwin and the Right', it would have been difficult to 'sell' a strong defence policy to the British public during the early nineteen-thirties, but the point was that Baldwin never really tried. He was 'never a man to take an awkward fence till he had to'[4]—although he himself did see some of the dangers of a weak military position. 'Don't rock the boat' has always tended, in varying proportions, to characterize the British party mind, and especially the Tory mind.

If the facts of parliamentary life placed a premium on loyalty, discipline, and the spirit of co-operation, the position of the bureaucracy demanded the same attributes in the Civil Servant. Men of the bureaucracy's management level, the Administrative

[1] L. S. Amery, op. cit., II, 352.
[2] Ibid., 241.
[3] Ibid., 226.
[4] John Raymond (ed.), *The Age of Baldwin*. cf. Lord Salter, *Memoirs of a Public Servant*, 249.

Class, holding lifetime positions, had to advise department heads who came and then left every few years. Confronted with a new minister holding political views that privately he might dislike, the senior civil servant faced the temptation of obstructing government policy. In fact, the Civil Service maintained a public school-type tradition of emotional detachment and deference to senior office.[1] There was little likelihood of the bureaucrat openly justifying disloyalty to his chief on grounds of community interest, since he recognized that public opinion should interpret the latter and that his political chief was supposed, at any rate, to represent public opinion. All in all, these attitudes were specially desirable in an organization where slow promotions and a well-defined hierarchy required a strong co-operative spirit.

The colonial services seem to have laid special emphasis on teamwork. Outnumbered by huge, alien populations, imperial administrators felt a strong desire for racial solidarity—exemplified in the British Clubs—and mutual reliability during rebellion. In his book on the East India College at Haileybury, a college run on public school lines, A. Lawrence Lowell suggested that, when the Indian Mutiny broke upon them, the men of Haileybury benefited from an *esprit de corps* founded in their youth.[2] Leonard Barnes, some time of the Colonial Office, noted in 1937 that 'the Public School spirit is greatly valued in the colonial service, and it is a matter of conscious policy to ensure that the supplies of it shall be constantly replenished'. For an explanation of what the 'Public School spirit' entailed, Barnes referred his readers to the Warren Fisher Report on the colonial service. The Report listed as desired qualities 'vision, high ideals of service, fearless devotion to duty born of a sense of responsibility and, *above all*, the team spirit'.[3]

In his concern with historical continuity and his consequent attitude towards the individual, the bureaucrat had some affinity —if modified—with the ethos of public school England. H. E. Dale, the analyst of British bureaucracy and himself a former

[1] H. E. Dale, *The Higher Civil Service*, 81.
[2] A. Lawrence Lowell, *The Colonial Civil Service: The East India College at Haileybury*, 335–6.
[3] W. A. Robson (ed.), *The British Civil Servant* (1937), 245.

Principal Assistant Secretary, has noted a certain difference in this regard between the English Civil Servant and the Labour minister of working-class origins. Whereas the latter feels that 'the present and the individual are self-existent', the Civil Servant sees them more as part of a continuum of history and even as 'cells' of an organization. The writer attributes the second viewpoint not only to occupational background but to an education focusing very much on history and tradition.[1]

The Civil Servant, in other words, has displayed somewhat the same sense of historic community that we observed in the Tory Party and, most strongly of all, in the public school. To say that education created this historic sense would be fatuous: the nature of English *law*, its piecemeal development from precedent to precedent, suggests that reliance on traditional wisdom is a deep-rooted element in the British social character. Yet the fact remains that the public schools did their bit to a social characteristic: they cemented it, tempered it a little with ideals of restraint and moderation, and left it fundamentally unquestioned.

[1] H. E. Dale, op. cit., 139.

Chapter 5

Dignified Government

In their private affairs, the English try to be undemonstrative, but in public manners they do what the drill sergeant says. They march down the years to the twirl of the bandmaster's silver stick and with bags and bags of swank. —JAMES MORRIS, *New York Times Magazine*, 13 November 1960

Nearly all governments seek dignity by creating for themselves a magical aura, but in this Britain has gone further than most. Her elaboration of ceremonial and ritual, her attention to the style of political command serve three closely related functions. First, the distinctive bearing they give the ruler helps him to earn the respect of others for what he is and how he acts as well as merely what he does. Secondly, they channel men's passions into communal means of expression—'public manners', and pageantry identified with the State. Like the manners of private life, public ceremonial replaces spontaneity with the aesthetic appeal of a formalized style. Hence, as James Morris says, the English are privately undemonstrative; when they do want glamour, they are content to follow the drill sergeant. Equally important, the Englishman can find emotional outlets in an elaboration of form rather than substantive and possibly violent action.

The third function of ceremonial is a symbolic one, centred—at national level—on the Crown. Symbolizing morality both in family life and in politics[1] the Crown faces the community as a religious institution;[2] it hallows the past and subtly compels the orderly succession of power; it subordinates the ruler to the State. Under a constitutional monarchy, no executive can very well say, '*l'etat; c'est moi*'. It is no coincidence, in this respect, that the

[1] Walter Bagehot, *The English Constitution*, 35, 47.
[2] Edmund Burke, *Reflections on the Revolution in France*, 102, 111–12.

Serjeant-at-Arms, the House of Commons' own disciplinary officer, was originally a court official. Today he symbolizes the self-restraint induced by hallowed institutions of government—not only the Houses of Parliament with their almost living atmosphere of dignity, but the monarchy itself.

Public school government employed magic in all three functions. First, the special differences which bolstered prefectorial authority included aesthetic distinctions of dress—the right to wear a gaily coloured waistcoat, to sport an unrolled umbrella, to wear a boater at a rakish angle—as much as more useful advantages like a special study or the service of fags. The very fact, possibly, that a privilege lacked immediate utility invested it with a slightly mysterious property; if it could not be *used* it must surely be a symbol of something greater.

In the second place, school tradition made much of community ritual. Some of it was carried by great events like the Harrow Speeches and Eton's Procession of Boats. Other ceremonies occurred more frequently, as, for example, the rite at Westminster exempting from fagging duties the two students who stood top respectively of the first- and second-year forms.[1]

Finally, Chapel performed for the public school some of the function that the Crown performed for the nation: there it stood, a symbol of 'Character', a monument to the community's supposed rebirth in Arnoldian morality. Supported by an array of architectural emblems—gates, walls, arches, and plaques commemorating school heroes from the past—Chapel symbolized the historical continuum and provided a focal point of loyalty. One has only to read Sir Henry Newbolt's jingoist poem, *Clifton Chapel*, to realize how emotional a focal point it could indeed become. In the public school Chapel, wrote a Harrow headmaster, the school 'learns that it has a corporate life; there it stands face to face with its chief, and there the lessons of brotherhood can be enforced'.[2] On a more worldly level, Chapel services at several public schools provided splendidly solemn occasions

[1] C. E. Pascoe, *Everyday Life in Our Public Schools*, 1881, 'Westminster' by W. A. Peck, 115.
[2] J. E. C. Welldon (former Headmaster of Harrow), 'Schoolmasters', in E. H. Pitcairn, *Unwritten Laws and Ideals of Active Careers*.

for a leadership ritual in which senior prefects only trooped in after everyone else was seated.

How did British government actually perform the three functions of magic? With regard to distinctive style, a public school accent and bearing helped a man win promotion in most branches of public service. Not only did public school life breed self-assurance and a relaxed air of command, but the public schoolboy's speech set him apart from others. Compared with the regional accents of most non-public schoolboys, the English spoken by the cross-regional clientele of boarding schools carried a cosmopolitan flavour. It was different; and, by the aesthetic standards of the English gentleman, it was superior. This was not surprising. For the essence of the gentleman-amateur ideal was to attach low prestige to specialization, whether technical specialization or regional 'specialization'. A public school accent was the aesthetic counterpart of the gentleman's emphasis on the well-rounded man. (To talk about accents at all, of course, is highly ungentlemanly.)

Among the different branches of government, the public schoolboy's accent and social poise probably carried most weight with the Foreign Office;[1] but if so, the military ran it a close second. Many units engaged in heavy rounds of social entertaining and, besides, the military profession wanted men who could inspire emotionally as well as make rational decisions. In the older services particularly, the prescription for finding men who could inspire was to insist on 'officer qualities', attributes which included a crisp, confident manner and an air of command. Such attributes were not to be confined to office-hours; an officer should be a leader instinctively and at all times.

Other spheres of government, too, rewarded the gentlemanly graces. During the nineteen-twenties, an oral interview that weighed these qualities heavily, though not exclusively, counted for about one-sixth of the Civil Service entrance examination.[2] In Parliament, where ministers were promoted from the ranks of debaters, a compelling style of speech, tuned to an educated

[1] See Chap. 2.   [2] Herman Finer, *The British Civil Service*, 101.

audience, helped the young M.P. to qualify for future, executive office. As the only legislative-relations men for their department, the Cabinet minister and his parliamentary secretary had to pay special attention to *how* they acted, quite aside from *what* they did.

Preoccupation with style, of course, was not without its political hazards. Just as Sir William Gilbert's aristocracy 'did nothing in particular and did it very well', so the gentlemanly politician of more recent years has been sometimes tempted into a policy of elegant inaction. For one thing, concern with manners and style may simply distract the leader from concentrating on substantive action. For another, the politician with charm and a magic touch may persuade others, as well as himself, that he is doing much more than he really is. Lord Salter made this charge about Sir Thomas Inskip, the co-ordinating minister responsible for Food Defence plans, in 1936.

Massive in figure, impressive in delivery, imperturbable in manner; no strength in the attack disturbed his equanimity. He was helped by his transparent sincerity. Others might be suspected of deceiving their audience, but not Sir Thomas. . . . He could look with frank and fearless gaze at any prospect, however appalling—and fail to see it.[1]

L. S. Amery made a milder, but somewhat similar point about Herbert Asquith, arguing that his great parliamentary gifts enabled him to avoid real decisions over the Irish question.[2]

The same observation about the potential conflict between style and achievement, has even been extended to the field of sport. 'One of the chief weaknesses of British sport', writes the outspoken runner, Christopher Brasher, 'has been, and still is, the importance which is attached to style. In athletics we have the most stylish hurdlers in the world, but unfortunately they can't run fast enough between the hurdles. A coach at Henley can hold up his head proudly if his crew go over the course smoothly and rhythmically at 32 strokes per minute, even if they have been beaten by three lengths by a foreign crew, bashing along at 36 to 38 strokes.'[3]

[1] Arthur Salter, *Memoirs of a Public Servant*, 255–6.
[2] L. S. Amery, *My Political Life*, Vol. II, 458.   [3] *Observer*, 1 July 62.

It should not be thought, however, that impressive style and energetic action are intrinsically opposed. One tendency of public school life, in fact, was to encourage vigorous activity, but to cloak it in a style of leisureliness. To sit in Parliament and at the same time to run a department, the minister had to show considerable appetite for long hours of hard work. Admittedly, there are different kinds of hard work: maintaining the Government's dignity at Question Time and supervising a department do not *necessarily* involve dynamic policy-making. None the less, it obviously requires great energies of mind.

With regard to the second function of magic, the channelling of emotion into formal occasions, British public life at all levels made great use of pomp and circumstance, from the Lord Mayor's Banquet to local processions of town aldermen. For its part the State maintained a whole medley of ceremonial, 'Changing the Guard', the Opening of Parliament, and so on. The House of Commons was particularly prone to the use of magic. Before the First World War, the new M.P. had to pay his respects to the House by undergoing a short initiation rite: five steps and bow to the Speaker, five steps and bow again, three steps more and bow at the table, take the oath, sign the book, and shake the Speaker's hand.

As the last example shows, the same magical device may serve both to direct emotions into communal expression and to symbolize certain values, especially the value of self-restraint. The same device, in other words, may perform both the second and third political functions of magic. Thus, the initiation rite undergone by new M.P.s provided a colourful spectacle and, at the same time, dramatized the idea that legislators should venerate historic institutions. The Crown itself did likewise, providing spectacular events and all the while comprising a moral symbol. In both functions, the monarchy benefited from close ties with the Church of England: the Coronation service, for example, simultaneously stirred patriotic emotions and invested the monarch with a religious aura.[1]

Throughout this book it has been suggested that public school

[1] cf. Christopher Dawson, 'Tradition of a Christian Monarchy', *The Month*, May 1953.

authority and the British Constitution alike relied heavily on aesthetic pressures to control the individual. Self-restraint, no less than public duty, was made a matter of 'good form' and backed by etiquette. For this reason it is impossible to make a sharp distinction between the manners that made the ruler responsible and the manners which gave him a magical air of authority, a *differentness*. Manners of courtesy and duty, in other words, were inseparable from manners of dignity and command. Both rested on emotions which involved the mystical and the beautiful.

Like public pageant and ceremonial, the elegant manners of the gentlemanly leader emphasize the group above the individual. Manners restrain spontaneous demonstrations of feeling and put in their place custom-decreed channels of expression. They tend, therefore, to collectivize emotion. Not only is it their role to effect harmony among individuals, but the criteria of what makes good manners depend, almost by definition, on group standards of taste. These characteristics of manners probably apply in any society, but they are obviously most potent where manners are most emphasized. Certainly the group nature of stylistic elegance has been noted in other fields than in politics. To cite Christopher Brasher again—'many of our top [British] tennis coaches place too much emphasis on a classical style without regard to the individual's temperament and natural ability'.[1]

As in athletics, so in politics and social behaviour. The whole tenor of gentlemanly manners was to stress group harmony and co-operation by the same token that it inhibited individual, private demonstration. The courtesies that the gentleman performed were courtesies of duty and command; to a much lesser extent were they courtesies of intimate friendliness and emotional warmth. Nor—to use David Riesman's term—was the public schoolboy-gentleman figure 'other-directed': he practised manners less to win the approval of others than because his manners were both the obligation and distinction of his class.

At first this may appear to be a contradiction. Already we have described at some length the degree to which group opinion dominated public school behaviour. Who, one might ask, could

[1] *Observer*, 1 July 62.

be more 'other-directed' than the schoolboy who shied away from walking to class alone or the Tory M.P. who voted in line because he didn't want his benchmates to think him a traitor? In a sense such a question is valid, but only in the sense that nearly all men are partly other-directed: nearly all seek the approval of their peers and are swayed by their opinions and judgements.

The fact remains that the Victorian public schoolboy was basically tradition-directed and community-directed rather than other-directed. There is more to this distinction than semantic quibble. One of the character-traits that William Whyte describes in *The Organization Man*, his analysis of American industry's professional manager, is the quality of *rootlessness*. The 'organization man' is not an individualist entrepreneur, he conforms to group style and opinions; he worships the idea of group harmony, group thinking, and group effort; he co-ordinates rather than commands, he is a good committeeman and he does not pound his desk. He is, in short, other-directed. He seeks *belonging* in social organization, the corporation or the club, and like the public schoolboy he places a high premium on social co-operation. Yet—and here lies the difference—he frequently does not forge deep-rooted loyalties to one company. 'According to a study by the management-consultant firm Booz, Allen, & Hamilton', reports Whyte, 'there are now twenty-nine more personnel changes per hundred management jobs than before the war, and a great part of the increase is caused by switches from one company to another.' Whyte goes on to observe that a 'hefty majority' of businessmen who graduated from college in the nineteen-thirties have changed jobs two or three times.[1]

By contrast with this picture of the industrial organization man, the public schoolboy identified himself strongly with his community, quite aside from his bonds with other men in that community. Like the organization man he followed group opinion, but he did so at least partly because group opinion and group taste represented the community and its traditions. These traditions he largely internalized: they became internal obligations.

[1] William H. Whyte, *The Organization Man*, 153 (Penguin ed.).

The public schoolboy felt *obliged* to co-operate as an act of 'good taste', just as he felt *obliged* to honour the community. He frequently enjoyed performing such obligations, but the psychology behind them was somewhat different from the psychology of 'togetherness', the organization man's constant quest for friendship and personal approval.

When the public schoolboy left his school community, he carried part of it away with him. He might acquire new loyalties to new communities, but these did not replace the old. The result was a sense of belonging and a self-reliance: a Royal Canadian Mounted Police officer told L. S. Amery in 1928 that British old public schoolboys made the best personnel for 'single-handed jobs'.[1] In a way, the self-assurance bequeathed by the public school to its members resembled the certainties generated by the aristocratic family. Members of both types of community grew up amid assumptions of social superiority. Such assumptions carried all the more weight for being handed down from generation to generation. It was superiority *conferred*—and conferred by tradition—rather than superiority individually earned.

This brings us back to the question of style. A prime assumption of the gentleman was the notion that outer actions could strengthen inner faith. It was an assumption that seems to have contained some truth: by all indications the style of effortlessness did bolster self-assurance, and attention to prescribed courtesies did enhance moral self-esteem. What is more, the following of a set etiquette, ordained not by the individual but by community tradition and group standards of taste, increased a man's sense of social belonging. As Erich Fromm has pointed out, the lone Englishman in the jungle who still 'dressed for dinner' could, by so doing, feel at one with his home community.[2] And when the etiquette followed was that of a traditionally superior class—in this case, the gentry—so much the better for the individual's confidence. The best illustration of this psychological process is the highly apocryphal story of the old public schoolboy caught by cannibals. He is placed in the pot, but he has last moments of

[1] L. S. Amery, op. cit., 457.
[2] Erich Fromm, *Fear of Freedom*, 17 (Routledge paperback ed.).

happiness when he sees that his enemies have 'bad' table manners.[1]

Behind the gentleman's predilection with manners and style lay an emphasis on *harmony*. Harmony has both an aesthetic and a moral value, for gentlemanly standards of excellence—like the *ching* ideal in China and, perhaps, the Athenian notion of *arete*—make little real distinction between the beautiful and the good. In theory, beautiful manners were meant to symbolize moral virtue, but in most gentleman's minds the two became inextricably fused.

The value of harmony, then, implied both beauty and good-ness; and it applied equally to individual character and to society as a whole. In its social application, the emphasis on harmony implied moderation, compromise, and self-restraint. Politically, it seemed best suited to a minimal concept of government, an outlook which saw the ruler as guardian rather than innovator. New ideas and methods nearly always appear to disrupt, how-ever much they may serve the long-run interests of social har-mony. Certainly the guardian outlook on government was well in tune with the public school prefect's style of leadership: the prefect's main task was to keep order rather than initiate major new schemes. On the other hand, the value of harmony did encourage political flexibility—piecemeal adjustment to changing factors and circumstances. When new forces arose to threaten the old order—in the Empire, forces of nationalism; at home, forces of democracy—the prevailing instinct of British leadership was to accommodate and contain rather than suppress. On those oc-casions when the guardians of harmony did turn to the sword, as in Ireland, the period of bloodshed, if not of bitterness, was relatively short. There was nothing like the protraction of conflict which characterizes the French Union today.

On a personal plane, the value of harmony meant gentle-ness: the curbing of base and selfish passions, the 'stiff upper lip Britisher'. As we have suggested before, it was a quality very much bound up with the amateur ideal of the well-rounded

---

[1] A story told me in a crowded lift by George Baron of the London University Institute of Education.

man, for it strove to secure moderation by balancing virtues and aptitudes against one another. 'Respectfulness, without the rules of propriety' (good form), 'becomes laborious bustle', wrote a Chinese sage on gentlemanliness, '. . . carefulness [becomes] timidity; straightforwardness [becomes] rudeness.'[1] Ideally, the well-rounded man sought harmony in what the Chinese called *ching*, a balance between fine sentiment and classically educated reason.

[1] *Lun Yu*, Part xiv, Chap. 29.

Chapter 6

The Amateur Ideal

The curriculum of the Victorian public school reflected traditional gentry prejudices about education. Education, for the gentleman, meant general education: only people who were not gentlemen went in for practical, vocational training at secondary school level. In fact, the possession of general culture was a traditional status-symbol, signifying that a man had leisure and wealth to pursue learning for its own sake. Two centuries before, John Locke had written,

Knowledge and science in general are the business only of those who are at ease and leisure, (who) by the industry and parts of their ancestors have been set free from a constant drudge to their backs and bellies.[1]

Yet, when Civil Service reform challenged the public school curriculum by setting up 'open competition' examinations, statesmen and educators alike were quick to argue that for would-be rulers a general education made the best 'vocational' training. In his 1854 report on the Civil Service, Thomas Macaulay asserted that general studies, far more than a specialized education, invigorated, opened, and enriched the mind.[2]

Historian, essayist, poet, M.P., and Indian administrator, Macaulay was an all-rounder himself if ever there was one, but like public school headmasters, he tended to equate general education with classical education. From the days when Latin was the unifying tongue of educated men, knowledge of the classics had carried 'snob value' as a sign of gentility. This property the winds of Civil Service reform did nothing to destroy.[3] Although the competitive examinations offered a choice of other subjects

[1] J. D. Kingsley, *Representative Bureaucracy*, 70.
[2] Herman Finer, *The British Civil Service*, 21.
[3] Vivian Ogilvie, *The English Public School*, 179.

64

besides Latin and Greek, they did not dispel the traditional notion that classical education and a broad education were synonymous. A majority of successful Administrative Class candidates came from Oxford and Cambridge where classical studies were still considered the most important field. The result was that Latin, and to a lesser extent Greek, remained the king subjects in public school education—a specialist bias that lasted until well past the First World War.

In 1884, Eton employed twenty-eight classics masters, six mathematics masters, no modern language teachers, no scientists, and one historian.[1] This classical preponderance was fairly typical, especially of the older public schools. By 1900, admittedly, most leading public schools had extended their curricula to languages and—partly under the pressure of Boer War reversals and German industrial competition[2]—to science. At Uppingham, Edward Thring (headmaster 1853–87), introduced fine arts,[3] and in many schools the Chapel became the music master's stronghold. Among the establishments founded in the nineteenth century, schools like Cheltenham and Rossall created strong modern departments.[4] Nevertheless, in academic matters as in social organization the newer boarding schools tended to imitate the older few; and so the classics remained supreme, both in hours devoted to them and in the weighting of marks.[5] In 1905, classics masters at Eton still formed over half the teaching staff, and entrance examinations to many schools made Latin the most important subject.

The treatment of the classics themselves hardly fulfilled the ideal of a broad, liberal arts education. For all, save the very brightest students, classical studies usually meant long hours of translation that left little time to consider literary content and meaning.[6] 'They laboriously toiled at the scaffolding and never built the house', said a Marlborough master of his pupils in 1895.[7]

1 Edward Mack, *Public Schools and British Opinion Since 1860*, 366.
2 Ibid., 180–1.
3 Vivian Ogilvie, op. cit., 179.
4 G. Kitson Clark, *The Making of Victorian England*, 269–70.
5 Ibid., 270, 272.
6 Edward Mack, op. cit., 125.
7 Frederick Malim, *Almae Matres*, 124. Matthew Arnold made a striking comparison in the same context between the Prussian 'higher schools' and the public schools: 'the great

Admittedly, the few very bright Sixth Formers who did experience the literary joys were disproportionately the ones to gain university scholarships and pass the stiff Civil Service examinations. But their exposure to a truly liberal education was generally brief, at the end of the long climb through junior forms. Nor should it be thought that subsequent study at Oxford or Cambridge would inevitably widen the students' horizon. Formal requirements for undergraduates were at least as specialized as the public school syllabus.

Viewed as history, likewise, the voyages of Aeneas and the campaigns of Caesar provided opportunities that were largely missed. A nice miniature of this failing occurs in a recent novel, *A Fleece of Lambs* by an author who was at Charterhouse just after the First World War. The portrait is of a fictitious London girls' school, but its inspiration must surely come from the author, Lionel Hale's, own schooldays.

. . . It had never occurred to Sophia, nor to any of the other girls in the Latin class, to connect the words on the printed page with anything that ever really happened. Men marched, camps were struck, winter quarters were gone into; but to Sophia the Latin language did not concern men, camps, winter quarters and cavalry. It existed to provide Subjunctives, and Past Participles, and (oh golly!) Gerunds.[1]

If the public school syllabus, taken as a whole, did not carry a well-rounded portfolio of subjects, the rigours of Latin translation did provide a general training of the mind, an exercise in logic and analysis. Like secondary school mathematics, Latin demanded a disciplined manner of thought following set rules; it is significant in this respect to note that many public schools, including Eton and Marlborough, employed more teachers in mathematics than any other field except classics. Modern languages, especially as they were taught at public schools, provided their own mental discipline: again, it is interesting to observe a

superiority of the Germans' . . . is in their far broader notion of treating, even in their schools, the ancient authors as *literature*' (his italics), 'and conceiving the place and significance of an author in his country's literature and in that of the world'. Arnold, *Higher Schools and Universities in Germany*, 1882.

[1] Lionel Hale, *A Fleece of Lambs*, 38.

school like Shrewsbury, with a strong classical tradition, gradually giving an important place to French and German.[1]

Even here, however, the public school achievement in providing general education was limited. As Jerome Bruner, the cognitive psychologist, points out, a child will get most benefit out of learning a new discipline when he is made conscious of the basic logical principles underlying the discipline.[2] He will get even more benefit if he is encouraged to relate those principles to other fields of thought. There is some evidence to suggest that without this basic approach, the child who, say, acquires skill at breaking down Latin sentences will only be able to use that logical ability in other fields to a limited extent. It is by no means certain that practice in one logical system, here Latin, will by itself increase a student's ability to solve problems in other areas where a different form of reasoning may be involved.

The trouble with the public school treatment of Latin was that most teachers never seemed to view it with any great persistence as sheer logical training. It was always being bathed in a romantic hue and justified as literature or history—which for most students it was not, as we have already seen. Through the classics, wrote T. E. Page, a Charterhouse master, in 1906, 'we are connected in an unbroken and living union with Greece and Rome. . . . Their words breathe on our lips.'[3]

As a result of such romanticism, public school Latin and Greek fell between two stools: the subjects served limited usefulness as literature or history, and yet they were seldom objectively scrutinized as logical training. If they had been so scrutinized, more educators might have concluded that the time spent on Latin translation would have been better spent in analytical fields of equal rigour but whose contents were nearer to the problem that the public schoolboy would actually face in adult life—science, say, or political philosophy. But such a conclusion would have been alien to the whole amateur-classicist mentality. T. E. Page, whose rhapsody about Greece and Rome we have just quoted, justified classical training first and foremost for its virtual inability to be

[1] C. E. Pascoe, Everyday Life in Our Public Schools, 143.
[2] Jerome Bruner, The Process of Education, especially Chap. 2.
[3] 'The Classics' by T. E. Page in Public Schools from Within (1906).

used for any utilitarian purpose: non-usefulness, in the immediate, practical sense of the word, made it an effective bulwark against vocationalism in education.[1]

All this is not to say that Latin exercises were unproductive; they were only *relatively* unproductive in the light of modern, but still very primitive, knowledge about how men learn and think. The main harm done by the public school obsession with classics was that it devoured time that might have been given to other kinds of thinking such as speculative thinking and intuition. Not only are there different types of thought-process, but recent cognitive research suggests that excessive attention to one logical system, e.g. Latin or algebra, may actually stifle creative thinking, e.g. literary imagination or historical synthesis, that proceeds on different principles to that system.[2]

Judged on its own merits alone, however, classical training possibly did foster a detached, orderly *approach* to problems that could be successfully transferred to other subjects. Similarly, the detailed memory-work required by Latin and by public school history lessons probably nurtured a general readiness to master detail. But by the same token, most history teaching did relatively less for speculative thought: form-masters taught battle names and dates far more thoroughly than they did social trends and ideas.[3] In their attention to memory-work—learning dates, learning verse, learning genders and principal parts—the public school authorities seemed to make the assumption that adolescent memory could be usefully developed and stretched like a muscle. Today that assumption has been challenged, although the complete verdict is still in doubt.

The most glaring deficiency of the classically biased public school curriculum was the poor place it awarded science, especially applied science. To some extent this deficiency was the fault of Oxford and Cambridge: the two universities offered more scholarships in classics than in any other field, and scholarship-

---

[1] 'The Classics' by T. E. Page in *Public Schools from Within* (1906).

[2] I am indebted here to Roxanne Harvey and her work on an undergraduate honours thesis, 'Creativity', presented to the Harvard University Department of Social Relations in 1962.

[3] Edward Mack, op. cit., 123, 212.

winning provided schools with a major source of prestige.[1] In these circumstances the universities couldn't help but influence public school curricula, and influence them away from science. Not until 1875 did Cambridge produce more than twenty names for the Natural Science Tripos,[2] and for decades after that date, as Sir Charles Snow and Sir Eric Ashby have described, the two universities continued to class both technology and science as less interesting than the humanities.[3] In the nineteen-thirties, most of the scientific specialists in the Colonial Service came from universities other than Oxford and Cambridge;[4] and it will be remembered that the great majority of boys from the more famous public schools either went to Oxford and Cambridge or else did not go to university at all.

Sir Eric Ashby has pointed out two ironies in the public school-Oxbridge disdain for 'Stinks'. First, the scientist was frequently identified with a socially inferior specialization.[5] The irony here, of course, was that in fact the public school or university classicist might be just as specialized as any scientist. But a great number of public school headmasters were themselves classically trained Churchmen, and from their viewpoint a well-rounded syllabus was a syllabus that taught morals as well as the mind. Their error was to assume that long hours of Latin translation necessarily exposed the student in any real fashion to the moral wisdom of the ancients.

The second irony was that both the public schools and Oxford and Cambridge fostered a much greater respect for the 'pure' scientist and mathematician than for the applied scientist.[6] To an extent, this distinction stemmed from a healthy desire to do more than merely teach mechanical skills. But it was carried much farther than this. It led, in the public school science classroom, to a de-emphasis on experimentation, on letting the student make discoveries for himself. The irony, as Ashby describes it, is that in a sense the applied scientist is nearer to the humanities and the

[1] Vivian Ogilvie, op. cit., 179.   [2] G. Kitson Clark, op. cit., 272.
[3] C. P. Snow, *The Two Cultures and The Scientific Revolution*. Eric Ashby, *Technology and the Academics*.
[4] W. A. Robson, ed., *The British Civil Servant*, 'The Colonial Civil Service' by Leonard Barnes.
[5] Eric Ashby, op. cit., Chapter 3.   [6] Ibid.

social sciences than is the pure scientist. To use Ashby's own illustration, the civil engineer who goes to an Indian village must know something of anthropology for his work to be most effective.

The tragedy of the prevailing public school attitude towards applied science was that it helped create an artificial breach between pure science and technology, and thus between theory and experience. It reduced vital cross-feeding between the two. Worse, it ignored the fact that aspects of applied science may provide as good a general mental training as more so-called 'pure' fields. The result was that Britain's public managers—the politician, the general, the administrative class bureaucrat—were in great measure educated well apart from the technologists. The former largely came from public schools; the latter largely didn't. As late as 1943 this pattern was officially sanctioned by a commission on education, headed by the Harrow headmaster, Sir Cyril Norwood. For the purposes of schooling, said the Norwood Report, children could be divided into three groups: first, pupils with practical aptitudes; secondly, pupils with insight into applied science and mechanical intricacies; and thirdly pupils 'interested in learning for its own sake, who can grasp argument . . . (and who are) interested in causes'. The student in the second group, argued the report, often found 'subtleties of language construction too delicate for him'.[1] Norwood wanted a separate school system for each group. Although he also wanted easy transfer between the different systems, his viewpoint reflected two public school tendencies: the tendency to overlook the importance of exposing all scholars and leaders to technology; and the assumption that technologists themselves (the second group) were not 'interested in learning for its own sake'.

So much for the amateur ideal as it was reflected by the curriculum. In athletics, the schools did produce an all-rounder: the more games a boy excelled at, the more 'colours'—fancy stockings, caps, sweaters, ties, &c.—he stood to win, and the footballer or rower usually found time in the same season to join cross-country

[1] H. C. Barnard, *A Short History of English Education*, 309–10.

runs and possibly play a court game as well. On the larger scale, however, public school life could be a narrowing experience. Athletics won far more prestige, decorations, and prefectorial posts than other activities; and public school isolation, backed by snobbery and a network of rules and regulations, gave the student little chance to see how men lived beyond his tiny world.[1]

Despite these limitations, the public school did give its members an admiration for versatility. It encouraged them to believe that what the leader needed for his role, above all, were general qualities of mind. Embued with these, the leader might forgo specialized training, the techniques of theorizing in advance. B. H. Liddell Hart sums up this point of view in his short analysis of the First World War:

Generals need to be truly general in their knowledge, and understanding. . . . The higher the plane of war, the more the solution depends on wide knowledge, broad outlook, and depth of thought: and the less, comparatively, on technical experience. This does not mean that knowledge of military technique is unnecessary. . . . The better a man's mental equipment, however, the less time he will take to acquire an adequate knowledge of such technique.[2]

As Liddell Hart goes on to point out, the danger of selecting leaders according to their technical training increases enormously where promotion is slow—conditions typical to bureaucracy and the military. Specialized knowledge may become obsolete; general qualities of mind cannot.

British parliamentary government posed a special need for the versatile leader. As an M.P. or member of the House of Lords, the Cabinet minister had to debate legislation as well as run his own department. Every few years he might have to change portfolio, and since the Cabinet took collective responsibility for major decisions, the minister was called upon to show a quick grasp of problems confronting his colleagues. To a smaller extent, the backbencher was a generalist also: Parliament has made less use of specialized committees than have either the French or the American legislature.

[1] Edward Mack, op. cit., 123–4.
[2] B. H. Liddell Hart, *The War in Outline*, Preface, xii.

In British bureaucracy, the generalist backgrounds of the top men have shown an interesting relation to professional procedure. Compared with the German bureaucrat whose education was largely technical with a heavy emphasis on exact knowledge and reference to authorities, the British civil servant generally showed flexibility in legal interpretation.[1] The Home Civil Service, moreover, recognized the generalist principle by officially regarding itself as one service, with its Head in the Treasury and its top men liable to cross-departmental appointments.[2] Abroad, the Colonial and Indian Civil Services demanded their own brand of versatility: the young district officer had to be judge as well as administrator; he had to learn agriculture, sanitation, and public accounting, and learn them all on the job.[3]

But there was another side to the coin. The very qualities which made the civil servant flexible and versatile made him distrust expert theory, especially when it was applied to matters of organization. Like public school authority, like the Constitution itself, he saw leadership in terms of men and honour and common sense. He was not generally interested in *method* for its own sake, in institutional engineering. Being brought up to lead, he found it difficult to view leadership as a science. He tended to shy away from academic studies of administrative technique, and this inhibited organizational improvements.[4]

As long as the demands on bureaucracy seemed to change but slowly, Civil Service organization could maintain efficiency through piecemeal adjustment, through the personal flexibility of its men. It was only when new challenges crowded thick and fast upon government that the absence of long-term administrative planning was felt. The outbreak of the First World War, for example, found the Admiralty's Transport Department completely unprepared for its wartime task of controlling transport shipping. It lacked plans, it lacked personnel, and it was handicapped by its traditional status as part of the Admiralty. In fact,

---

1 H. M. Stout, *Public Service in Great Britain*, 90–91.
2 Ivor Jennings, *Cabinet Government*, 145.
3 Philip Woodruff, *The Men Who Ruled India*, Vol. II, *The Guardians*, 80–82.
4 H. M. Stout, op. cit., Introduction by W. Y. Elliott. C. H. Sisson, *The Spirit of British Administration*, Introduction.

much of its wartime business concerned the Board of Trade. The Department's organizational inadequacies continued for at least a year after the outbreak of war.[1] In fairness, it must be said that the state of the Transport Department reflected official pre-war opinion that the war would be short and Britain's part in it small. But the criticism is still valid. For one of the advantages of administrative reviewing is that thought can be given to a range of future contingencies. Had this been done one of the contingencies considered might have been the one which actually became reality— a costly and prolonged war.

Among the most oft-cited examples of bureaucratic disdain for expert method has been the Treasury—which controls the Civil Service by controlling its purse-strings—and the Bank of England. The Treasury has employed an old-fashioned and cumbersome accounting system, and until recently has hesitated to become heavily involved in economic research and prediction. It never really took steps to anticipate the sophisticated, fiscal role that a modern industrial State would thrust upon it.[2]

The Bank of England, likewise, has accrued over the years a reputation for disliking or ignoring expertise. In the nineteenth century the Bank was a pioneer of central banking and it succeeded as that pioneer through the 'inspired common sense' of its part-time merchant directors.[3] But the amateur spirit proved less good at the subsequent follow-through amid conditions of mounting economic complexity. 'The tragedy of modern British society', wrote Hugh Massingham in an article on the Bank of England, 'is that the inspirations of yesterday turn into the numbing conventions of today.'

The Americans and the West Germans have taken over where we left off and have perfected a system that is far more advanced and far better suited to the complications of our times. High officials in the Bank sometimes use words that perfectly describe the amateur spirit which still animates Threadneedle Street. They talk about 'Fingerspitz Gefühl', a witticism very appropriate to an Oxford Common-room and curiously frivolous when used by practical people engaged in

1 Arthur Salter, *Memoirs of a Public Servant*, 73–80.
2 cf. Anthony Sampson, *The Anatomy of Britain*, 270–86.
3 Hugh Massingham, 'Our Man in Threadneedle Street', *The Queen*, 6 February 1962.

serious business. Roughly it means intuition, though no translation can do justice to the rich and snobbish jargon of the original. Or take two revealing sentences from an official pamphlet appealing for recruits. 'All-round ability', it says, 'including personality, power of leadership and keenness for games, is given considerable weight in choosing candidates. A boy who, though not brilliant, is a good all round type with character and a sense of responsibility is likely to be an acceptable candidate.' It reads like a headmaster's report.[1]

It would be ridiculous, of course, to declare the public schools solely responsible for amateurism in high places. The British legal system—to use an example we have used before—suggests that trust in the amateur is a part of the nation's social character. What could be truer to the amateur spirit than the jury system and the citation as legal authority of past court cases, of specific decisions based partly on sheer common sense. Nor is there much evidence that non-public school civil servants were any less amateurist than those from public schools.

To defend the public schools, however, by saying that they did not do any more harm than other institutions is not a very compelling defence—even if it were true. With their self-declared duty to provide leaders, and their ability to attract high-calibre teaching staff, the public schools should have been expected to display *more* intellectual enlightenment than other schools and other institutions. If the prevailing national tendency was to amateurism, they might have done more than they did to counter that tendency, or rather, to counter the harmful side of that tendency. Such countervailing action would not have been out of social context: the Dissenting Academies of the eighteenth century and the Industrial Revolution itself supplied enough social roots for educational attention to science and technology. Unfortunately, most public school headmasters failed to realize that a school curriculum can respect both science and classical literature. And Oxford and Cambridge, for their part, failed to realize that a well-organized undergraduate curriculum can offer a reasonably well-rounded syllabus and still leave room for specialized work in one area. Educators felt that they had to choose between turning out well-

[1] Hugh Massingham, op. cit.; cf. Anthony Sampson, op. cit., 355–68.

74

rounded men and producing technical experts; they chose the former, and ended up by creating classical specialists.

These attitudes helped confirm amateurism in government, for the classical specialists did not think of themselves as specialists. Their hesitance to use administrative expertise was closely linked with their lack of real enthusiasm about any sort of technical expertise. Thus, the Treasury, which as we saw has been criticized for old-fashioned method, has also been criticized for failing to put scientists on committees even where highly complex, technological projects were under discussion.[1] Throughout the bureaucracy as a whole, the public school background of individual men supported an attitude that British government was prone to anyway. Nor did those civil servants who came from grammar schools, where science was generally far more stressed than at public schools,[2] seem to form any recognizable bloc against the amateur spirit. Without further research into civil servant backgrounds and attitudes, it is difficult to tell whether non-public school entrants to bureaucracy were as a group initially more friendly to technology and expertise than were old public schoolboys. But one should not underestimate the extent to which members of an organization unconsciously take on the 'establishment' point of view, especially when that point of view is associated with a whole upper-class style.[3]

In criticizing public school belittlement of science, it must be recognized that the schools did produce some unusually inventive minds—in science, as in politics and the arts. This point by itself, however, is no real defence of public school education; certainly it is no defence in terms of the system's principal purpose, the production of effective leaders. Highly creative minds may indeed survive virtually any education system.[4] But there are few of these. What counts for political education is the number of

[1] Hugh Massingham, op. cit., 278.

[2] George Whitfield, 'The Grammar School Through Half a Century', *British Journal of Educational Studies*, May 1957.

[3] The Administrative Class official from a grammar school or minor public school usually moved up a social notch, sending his son to a more famous school and himself often joining a distinguished London club.—H. E. Dale, Chapter 3, especially pp. 49–54.

[4] Particularly—in the case of a restrictive education system—when the society as a whole offers academic freedom and creative stimulus. In such cases creativity may be encouraged by experiences outside the school, at home or in adult years.

leaders it produces who are willing and able to *implement* the ideas of the truly inventive few. And it is here, particularly in the field of science and technology, that public school limitations were most felt. The story of the jet engine and, more recently, the story of electronic computors are just two examples of technical innovation in which Britain led at the invention stage but lagged at the subsequent development and exploitation phases.

Today the amateur spirit in government—and allegedly, in industry—is a favourite target for writers of varying political persuasions. Their criticism would be more constructive, however, if they admitted certain advantages that the amateur spirit, or generalism, confers on government. One such advantage is the support it gives to democratic responsibility. On the part of the M.P., an amateur air appeared to increase public trust in government: the politician did not seem as much a 'man apart' from the people as otherwise he might have.[1]

In the Civil Service, the fact that bureaucrat and politician had frequently shared the same general educational background helped produce an administration responsive to political control. The general part of the Civil Service entrance examination—a requirement that included a free-roving essay—played a role in providing bureaucrats who could communicate with other professions in government.

It should not be thought, of course, that the Administrative Class has always shown responsiveness to outside advice. Strong *esprit de corps*, added to the sheltered backgrounds of most officials —boarding school, then university, then the Department—have at times fostered a 'nice-mannered arrogance and exclusiveness' to outsiders and to lower grades of the bureaucracy.[2] The Treasury has been especially criticized for keeping information unnecessarily to itself. But at least the civil servant accepted changes in ministerial command and, with them, change in policy: if minister and parliamentary secretaries were amateurs at departmental affairs, this did not make them objects for

[1] H. M. Stout, op. cit., 74.
[2] Herman Finer, *The British Civil Service*, 43. cf. W. A. Robson, op. cit., 53, 55.

professional contempt. Public opinion influenced the workability of most programmes, and it was clear to the civil servant that the men who knew about public opinion were the political generalists, the M.P.s. In short, the generalist attitude had a twofold effect on bureaucracy. First, it influenced the civil servant's training. Secondly and consequently—it encouraged the civil servant to accept a political chief whose experience was refreshingly different from his own.

The same applied to the military. Despite its high status, the military profession has never in recent times become a *junta*, openly flouting civilian authority. One reason for this, as Simon Raven suggests, may be that the officer felt himself to be a gentleman first and a professional only second: he derived status and self-esteem not so much from expertise as from membership in a social class which cut across professions.[1]

Even the amateur's treatment of the scientist had its democratic advantages. The complexities of industrialization tend to produce the technocrat, the technical administrator whose monopoly of certain areas of knowledge precludes political responsibility. Under Macaulay's ghost, however, the generalist continued to run Whitehall, and the specialist was usually to be found in an advisory role, away from the command hierarchy.

This is not to say that a midway point could not have been found between technocracy, on the one hand, and on the other, dangerous belittlement of the technologist. The ideal solution was and still is partly an educational one: to produce scientists who are also educated in non-science fields, and to produce non-scientists who have at least a developed feeling for technical innovation. But, as we have already suggested, such an approach would have been quite alien to the men who ran the Victorian public schools.

In his account of the First World War, B. H. Liddell Hart showed what could happen when the principle of leadership by amateurs did *not* prevail. The result, ironically, was that British policy-making suffered the worst effects of both amateurism and specialization. Lloyd George, it is true, respected the generalist

[1] Simon Raven, 'Perish By the Sword', *Encounter*, May 1959.

concept by creating a small War Cabinet whose members, freed from departmental chores, could concentrate on the war as a whole. Unfortunately, the Conservative M.P.s on whom the Premier's political strength depended appreciated the amateur of war less than they did the amateur of peacetime. They 'tended to have the instinctive conviction that in war the soldier and sailor in authority must always be right. This produced in practice a definite limitation of the War Cabinet's powers in a most important sphere'—a limitation increased by lack of frank reporting between professional commanders and their civilian chiefs.[1] Unlike their successors of the Second World War, moreover, the British and French generals failed to promote temporary soldiers to planning posts where general ability counted more than technical training.[2]

What price did Britain pay for wasting civilian aptitudes, for deserting her peacetime attachment to the generalist? Some answer can be given by noting key innovations that civilians introduced and senior professionals obstructed. Behind the convoy system, the machine-gun, the tank, and the mortar lay the hand of Lloyd George, sometimes aided by his Cabinet Secretary, Maurice Hankey, sometimes by an energetic temporary soldier or a few junior officers.[3] We should also note that Field-Marshal Haig carried out the disastrous Passchendaele offensive against the gravest doubts of the War Cabinet,[4] and at the top policy-making level the main questioning of a frontal offensive strategy came from civilians.[5]

As we have already suggested, the general and admiral of the First World War really suffered the worst of both amateurism and specialization. On the one hand, the social preoccupations of regimental life precluded full attention to military technology:[6] if he ever dreamed of questioning his right to command, the officer sought credentials in a gentlemanly style and social status

---

[1] L. S. Amery, *My Political Life*, II, 96–97. B. H. Liddell Hart, op. cit., 151.
[2] Ibid., Preface, xi–xii. Success of amateur soldiers in the Dominion forces—xiii.
[3] L. S. Amery, op. cit., II, 119–20. J. F. C. Fuller, *The Army in My Time*, 135–40. B. H. Liddell Hart, op. cit., 127, 168–70.
[4] Ibid., 176.
[5] cf. J. M. Keynes, *Essays in Biography*, 57.
[6] J. F. C. Fuller, op. cit., 36–41. T. C. Worsley, *Barbarians and Philistines*, 124–5.

per se rather than professional efficiency.[1] On the other hand, the special techniques that the senior commander had once learned in the field suddenly became obsolete with the advent of war. His reluctance to discard these techniques was unlikely to be lessened by a public school outlook. If he was one of the many who had gone to a public school, his schooldays, as we have seen, would have taught him little respect for technology. Moreover, the public school Rifle Corps and Army Class—the latter created during the Victorian period to prepare boys for Sandhurst—taught an old-fashioned brand of warfare; they represented the one exception to the public school horror of technical, vocational training. Public school life itself, of course, was full of military overtones and perhaps this contributed to the Tory trust in admirals and generals which Liddell Hart found so misplaced.

[1] Keir, *A Soldier's Eye View of Our Armies*, 5.

Chapter 7

Adjustment to Change

It is my contention that the public schools bred mental flexibility rather than imaginative foresight. Faced with an urgent need to change, the old public schoolboy was usually resourceful in his adjustment; confronted by crisis, he would 'muddle through'. What he frequently lacked was the interest in new ideas that would have helped him to avoid crisis by looking ahead. If he possessed intelligence, he was also apt to be complacent.

A curriculum that focused heavily on Latin translation might do something for memory and logical thinking but it did little to awaken the imagination. Beneath the Sixth Form most masters accepted the unpopularity of studying.[1] Possessing little faith in schoolboy curiosity, they justified Latin as a moral, as well as mental, discipline. In order to supply leaders for a newly industrialized state, the public schools grafted the Samuel Smiles Gospel of Work on to the leisurely style of the gentleman by the same token that they fused the ambitious middle classes with the landed gentry.[2] By the late Victorian era Smiles had entered the classroom; hard work—especially painful work, since hardship 'built Character'—became a moral good.

The same moral concern which made the receipt of learning so unappetizing a task embued the whole of public school life with a non-intellectual bias.[3] In *A Schoolmaster's Apology*, the headmaster, Cyril Alington, confessed that he was 'more anxious that a boy should have to deal, and know that he is dealing, with gentlemen than that he should be taught the best subjects by the best

[1] Edward Mack, *Public Schools and British Opinion since 1860*, p. 169. cf. G. M. Young, *Victorian England: Portrait of an Age*, 158.
[2] Asa Briggs, *Victorian People*, chapter on Samuel Smiles, especially pp. 134, 139.
[3] Edward Mack, op. cit., 125.

methods'.[1] Long before he wrote this, Alington's predecessors had permitted the growth of athleticism by downgrading intellectual inquiry for its own sake. Once character was made the prime public school goal, games could become as worthy a pursuit as learning—rather more so, in fact, since character was largely seen in terms of 'muscular Christianity'.[2] An Etonian reported in 1881 that his contemporaries rapidly acquired 'enmity to masters', a 'profound aversion to Collegers' (scholarship students who lived in 'College'), and an 'intense veneration' for athletic heroes rather than for wealth or social rank. Admittedly, these attitudes seemed to become milder as the individual rose in the school, but the longest-remaining value was, according to this Etonian, the 'depreciation of mere scholastic merit'.[3] The same outlook prevailed in other schools besides Eton: during the eighteen-seventies and eighties prefectorial power in the public school system as a whole passed from the scholar to the athlete.[4]

But games provided only one way by which the public school tried to instil character. The etiquette and custom that it also employed were directly hostile to the imagination. Roping off vast sections of a schoolboy's life from the exercise of individual reason, the requirements of 'good form' demanded unquestioning faith in tradition and instinctive-seeming obedience to authority.[5] 'The business of a school', wrote a Harrow headmaster, 'is to work and get on with its life without bothering about whys and wherefores and abstract justice and the democratic principle.'[6] Denying that discipline and 'an atmosphere of free criticism' were incompatible, the writer claimed that the public school gave the individual every chance to learn what was thought of him; whether he was equally encouraged to criticize the community the writer did not say.

In fact, the climate of opinion inside the public schools was generally uncritical of school institutions. Despite surface criticisms

---

[1] Quoted by Edward Mack, op. cit., 299–300.
[2] See Chapter 3. Also David Newsome, *Godliness and Good Learning*, especially Chapter IV—'Godliness and Manliness'.
[3] C. E. Pascoe, *Everyday Life in Our Public Schools*, 39–40. 'Eton' by an Oppidan.
[4] John Corbin, *Schoolboy Life in England, 1898*, p. 97.
[5] cf. Edward Mack, op. cit., 124–5.
[6] Cyril Norwood, quoted by T. C. Worsley, *Barbarians and Philistines*, 133.

by school debating societies and the more weighty effects of individual reformers, most public schoolboys seemed unaffected in their outlook by the educational debates that livened late Victorian England. 'Schools have been invaded, schools have been operated upon, and schools have been dumb,' said Edward Thring in 1883.[1] Towards their dumbness Thring was by no means entirely hostile. The public school educator, he said, was like a 'skilled workman', too involved in action to take part in theoretical discussion.[2]

The schools' unquestioning approach to education stemmed in part from the English tendency to value experience above abstract speculation, to ask 'will it work?' rather than 'what is the best conceivable scheme?' But there was another factor behind the unself-critical nature of public school opinion. Vocationally, the public schools felt responsible for supplying a relatively small number of professions, centring on the government service occupations. In these circumstances it was all too easy for the schools to develop a standard and unquestioning image of the product they were meant to turn out. To a diminishing extent this tendency still characterizes the public schools; as recently as December 1958 it was recognized, and apparently accepted, by an anonymous writer in the Old Wykehamist periodical, *The Trusty Servant*:

A school must be a smoothly efficient organization that must deliver the goods, and that in return for a high fee, turns out men with the right qualifications, the required number of passes and all the right forms filled in. There is not much time for the striking of picturesque attitudes, dons cannot gadfly about taking potluck on what a sting here or there might produce, but must quietly and regularly practise the midwifery of their educative art. You cannot afford a major boob over somebody's career, and nobody would thank you if you ran a 'give-them-their-head-and-let-them-make-their-own-mistakes' sort of programme. You can see that an accepted pattern of what they should be has stamped itself upon the House dons, and this earnest, talented and busy breed are forced by circumstances to do too much and see to everything themselves.

---

[1] Edward Thring, *The Theory and Practice of Teaching*, 2.   [2] Ibid., 2.

There were more profound reasons, however, for the public school failure to encourage criticism and questioning. In the final analysis, the education system viewed the intellect itself as hostile to loyalty. We have already seen how the system instilled loyalty not by explicit dogma but by custom and etiquette, devices that played on a community mysticism and the aesthetic emotion of 'good form' rather than on reason. To the extent that the dictates of 'good form' were tacit dictates, influencing the individual unconsciously, their effects might even be called subliminal.

But it was not simply the *method* employed that made the public school treatment of loyalty anti-intellectual. Loyalty itself was considered a virtue which the exercise of reason could easily destroy. In Chapter 3 we saw how public school headmasters related Character to athletic vigour rather than to intellectual activity; in Chapter 4 we noted *The Times*'s defence of 'school spirit' as a force which induced boys to *distrust their individual intellects and do an unselfish job*. Public school loyalties formed part of a faith rooted firmly in unquestioned assumptions about the gentleman's moral duty and his relation to the society about him. The same faith provided the public schoolboy with self-assurance and decisiveness. He took command easily because he did not often question either his right or his worthiness to take command. Self-assurance and rational inquiry were kept well apart.

'Doubt is unnerving save to philosophic minds,' wrote B. H. Liddell Hart on the lack of military imagination in the First World War, 'and armies are not composed of philosophers either at top or bottom'.[1] Nor, one might add, are most professions, especially where the leadership of men is involved. The old dictum that men of deepest thought are seldom men of action is in no case more true than in that of the leader. For if the leader obviously depends on intelligence, he can also be hurt by it, his decisiveness sapped by a mind that sees many sides to every question, many obstacles to every plan. The intellectual leader may indeed be imprisoned in subtlety.

This is not to say that leadership and intellectual inquiry are *necessarily* subversive to one another, nor that education should

---

[1] B. H. Liddell, Hart, *The War in Outline*. 69.

not try to bring the two together. In the case of the public schools, however, the prevailing concept of leadership derived an anti-intellectual bias from the leader's social situation. The English gentleman assumed by instinct—or, more precisely, by the acquired instinct which upbringing imposed—that high social status conferred the right to give orders. Furthermore, it was instinct, not calculation, that created the distinctive bearing which, in a class society, excited respect from lower status groups. Because of its emphasis on the instinctive, therefore, the public school concept of leadership depended heavily on irrational indoctrination, the appeal to custom and aesthetic taste. Through these means it could also make gentlemen of its new middle-class clientele—a process which had mixed merits. If public school indoctrination directed the young bourgeois towards public service, it did so at a price. In return for good manners and a public school accent, the new gentleman lost any marks of the liberal rationalism that his middle-class background might have left on him.[1] Usually, however, his parents had already become good conservatives, too.

Politically, this phenomenon was very noticeable. According to one witness, the Wellington headmaster who married Gladstone's daughter found that his marriage 'was not an advantage to the Master of a school whose boys came largely from Conservative families, to whom distrust and dislike of the great Liberal leader was almost *an article of faith*'.[2] (Italics mine.) Somewhat earlier, a headmaster of Clifton who was himself a Liberal incurred similar unpopularity.[3] We should also note that of the 1934 Parliamentary Liberal Party, only nine among the seventy-one members were old public schoolboys.[4]

Intellectual conformity was not confined to political views. Isolation from the contrasts of the outside world coupled with lack of privacy were hardly conditions that favoured the eccentric opinion in anything. To the extent, therefore, that conflict of

[1] G. M. Young, op. cit., 158. Edward Mack, op. cit., 104, 122. T. C. Worsley, op. cit., 80–82. For an account of the general English bourgeois tendency to forget liberalism with material success, see R. Lewis and A. Maude, *The English Middle Classes*, 44–45.
[2] Frederick Malim, *Almae Matres*, 83.
[3] T. C. Worsley, op. cit., 98.
[4] H. M. Stout, *Public Service in Great Britain*, 64.

ideas develops the imagination, the late Victorian public school bred complacence—in thought, if not in action. It would be wrong, however, to charge the schools with doing nothing whatever to produce adaptability when conditions quite obviously required it. The unwritten nature of public school tradition did enable it to change gradually, to invest new institutions with a false aura of antiquity. Criticism and minor reform did stem from internal sources: alumni rebels and strong headmasters. And certain features of extracurricular life—debating clubs, for instance, and the Rifle Training Corps—undoubtedly induced quick thinking and initiative.

But sometimes it seemed as if those very qualities of adaptability, added to vast reserves of self-assurance, discouraged the public school graduate from showing imaginative foresight. The confidence that he could handle crises when they came along reduced his efforts to avoid them in the first place: hence the *pride* underlying such sayings as 'the Englishman loses every battle but the last' and 'Britain somehow muddles through'. Behind the Civil Service concept of generalism, after all, lay the belief that a properly educated man did not need to indulge in advance theorizing; a developed memory and a quick mind should enable him to grasp the practical essentials of each problem as it arose.

This point of view comes out very strongly in the speeches of Stanley Baldwin. First, Baldwin possessed an unusual capacity to sense national moods and attitudes.[1] Secondly, he was the very epitome of the public school gentleman: a countryman; a classicist; an Anglican, despite his Methodist forebears; the heir to a steel fortune who himself cared less for money-making than for public office as J.P. and politician; and, finally, an Old Harrovian —although one who remembered his schooldays with distaste.[2] Thirdly, it is significant that a man of his position felt he could express such views in public, and with such obvious relish:

The English schoolboy, for his eternal salvation, is impervious to the receipt of learning, and by that means preserves his mental faculties

---

[1] Ivor Jennings, *Cabinet Government*, 472.
[2] Robert Blake, 'Baldwin and the Right' in *The Age of Baldwin*, ed. by John Raymond, 25–30.

further into middle age and old age than he otherwise would. . . .

The Englishman is made for a time of crisis, and for a time of emergency. He is serene in difficulties but may seem to be indifferent when times are easy. He may not look ahead, he may not heed warnings, he may not prepare, but when once he starts he is persistent to the death and he is ruthless in action. It is these gifts that have made the Englishman what he is, and that have enabled the Englishman to make England what it is.

It is in staying power that he is supreme, and fortunately, being as I have said, to some extent impervious to criticism—a most useful thing for an English statesman. That may be the reason why English statesmen sometimes last longer than those who are not English.[1]

To assess British institutions and public policies for their general adaptability since the Victorian period would obviously demand a complete twentieth-century history of England. If we were able to make such an assessment we would probably conclude that as a political society Britain did retain stable and effective government amid a changing environment. As the latter posed new goals, the government provided a focal point of agreement on these goals and moved with some efficiency to meet them. At home, the Constitution adjusted to the implications of political democracy, while the Civil Service and even the Conservative Party accepted greater State responsibility for public welfare.

Abroad, Britain gradually modified her colonial notions with the idea of voluntary commonwealth. If the Colonial Service underestimated the rapid growth of nationalism,[2] especially African nationalism, there is little evidence that any other European power did better at preparing her African colonies for independence; there is some evidence that no other power did as well.[3] Nor can it be said that the British Empire only showed piecemeal adjustment to change, that it never attempted long-range planning. When time and experience were on the side of British authority, it sometimes made systematic attempts to prepare and predict. These achievements were largely carried

[1] Stanley Baldwin, *On England (and Other Speeches)*, 12–13. This was an address made to the Royal Society of St. George in 1924.
[2] Margery Perham, *The Colonial Reckoning*, 114.
[3] Ibid., 131–2. See Chapter 9 for a fuller treatment of Britain's colonial pattern.

through by men from the Victorian public schools, men like Frederick Lugard whose educational plan for Nigeria was based on systematic analysis and planning. The Colonial Office, admittedly, blocked many of Lugard's plans, but as his biographer, Margery Perham, points out, the Office had enough ability to promote him, 'even if they had not enough to make fullest use of him'.[1]

Where time and experience, however, were not so clearly on Britain's side, when the making of successful policy depended on the swift perception of completely new concepts, the defects of British leadership were exposed. The exposure was most vivid in two great failures of the national authority: the military policy of the First World War, with its appalling and unnecessarily high losses, and the 'appeasement' policy of the nineteen-thirties. The two failures, in fact, were slightly related, for not only did the First World War kill an unusually high number of young officers, including men who might have become statesmen, but the casualties left a horror of war that helped blind the British people to the warnings of Churchill. In both cases, entirely novel conditions appeared so rapidly that only the most vigorous imagination could have appreciated them in time to avert disaster. In both cases, too, attitudes engendered by public school education reinforced rather than offset a shortsightedness that British leadership may have possessed anyway. To put it differently—the intellectual shortcomings of the public schools comprised one factor, and only one, in the two great failures of British national leadership.

During the First World War, the public school characteristic of instinctive loyalty and unquestioning obedience found its counterpart in similar attitudes that the military profession tends to instil anyway. 'Faith matters so much to a soldier in the stress of war that military training inculcates a habit of unquestioning obedience which in turn fosters an unquestioning acceptance of the prevailing doctrine.'[2] Before the Somme offensive, for example, considerations of loyalty seem to have inhibited Haig's

---

[1] Margery Perham, *Lugard*, Volume II, 496, 638.
[2] B. H. Liddell Hart, op. cit., 69.

army commander, General Rawlinson, from criticizing the plans of attack, though 'privately he was convinced that they were based on false premises'.[1] Furthermore, as we have already suggested, few—if any—of the top commanders possessed either the imagination or the scientific background to understand new technological conditions. With the generalist influence of civilian authority weakened, the other generalist factor—the so-called general education which many commanders had received in their youth—was not enough to temper the glorification of tradition instilled by public school and British regiment alike.

Please note, however, that we are not singling out the public schools as the sole source of World War folly. All we can say is that the education system failed to offset the intellectual shortcomings that military habits tend to breed. The failure was particularly disastrous in the First World War where the British generals and admirals wielded more power *vis-à-vis* civilian authority than they did in the Second.

The failure, in short, of the public schools was that they mirrored too faithfully the professional life that many of its members would later lead in the armed forces. The same applied to those public schoolboys who went into Parliament. In the political party, as in the regiment, the old public schoolboy found a mere extension of the pressures to conform which he had experienced at school. The likeness between boyhood and adulthood was unfortunate, for one duty of education is to widen the individual's horizons before the burdens and restrictions of manhood close in. Had the public schools provided an intellectual experience which *complemented* rather than largely duplicated the experience of the soldier and the politician, they might have done more for the country's leadership. It was significant, even so, that the more outstanding leaders were frequently outsiders, men whose experience extended beyond the discipline of one group or profession. Certainly this was true in politics where, as Lord Salter says,

the dynamic energy has come from leaders who have changed their party allegiance, like Gladstone, Joseph Chamberlain and Churchill; who have disrupted their parties like Peel and Lloyd George; who have

[1] *Official History of World War One*, quoted by B. H. Liddell Hart, op. cit., 122.

headed coalitions, in peace as well as war, like Lord Randolph Churchill and his 'fourth-party' associate, Balfour; or have 'dished the Whigs' like Disraeli by going one better on their policy.[1]

For us, the moral of this story is that education, however much it is servant to certain professions, will serve those professions best if it provides some of the perspective of the outsider. In the case of the First World War, the public schools would have supplied the most refreshing perspective if they had done more for science and independent thinking and less for the worship of tradition.

During the nineteen-thirties, the novel conditions facing British policy-makers were at first political rather than technological. The threat of Nazism called for a special display of imagination by the British Government since England herself had not known a dictator since Cromwell. Here, again, attitudes which the public schools endorsed formed a fatal combination with other beliefs and values. To the latter—the pacifist principles of a George Lansbury, for instance, and the desire for comfort of war-sickened people—were added opinions more typical of a public school outlook: the over-confidence and narrow vision created by what Lord Salter termed the 'psychology of island immunity'; the premium placed by some leaders on political stability and, consequently, their respect during 1934 and 1935 for German rebuilding; the Conservative tendency to fear Communism more than Fascism.[2] At crucial points, the public school set of values failed to perform countervailing functions that might have produced a quicker national response to the German threat. In other words, attitudes fostered by public school life reinforced, rather than countered, attitudes that sprang from other factors in the social environment. The 'psychology of island immunity' could originate with monastic schooldays no less than with the facts of national geography and a proud naval tradition. To take another example—Neville Chamberlain's great confidence in negotiation and contract possibly stemmed from his business background,[3]

---

[1] Lord Salter, *Memoirs of a Public Servant*, 245–6.
[2] John F. Kennedy, *Why England Slept*, 27–28, 52, 172–3.
[3] Keith Feiling, *Life of Neville Chamberlain*, 39, 41, 55.

but it was certainly not weakened by the public school emphasis on 'fair play', by Alington's precept that schoolboys should learn to deal with others as gentlemen.

Finally, public school attitudes joined with democracy itself in obstructing peacetime rearmament. The penchant for *voluntary* co-operation which delayed the introduction of conscription characterized the public school as much as it did democracy and the whole British character.[1] Likewise, a passive responsiveness to public opinion deterred the Government from introducing the consumption controls needed to finance defence outlays without cutting vital export production.

This argument can easily be misinterpreted. I do not say that public school respect for public opinion, any more than the public school emphasis on 'fair play', were in themselves harmful to efficient leadership. Far from it. They only *became* harmful when they were not accompanied by a critical attitude, by a mentality which would have seen that 'fair play' did not characterize Hitler and that an untutored public opinion would by itself be much too complacent to avert war. But the public school outlook was itself complacent; it saw problems excessively in terms of its own first-hand experience. And here lay the tragedy.

The most successful education system, suggests David Riesman, is the one that performs a 'counter-cyclical' function. Education should be, in other words, a stabilizing factor, a counterforce against constantly changing trends that may harm the society if they are pursued too far. Riesman applied the 'counter-cyclical' notion mainly to one sphere—American society's changing treatment of academic freedom[2]—but there is no reason why it should not be applied in other contexts as well. Now, in some senses the Victorian public schools did perform a countervailing role. During the late nineteenth century the schools undoubtedly formed a citadel against the materialism and selfishness generated by the new capitalism of the Industrial Revolution. But when

---

[1] 'We alone among the great European Powers . . . recruit our army by voluntary enlistment'—T. H. Escott, *England: Its People, Polity and Pursuits*, 1885, p. 441.

[2] David Riesman, *Constraint and Variety in American Education*, Chap. III. In using the word 'counter-cyclical' I refer more to 'counter' than to 'cyclical'. I do not necessarily imply that the changing trends in English society followed a cyclical or 'zig-zag' pattern, although there may indeed be a pattern of alternation between criticism and contentment.

they performed this offsetting function, they did so by stressing tradition rather than supporting intellectual criticism and imagination. They chose to make themselves an anchor of stability, a guardian of conservatism, in such a way that they were unable also to serve the cause of intellectual enlightenment. As a result, they produced leaders whose good sense was too often not accompanied by vision, and whose insularity and complacence matched too perfectly the insularity and complacence of their island people.

Part Three

THE POLITICAL OUTLOOK

Chapter 8

Tory Democracy

One of the most familiar charges levied against the public schools is that they are undemocratic. In fact, this charge is more relevant to the public schools of recent decades than it was to the system between 1870 and 1914. For during the late Victorian-Edwardian era, the public schools did assist in the extension of political power from the landed families, Britain's traditional rulers, to the new middle classes.

It must be remembered that the eighteenth-century public schools were largely the preserve of the gentry and aristocracy. The opening of their gates to professional and commercial families was a corollary of Britain's gradual transition from oligarchy to democracy. If the public schools failed to open their gates still wider, to extend social opportunity to members of the working classes, that was more the fault of the system after 1918. In the class-conscious society that comprised Victorian England, it would have been unrealistic to expect a *sudden* opening of the school gates to individuals, however talented, from all classes.

Admittedly, the Victorian public schools did their bit to create unequal opportunity: by helping to crystallize an 'Establishment' style and accent, they made it all the harder for a working-class person without that style and accent to be accepted in the top circles of power. Likewise, the emphasis on classics, however nobly viewed, provided the schools with a neat formula for offering free and reduced-fee scholarships and still excluding the lower-class boy. The formula worked because, at primary school level, Latin and Greek were a virtual monopoly of private education—the 'prep' school and the family tutor. By stressing Latin, public school entrance examinations deterred working-class families from even seeking entry to the schools.

Having said all this, the fact remains that in the social conditions of Victorian England it was practically impossible anyway for a working-class individual to attain high public office. For their part, the Victorian public schools did at least help set a pattern of extending the gentry's privileges to new classes. Had the public schools of more recent times developed the pattern still further, had they admitted talented individuals from the working class, they would not have been perpetrating revolution. Viewed against the full march of public school history, the extension of privilege would have been a restoration, for many of the oldest and most famous public schools were founded with the express purpose of providing a good education for poor scholars. But, as we all know, the restoration was never made.

For all their exclusion of the working-class youth, the Victorian public schools and their particular brand of élitism were curiously well suited to the ushering in of political democracy. The public school community, despite its ladder of rank and privilege and its servant class of 'fags', did little to undermine democratic ideals. On the contrary, we have already perceived that most public schoolboys respected majority opinion as the carrier of tradition. By limiting personal privacy, furthermore, the school authorities made popularity a valuable possession, a protection for the individual against the crowd. The general desire for popularity— or rather, popular respect—influenced the prefect and encouraged him to recognize a vaguely defined consensus of school or house opinion. In parliamentary life, the same responsiveness to consensus on the part of the executive allowed the House of Commons to influence government policy and thereby serve a democratic function, in spite of the fact that it was a mere deliberative body.

The self-restraint and lack of emotional demonstrativeness that the public school tended to inculcate was, again, particularly useful to democracy. For democratic politics demand the publicizing of issues and are apt to reward the demagogue, the man who discusses issues in emotional terms easily understood by the average voter. One tendency of democratic politics, therefore, is to make compromise and productive discussion difficult by driving opposed parties into well-publicized and implacable positions, fraught with prejudice. Against this tendency the public school spirit of moderation and mannerly dealing was a welcome counterforce. A keen sense of office, moreover, and respect for traditional etiquette infused government with a dignity that democracy itself cannot easily supply.

In his study of democracy, Joseph Schumpeter contended that, for at least two reasons, effective democratic government required the existence of a 'social stratum . . . that takes to politics as a matter of course'.[1] The first reason has been already mentioned: the need to attract into political life men 'who can make a success at anything else' and who might be inclined to find democratic politics repugnant.[2] Schumpeter's second reason was that 'the effective range of political decision should not be extended too far', since the elected executives and legislators could not be experts on any one administrative subject. Limitation of political decision, in turn, required 'the services of a well-trained bureaucracy of good standing and tradition, endowed with a strong sense of duty and a no less strong *esprit de corps*'. For such a bureaucracy the best source of recruits would again be a government-orientated social stratum.[3]

Judged by Schumpeter's standards, the public schools were obviously healthy for political democracy. They helped produce and preserve a social stratum that met all his requirements. As Schumpeter himself implied, however, this class could not long survive the advent of democracy and still consider government to be its special charge. To explain why this was so, Schumpeter pointed to the capitalism which helped produce democracy. Inevitably, society would award chief prominence to a bourgeois class, diverted from public service by private gain and lacking in the magic qualities that national rulers must have if they are to

[1] Joseph Schumpeter, *Capitalism, Socialism and Democracy*, 291.
[2] Ibid., 290. See Foreword.
[3] Joseph Schumpeter, op. cit., 291-4.

command loyalty as a social stratum.[1] What Schumpeter does not stress is that the very policies of democratic government, quite apart from the factor of capitalism and industrialization, tend to weaken the political stratum and reduce its political usefulness. Sooner or later, an elected government will move to increase economic equality, if not for reasons of justice, at least to please the majority of voters. Not only will the ruling class lose interest in serving the State which taxes it so heavily but it will be forced to seek commercial profit in order to maintain a differentiated way of life.[2]

In post-1918 Britain, the public schools might delay, but they could not prevent, the effects of democratic policy on their members' orientation to government. For the education system instilled the spirit of public service as part of a differentiated way of life, and once economic equality threatened the latter, the schools could no longer serve the political function that they had in the past. However much the public school taught its members individually to treat community service as a good in itself, it also taught them collectively to treat community service as the price of material privilege and the hallmark of social prestige. Under conditions of economic equality and progressive taxation, the public school class began to lose its distinctive standard of living. This, in turn, weakened its social prestige, its assumption of moral superiority,[3] and even its solidarity as a class.[4] With the assets of its former status dwindling, the public school class could not be expected to go on paying the same price—in public service—for those assets: nor did it possess the confidence in its superiority which once made it feel that government was its prerogative.[5]

The public schools, in short, contributed to the successful introduction of political democracy but, having made this contribution, their political usefulness began to wane. Yet long after the Victorian-Edwardian era they continued to defend

---

[1] Joseph Schumpeter, op. cit., 134–8, 298.
[2] cf. Alexis de Tocqueville, *Democracy in America*, I, 105.
[3] Even in post-Victorian England there still obtained some of the 'Protestant ethic' which saw material status as a sign at least of ability and industry, if not of grace.
[4] cf. R. Lewis and A. Maude, *The English Middle Classes*.
[5] cf. Peregrine Worsthorne, *Foreign Affairs*, April, 1959.

privilege—unequal social opportunity—although privilege and public service were no longer very firmly linked. The result was the anachronism of today: a class system of education in the midst of well-established political democracy.[1]

[1] This is not to say that the public schools are the only agent in Britain's class system of education. The grammar schools too, of course, are wedded to the principle of creating a leadership *élite*. And however much they claim to select by merit, to the extent that their entrance examinations penalize the 'late-developer', the grammar schools create unequal opportunity between individuals of equal (long-term) ability. It might well be argued, however, that the public schools helped create the élite outlook that influenced the development of the grammar schools. Certainly the grammar schools have imitated certain public school institutions, such as the prefectorial system and the house organization.

Chapter 9

The Guardian Imperialist

Much has been written by nostalgic owners of the Old School Tie, praising the 'Cheltenham and Haileybury and Marlborough chaps [who] went out to Boerland and Zululand' and there 'lived or died as gentlemen and officers'.[1] Certainly the imperialists of the nineties often mentioned England and their schooldays in the same breath; certainly many of them saw the public school as a generator of imperial enthusiasm.[2]

Just as certainly their eulogies were exaggerated. However much the songs of Harrow glorified games and hailed the strenuous life,[3] the late Victorian public schools could hardly be called hotbeds of evangelical fervour; nor did 'house spirit' carry a fiercely militant tone. Amid the new restrictions of school life, the evangelicalism of a Thomas Arnold had subsided into quieter, more comfortable form.[4]

But it is not the contention here that the Victorian public schools helped create an empire. Once the empire was mainly built, however, public school education did partly contribute a faith and a rationale to the men who were going to administer and defend that empire.

In her book, *The Colonial Reckoning*, Margery Perham suggests that towards the end of the nineteenth century five motives for empire had come together in Britain. These motives were trade, military security, emigration, the attainment of national power and prestige, and philanthropy.[5] For the last two motives on the

[1] John Pringle, 'The British Commune', *Encounter*, February 1961, quoting Rudyard Kipling.
[2] cf. J. G. C. Minchin, *Our Public Schools: Their Influence on British History*, 1899.
[3] L. S. Amery, *My Political Life*, Vol. II, 38.
[4] G. M. Young, *Victorian England: Portrait of an Age*, 4–5.
[5] Margery Perham, *The Colonial Reckoning*, 103, 110. This book is an expanded version of the 1961 Reith Lectures.

list the public schools provided a sounding-board. Behind the seeking of power and prestige, for instance, lay a nationalism which the public schools helped to foster. Nationalism, of course, does not automatically lead to imperialism, but it does marshal the individual energies and create the outlook that imperialism requires. The public school community was itself 'nationalist': the central place of games in house life induced the individual to seek personal pleasure in collective competition, in winning prestige for his group. He was taught, in other words, to seek *vicarious* enjoyment by identifying himself closely with his community. And this was the essence of nationalism.

On a wider plane, the public schools assisted nationalism by bringing together the classes which enjoyed most influence over the country's opinions—the taste-setters. During the early nineteen-hundreds, many middle-class liberals were already showing nationalist sympathies, and their nationalism drew nearer to the conservative version of the gentry as the century wore on.[1] It was in this trend that the public schools played their part, opening their gates to members of the middle classes and teaching them to identify love of the community with love of its traditions.

As well as merely inculcating nationalism, the public schools helped to create a fusion between the nationalist spirit and the motive of imperial philanthropy. The link between the two comes out strongly in the writing of J. E. Welldon, a Harrow headmaster who himself answered the call of imperial philanthropy and became an Indian bishop. In 1899 Welldon wrote:

An English Headmaster, as he looks to the future of his pupils, will not forget that they are destined to be the citizens of the greatest empire under heaven; he will teach them patriotism, not by his words only but by his example. . . .

. . . He will inspire them with faith in the divinely ordered mission of their country and their race; he will impress upon their young minds the convictions that the great principles upon which the happiness of England rests—the principles of truth, liberty, equality, and religion—are the principles which they must carry into the world; he will emphasise the fact, that no principles however splendid, can greatly or

[1] Frederick Watkins, *The Political Tradition of the West*, 288–91. T. C. Worsley, *Barbarians and Philistines*, 80–91.

permanently affect mankind, unless they are illustrated by bright personal examples of morality.[1]

As Welldon's words indicated, the British Empire satisfied both the patriotic impulse to seek national glory and the philanthropic impulse to do good to others. (And to inspire by setting examples of superior morality.) The connexion between the two impulses was to be found in an assumption of national—and racial— superiority. In the eyes of the imperial guardian, the 'white man's burden' signified moral status as well as moral duty. This psychological fusion between prestige and philanthropy was a familiar process to the public school gentleman who, as we saw earlier, showed much the same attitude to his place in British class society. From the standpoint of gentlemanly values, the principle of the 'white man's burden' was really an imperial extension of *noblesse oblige*. Both principles made status a reminder of duty; and both made duty a symbol of status.

The very curriculum of the public schools supported the Victorians' moral faith in empire. An approach to history which lauded Richard I and Henry V for the glory they won abroad and left virtually unquestioned their stewardship at home was unlikely to subvert the imperial spirit. On the contrary, it seems to have been widely assumed in Victorian classrooms that the British Empire was a splendid thing, for ruler and subject alike.[2]

Besides nurturing an imperial rationale, there were other ways in which public school education supported the British Empire. The schools also fostered personal attributes which were an important part of the British colonial administrator. Several of these qualities represented a combination of bourgeois and gentry traits—a combination which reflected public school England's merger between the rising middle-classes and the landed *élite*. The businessman's competitive instinct, for example, joined the gentry's sense of the community to accommodate imperial needs that stressed *both* self-reliance and close co-operation. By the

---

[1] E. H. Pitcairn, *Unwritten Laws and Ideals of Active Careers*, 1899, 'Schoolmasters' by J. E. C. Welldon, p. 284.
[2] cf. Margery Perham, op. cit., 14–15.

standards of Stalky and his band, the young district magistrate may not initially have possessed great individuality and imagination, but he soon had to develop a considerable capacity for independent judgement.[1] At the same time, he knew that farther up the ladder of his profession, he would have to adjust to all the restrictions of formal bureaucracy.

Another combination of bourgeois and the landed gentry appeared in the colonial officer's taste for hard work tempered by gentlemanly moderation and some tact, qualities especially needed where there was little military force available. In Hindustani there was a word for these qualities—*hikmatalami*. As Indian Civil Servants used it, *hikmatalami* meant tactful management, the light touch and a background hint of force.[2]

On the ethical plane, too, bourgeois and gentlemanly traits were fused. The remnant of middle-class evangelicalism, 'secularized as respectability',[3] merged with the gentleman's assumption of moral superiority. Together, they implanted in the imperial administrator a sense of moral obligation without the cruelty of the crusader. By the same token that they added to the white man's racial arrogance, they gave him the self-assurance he needed to control large populations with few troops, and to meet hardship and crisis with the conviction that his efforts were not wasted.

The result of these combinations was a character that fitted the lonely role of District Commissioner. Like the British Constitution itself, the 'D.C.'s' office depended for responsible government on a gentlemanly tradition of unwritten restraint. In a remote district far from higher authority, in a position of great power not simply as an administrator but also as a judge, the D.C. had every opportunity to be lazy, corrupt, and unjust. In fact, he was nearly always honest, humane, and hard-working. He was not, of course,

[1] Philip Woodruff also reports that quite a few Indian Civil Servants displayed original tastes, ranging from eccentric hobbies to the occasional man's living practice of 'going native'. At home, too, among the British landed classes, observers have commented on 'English eccentricity'. Originality in the adult's private pursuits and within the requirements of etiquette should not, however, be considered incompatible with some conformity in more serious matters of work and policy-making; perhaps latitude in the former even compensated for self-restriction in the latter. Philip Woodruff, *The Men Who Ruled India*, Vol. II. 'The Guardians', 15.
[2] Ibid., 179–80.   [3] G. M. Young, op. cit., 5.

a paragon of virtue—certainly not by modern ideals of racial equality. If he dedicated himself to his subjects, he usually did so as a superior being. As an Englishman and as a white man, he was apt to be arrogant, however quiet a form his arrogance took.

To his colour-consciousness, furthermore, the Englishman abroad often added the class-consciousness of his own people at home. Margery Perham has described how this process worked in the case of Kenya settlers.

It is often said that races are divided by a culture-bar as well as by a colour-bar. But is there not also a class-bar? Many Kenya settlers belonged to what we used to call the gentry, if not, indeed, to the aristocracy, and in earlier days they came from a country which still had strong class divisions.

They saw the African tribesmen living in their dark little huts; they were either naked or in greasy goat skins. At home these whites had had no social contact with their servants and labourers—how much less would contact seem possible where the barriers of race and mutual incomprehension were added to that of status.[1]

In the alliance between colour-consciousness and class-consciousness, the public schools played their part. The Englishman was accustomed to a society where a select system of monastic boarding schools had helped to form a single governing *élite*. The style and bearing of the governing *élite* was highly uniform, and at the same time sharply differentiated from the styles of the non-*élite*.

What this meant was that the Englishman, especially the public school Englishman, acquired a marked tendency to equate cultural differences with differences of status. In other words, he took differences of outlook and of style—differences of speech, or dress, or table manners—to imply social inferiority or superiority rather than mere differences of culture. When the Englishman went to Africa or India, therefore, he found it difficult to accept native ways of life as equal to his own; the simple fact that they were alien implied that they were socially beneath him.

Such an attitude was not, of course, restricted to old public schoolboys. The geographic insularity of Britain encouraged the

[1] Margery Perham, op. cit., 89. I am grateful to the author for permission to quote from her book.

whole population to view the peculiarities of 'frogs, wogs, and dagoes' as socially—and morally—inferior. When L. S. Amery visited Malta as Colonial Secretary in the nineteen-twenties, he found that the worst cases of racial arrogance were to be found not among senior British officials but among more lowly clerks.[1] Within the Colonial Service itself, moreover, not all administrators had been to public schools, and there is no evidence that non-public schoolboys were any less arrogant than those who wore an Old School Tie.

The fact remains that the public school-gentleman ethos was a predominant ethos among the men who governed the British Empire. In 1928, 33 out of 45 senior Indian Civil Servants and 30 out of 47 Colonial and Dominion Governors were old public schoolboys.[2] Nine years later, Leonard Barnes, sometime of the Colonial Office, wrote that the public schools, and Oxford and Cambridge, were more likely than any other institutions to give the Colonial Service the qualities it wanted. He added that it was a matter of 'conscious policy' that such qualities were 'replenished'.[3]

(More frivolous evidence of the public school-gentleman ethos in the empire's administration was given me recently by a retired colonial civil servant who joined the service in 1926. Between the World Wars, he noticed, there sprang up in Africa a 'country gentleman cult'. It consisted largely of shooting birds rather than buffalo and of having game dogs, and wives who wore tweeds even in fairly hot weather.[4])

Given the factor of public school influence on colonial government, it is not a very stirring defence of the system to say that old public schoolboys were no more racially arrogant than men from any other schools. As we have argued before, the public schools' special claim to produce leaders, added to their ability to attract relatively high-calibre teaching staff, placed the onus of fostering enlightened attitudes squarely on the public schools themselves rather than on any other type of British school.

[1] L. S. Amery, op. cit., 191.
[2] R. H. Tawney, *Equality*, 300–1.
[3] W. A. Robson (ed.), *The British Civil Servant*, 245–6.
[4] Commander Thomas Fox-Pitt, now Secretary of the Anti-Slavery Society.

Even when it is judged solely for its contribution to effective government, the arrogance of the white man abroad can be seen as a tragedy. By sowing resentment among peoples who would one day have to rule themselves, the British official's assumption of superiority mitigated against the efficient transfer of power, against a smooth transition from empire to voluntary commonwealth. Yet the tragedy was not a whole tragedy. In a curious way, assumptions of superiority helped to preserve a just and honest administration. The official who thought himself above his native subjects—above, that is, in civilization and in morality—generally thought himself above bribery and graft.

The same applied to the matter of women. On those occasions when the colonial administrator did take a native mistress—occasions more frequent than is popularly supposed—his liaison was rigorously separated from his work. He seldom departed from the impartial tenor of his rule to award special favours to his mistress or her family and friends.

Now, it can easily be seen that assumptions of racial superiority would support a 'proper' division between the administrator's private and professional spheres of life. At its most unattractive, this dividing process was described in a letter I once received from a colonial civil servant. On one of his first stations there was a District Commissioner

who had what the Provincial Commissioner's wife called 'the Oxford' manner. He always said the right thing. One day someone said he had gone to another man's house and found him in bed with a black woman.

'Disgraceful,' said the Oxford manner. 'Never let them into your bed. Keep them on the mat. Keep them on the mat.'

There was a subtlety in this because a man could say when confronted, 'I have never shared my bed with a black woman'.

The case must not be exaggerated. A vast majority, doubtless, of imperial servants remained celibate during the long, lonely years away from their homes; and those who did take native mistresses must surely have behaved, in nearly all cases, with less blatant arrogance than the above incident suggests. But whatever the sexual pattern of the colonial administrator's life, it was one well in keeping with the *mores* of the public school. For the essence of public school monasticism was to keep the individual's family life well separated from community service and professional obligations. Such a separation was useful to a bureaucracy whose codes stressed dedication, industry, and emotional detachment. This applied to the home Civil Servant as well as to the colonial officer. In his memoirs, Lord Salter recalls how, as a young civil servant, he lunched once or twice a week with his immediate superior and yet only learned years later that his chief was married.[1] Family and office simply did not meet.

If, in the home bureaucracy, the professional man was sovereign over the private man, still more so was this the case abroad. For the lonely District Officer in the Indian Civil Service, there was a special institution which channelled a man's drives either into his work or into outlets that would not infringe upon his work. The institution was pigsticking, and its psychological function is described by Philip Woodruff in his book, *The Men Who Ruled India*. Woodruff actually entitles one of his sub-chapters 'Pigsticking and the Purgation of Lusts'. As the author describes it, pigsticking served a function remarkably similar to that of public school Games. I.C.S. veterans claimed that it diverted a man's lusts away from women and power; it offset the sluggish effects of a hot climate; and it demanded crisis qualities—courage and quick judgement. This is not to say that men stuck pigs for any other reason than the fun of sticking pigs; but the motive for a sport should not be confused with its social effects. Woodruff, indeed, suggests that pigsticking also improved a District Officer's knowledge of his domain by leading him out among his villagers.[2]

Pigsticking, above all, was toughening. The sport did something to equip the colonial officer for a life of privation and hardship. And it *was* hardship—despite the servants and exotic travel. On several planes, a public school background helped the colonial officer to meet that hardship. Boarding school isolation inoculated the individual against extreme homesickness, and the Spartan conditions of dormitory and study-hall offered harsh contrast to the comforts of a middle- or upper-class household. If

[1] Lord Salter, *Memoirs of a Public Servant*, 44.   [2] Philip Woodruff, op. cit., 179.

public school values made distinctive manners and style a pre-requisite for leadership, they did not indulge human cravings for great physical luxury. 'I marvel that an English graduate can endure to live alone in such a place for £400 a year', wrote onè of the first Africans to become an Assistant District Commissioner, from a remote station.[1] His tribute was, in part at least a tribute to the public school system.

So far we have traced two ways in which the public school system influenced imperial government. We outlined, first, the public school contribution to the spirit of empire and its moral rationale; and we then looked at some of the governing charac-teristics of the colonial civil servant. A brief note remains to be added about the public school influence on imperial policy.

I do not wish to argue that the public schools were a powerful causal factor in the formulation of imperial policy. There was, however, one major policy characteristic which bore some resemblance to public school values. The policy of indirect rule was very much a public school-type balance between custom and efficiency. In the form it took after Lugard and others rationalized it, indirect rule meant a complex pattern of control by which British administration governed through native chiefs and leaders. It was applied not only in Africa but to Indian and Malayan States.

The essence of indirect rule was that it respected traditional communities and their traditional authorities. It was not without drawbacks: it deterred Britain from making radical efforts to train native bureaucracies and found education systems which would support democratic government.[2] Such innovations would have disrupted tribal authority; and many British officials felt personal loyalty to native chiefs and princes with whom they had closely worked.[3]

If the British style of indirect rule, however, gave inadequate preparation for self-government, it was at the time an efficient and flexible way of running an empire. It was highly suited to the public school concept of leadership which respected the guardian

---

[1] Margery Perham, op. cit., 128.   [2] Ibid., 115.   [3] Ibid., 116.

more than the innovator. A certain public school flavour could also be identified in the tolerance that British administrators showed towards native *traditions* and the personal *loyalty* they felt towards their subordinates and colleagues, the princes and chiefs.

All in all the pattern could have been worse. When the British Empire is compared with other empires in history, it might well be argued that the laggard development of native bureaucracies,[1] the quiet but enduring racial arrogance, and a failure to institute widespread technical education,[2] were but blemishes on a singularly unoppressive colonial rule.

[1] This applied more to Africa and the Middle East than it did to India.

[2] In India, the coming of British rule buttressed the traditional tendency of Indian education to belittle technical, expert training. The British, in any event, tended to export technicians to India rather than train Indians in technology. These points are made by S. Shukla in 'Formal Education and Modern Indian Elites', a paper given to the Fifth World Congress of Sociology, Washington D.C., September 1962.

Also relevant here is Margery Perham's point that British colonial administrators tended to look down on technical officers.—Margery Perham, op. cit., 128.

Chapter 10

Conservatism

Taken together, the attitudes and values inculcated by the Victorian public school very nearly comprise a definition of conservatism. They match practically item for item, the list of common beliefs held by Burke and 'acknowledged conservative thinkers' as compiled by H. McCloskey.[1] According to this definition, conservatives believe, first, that man is a creature of appetite and will, governed more by emotion than reason, and doomed to imperfection; secondly, that society derives from divine intent and is secured by religion; thirdly, that society is organic and complex, the product of long evolution and the collective wisdom of ancestors innumerable; fourthly, that tradition gives man a rich and mysterious heritage, not to be lightly cast away for abstract theories born of shallow reason; fifth, that social innovation destroys more easily than it creates; sixth, that men are naturally and inevitably unequal and that a class system benefits all; and seventh, that social duty, obedience to authority, loyalty to the community, and respect for stabilizing institutions—the church, the family and private property—are vital restraints on man's natural impulse to anarchy.

The connexion between most of these beliefs and the public school outlook is quite obvious, but special attention should be drawn to some of them. McCloskey's first category finds its public school counterpart in the irrational devices used to mould behaviour. It also appears in the official pessimism about the extent to which the schoolboy could enjoy intellectual subjects. In all fairness, however, we should recognize that neither prefectorial government nor the British Constitution were wholly

[1] H. McCloskey, 'Conservatism and Personality', *American Political Science Review*, March 1958.

characterized by pessimism concerning human nature. The very reliance on irrational means—demonstrations of magic and internalized restraints—to secure group loyalties meant a reliance on men and their character, rather than institutions, as the way to obtain responsible government. This reliance, however, is implicit in McCloskey's third category. If successful government institutions can only evolve slowly, rulers must have freedom to meet new problems and needs without having to resort to elaborate constitution-building and institutional modification. At the same time, those institutions which history *has* sanctioned must, from the Conservative standpoint, be far more respected than the easily-destructive reason of individuals.

Another tendency implicit in the third category is to view the workability of an institution as the main gauge of its value. Rather like the old Protestant ethic that made material success a sign of Grace, the mere survival of an institutional system shows that it personifies the accumulative wisdom of past ages. This explains, partly at any rate, the tendency of the public school Tory to revere the political system *per se*. It also explains his frequent *practicality* and his willingness to compromise for the sake of workable government.

Turning to the fourth category, we find a strong link between conservatism and the public school concept of a general education. Faith in Western traditions bred love for the classical origins of those traditions—and vice versa; distrust of abstract theorizing applied particularly to vocational subjects where past experience seemed teacher enough.

As in Confucian China, furthermore, respect for classical education was linked with the agrarian traditions of the ruling group. Gentry classes, compared with urban and business classes, seem to venerate tradition above the uncertain promises of change. In 'classic' literature and art, the gentleman finds his preferences fulfilled. For, by definition, a classic only becomes a classic when it gains a measure of antiquity; when it appears to conform to a well-ordered structure; and when it follows absolute and unquestionable rules.[1]

[1] *Concise Oxford Dictionary*. See under 'classic', 'classical' and, for contrast, 'romantic'.

The greatest discrepancy between public school values and conservatism seems, at first sight, to lie in the seventh category. What sort of tribute, the observer might ask, did dormitory and communal study hall pay to the principle of private property? What place did upper-class England—according to the proverbial Frenchman, 'a land of men, nannies, and horses'—give to the family, when it sent its sons away to boarding school at the age of eight? In fact, the conditions of public school life reflected faithfully and vividly the essential conservative attitude to duties and rights, and to property and the family. At its starkest, this attitude might be summed up as follows. There are no natural, only prescriptive rights. These, being given by the community, must serve the community, granting it cohesion and stability. Private property, like any public school privilege, is merely a prescriptive right; it only exists when it directly serves the community.[1] Again like public school privilege, its main service is to check tendencies to anarchy, including the arbitrary acts of rulers.[2]

Two conclusions can be drawn from this belief. First, the public school conservative put duty before rights, since society gives the latter and rests on the former.[3] Secondly, even the family should be treated as a stabilizing institution, whose pattern is subject to communal needs.

In moderate form, and excluding the notion of natural inequality, the conservative attitude becomes that of the senior Civil Servant. This shows that the general conservative of our definition need not, in politics, espouse the Conservative Party. H. E. Dale estimated that, just before the Second World War, about half the higher Civil Service was nearest to the Liberal Party, perhaps a quarter was Tory, and slightly less, Labour.[4] Despite these propor-

[1] It only exists—and it only *should* exist, according to the public school ethos. 'Is' becomes 'ought' when the survival of social institutions proves their moral value.
[2] cf. McCloskey, op. cit.
[3] According to McCloskey's study, a poll of self-styled conservatives in America reflected this preference.
[4] H. E. Dale, *The Higher Civil Service*, 50. To account for the low Tory representation in the Civil Service, one might cite these facts drawn from Dale's analysis: (1) fewer top civil servants came from the most fashionable and famous public schools than did Tory M.P.'s, Cabinet personnel or diplomats; (2) a bare majority were born into the upper and upper-middle classes.

tions, Dale found that bureaucratic life was a conservatizing experience: 'Most of them have a keen sense of national improvements that are required and possible . . . but they have seen too much of government to believe in the indefinite extension of its functions.'[1]

Notably, Dale's list of characteristics displayed by the British civil servant bears some similarity to McCloskey's list of conservative beliefs. According to Dale, the civil servant was inclined to feel that pure reason was not the most important factor in human affairs and wants, that great economic and political change could not be made without causing opposition and suffering, and that no one could predict all the results that major innovation would bring. Concerned with effective action and precise information, the civil servant usually had little time for 'vague generalities'; and the requirements of impartiality and administrative continuity enhanced his respect for precedent. If awareness of social complexity made him doubt the efficacy of general theories and extensive reforms, it also helped him to see both sides of questions and to maintain political neutrality. (The conservative distrust of individual reason, he showed, need not breed blind faith; it could just as well produce intellectual humility and, thence, the open mind.) Finally, the civil servant backed his famous qualities of loyalty and discretion with a consciousness of rank as marked as that of any public schoolboy.

Although British bureaucracy showed that a man could have a largely conservative outlook and still be 'Left Centre' in his political sympathies,[2] public school conservatism did lend itself to the defence of class privilege.[3] McClosky's sixth category—the notion of natural inequality—included the belief that only a social class as such, rather than individual leaders, could satisfy men's longing for leadership—Dignified leadership as well as Efficient leadership. On a more cynical level conservatism was the argument which the group in power could put forward for its retention of that power. In Victorian England, this group was the

---

[1] H. E. Dale, op. cit., 107. [2] Ibid., 107.
[3] It must be recognized, however, that in McCloskey's poll conservatism and upper-class status did not seem to be exclusively linked. Rural backgrounds and extreme *lack* of education also appeared to produce conservatism.

landed gentry, and to stay in power it had to do two things. First, it had to 'capture' its competitors, to extend its social and political privileges to leaders of the potentially liberal business classes. Secondly, it had to show that it deserved to govern by merit as well as by birth. The instrument for accomplishing both of these operations was the gentry's education system, the public schools. In this regard, then, the public schools were not merely the propagators of conservatism; they became its logical expression.

Chapter 11

Conclusions About the Victorian
Public School

With institutions, as with people, vices are frequently but the
shadows of corresponding virtues. Certainly this was so in the
case of the late Victorian public schools. Assets they had, but every
asset seemed to have its price, every advantage a drawback
with which that advantage was subtly linked. We have noted,
for example, that the same public school devices which produced decisive yet restrained leaders also tended to produce
uninquiring minds. Self-assurance and responsibility, on the
one hand, and intellectual complacence, on the other, were
interrelated traits.

The lesson of this example is that when we assess the public
schools for their contribution to effective, national leadership, it
will not be very intelligent if we merely draw up a ledger with
assets on one side and liabilities on the other. It will be even less
intelligent if we assume that the schools might have removed all
liabilities and still preserved without difficulty their assets. A more
sensible way to appraise the public schools is to ask whether the
system paid an *unnecessarily* high price for its undoubted achievements. Could it have shown far smaller defects and still made the
contributions it did make? My own guess is that in fact the system
could have done so, that in this sense the public schools might have
been more efficient, but that the problem was far more complex
than most public school critics indicate.

The paramount achievement of the Victorian public schools
was that they maintained and expanded a core of public servants
at a time when capitalism was still irresponsible and the electorate
untutored. By indoctrinating bourgeois as gentlemen, the schools

made sure that competitive pursuits of private gain did not swamp the gentry's tradition of national service. England remained a class society, and opportunity remained harshly unequal, but the public schools could claim credit for preserving strong links between social duty and high social status.

Today we easily underestimate such achievements, for by their very success they have blended undramatically into Britain's social past. It is only when we look abroad—to societies where public service has held less prestige;[1] or to new nations where democracy and urbanization have uprooted and sown strife— that we can realize fully the political worth of a system like the public schools.

What was the price of these achievements? First, there was the personal price. One wonders how furiously a prison commission would react if it found in today's prisons the living conditions which characterized the public schools around the turn of the century. More serious, however, than poor food and cold, damp study-halls was the factor of emotional development. 'School spirit' did little to foster emotional warmth and the expression of fine shades of feeling. If the public school 'new boy' was sensitive, he was hurt; if he was artistic, he was frequently thwarted. Above all, he was exposed to sexual privation. The public school age group covers the years of puberty and adolescence when, in natural circumstances, it hardly needs saying that interests turn to the opposite sex. Such interests the public school blocked; it cut the individual off from the companionship of women and for normal sexual feeling it offered a temporary substitute— homosexuality. As a result, one suspects, the schools produced better leaders than lovers, men of duty and fellowship rather than men who took easily to family warmth and feminine intimacy.

The personal price was high, but set in context it does not seem excessive. Certainly it does not seem so in terms of happiness, a property impossible to measure with any precision. By all

[1] According to Vance Packard, less than 1 per cent. of the graduates from seventeen major American 'prep schools' (private, secondary schools) have gone into government professions since 1900. cf. Robert Gutwillig, 'The Select Seventeen', *Esquire*, November 1960.

accounts, most Victorian public schoolboys seem to have enjoyed their schooldays: the community genuinely did make the individual enjoy group activities. Long after he left school, he retained an unusual capacity to take vicarious pleasure in the fortunes of his group—his profession, his nation. If he lost in the process an undefinable quality, a capacity for warmth and intimacy, such loss was perhaps the necessary price of national prestige and glory. With sparse material resources, Britain could only meet her great aspirations as a commercial and military power by making heavy demands on her human resources. And that meant the provision of leaders dedicated to hard work and public service. In terms of happiness, the main losers were probably Britain's upper-class women—the 'grass widows' of imperial servants; the mothers who lost eight-year-old sons to preparatory boarding schools. Public school England was indeed a country of men.

So much for the personal price. But there was also a national price. Philosophically it might be summarized by a series of questions.

How far can a system try too hard and too directly to achieve its ends? Can education, like generalship, profit from a strategy of 'indirect approach'? To make the questions more specific—as an institution geared to produce effective, national leadership, did the public school pursue its goal too directly and, thereby, too narrowly? By focusing on the government professions, did it starve those private professions which also nourished the nation and thus furthered the ends of government? And by focusing exclusively on the moulding of leaders, by giving the individual little freedom or privacy for *self*-development, did the schools deprive their youth of certain intellectual qualities that leaders themselves should have? The same question might be applied to government or, indeed, to any system of human control. Will it not benefit authority to grant considerable freedom to the individual, not simply because it values consent and shuns revolution, but because freedom stimulates the creative abilities of the men it must employ?

Let us take these last questions in order. First, did the public schools starve key private occupations which vitally nourished the nation? In science and technology, they probably did; certainly they supported a type of leadership which failed to *implement* new technical ideas. Whether they stunted scientific invention itself—as opposed to its implementation—is more debatable. As we have already suggested, the truly inventive few may survive practically any education system.

In commerce and industry, there is no evidence that recruitment suffered inordinately from the low prestige that public school values conferred on the business professions.[1] Public schoolboys, and able public schoolboys, did go into business, however much more gentlemanly the Church, or the Army, or the Civil Service might seem. The high status awarded public service did no more than provide a healthy counterbalance to the material inducements of private enterprise. One factor in this balance was the amateur ideal, which encouraged men to combine private money-making with 'nobler' service as M.P. or local magistrate.

What I am really arguing here is that the award of highest status to public service occupations will not *necessarily* starve a nation's industry of talent. To the extent that private employers can offer higher material rewards than can government, the latter must find equivalent appeals of its own. Such appeals will be most effective if they play on self-interest as well as altruism. To put it brutally—if commerce offers more pay, government should offer more status.

The question, of course, is one of balance. When we look at Confucian China we will see what happens when public service is awarded *excessive* status, far more than simply balancing the material inducements of trade.[2] But the argument for giving government professions some superiority of status carries a lesson that we need to remember today. In the current, educational debates about British 'meritocracy', much thought is directed to

---

[1] This is not to deny that public school education may have induced unsuitable qualities in those who *did* go into business: see below.

[2] In China, it must be pointed out, government employment offered other advantages besides high occupational status. Not only did it offer relatively high material rewards, but a post in the bureaucracy awarded some security versus arbitrary Imperial power. With so many factors in its favour, it was all the easier for government recruitment to starve private professions. See Chapter 12.

the efficient selection of leadership. Less thought, however, is directed to the political allocation of that leadership—to the problem of attracting enough able leaders into government. Yet how important the problem is.

It is quite conceivable that in fifty years time our schools will produce a far richer national aggregate of skills and ability and leadership than did Victorian education; it is equally conceivable that they will do no more than did the Victorians to select able *political* leadership. The national cake may get bigger, and the political slice remain the same. As a system for producing public servants, the Victorian public schools stand or fall on the assumption that before one talks of selecting political ability one must talk of producing political motivation, of inducing men to take on public responsibility in the first place. That they produced strong political motivation we have already established. We have also established that the public schools paid an intellectual price for producing political motivation, that the devices used to foster a sense of public service actively opposed certain intellectual qualities that the effective leader should have. We must now decide whether this intellectual price was excessive—or whether it was unavoidable, an inevitable corollary of the public school achievement.

If the public school system did not starve industry of recruits, it did tend to induce unsuitable traits in those who entered industry. Public school life mitigated against entrepreneur qualities—creative imagination; friendliness to innovation—which would, in fact, have benefited government professions as well as business.

Could more have been done to induce these entrepreneur qualities? As far as the curriculum was concerned, the answer is immediately 'yes'. Despite Divinity lessons, despite Samuel Smiles and his gospel of hard work, the classroom side to public school life did not carry the main brunt of moral indoctrination in the schools. Curricular reform seemed to have little effect on the prevailing public schoolboy ethos. This being the case, the curriculum might have done much more than it did for intuitive thinking and creative speculation—*vis-à-vis* memory-work and Latin analysis—without sapping gentry traditions of public service. Had the public school classroom made more of literature and essay-writing, had public school history lessons been less *uncritically* patriotic, had they set store by ideas as well as detailed events, they might have produced a richer supply of imaginative leadership.

When we turn to the social side of public school life, the side mainly responsible for moral training, we find a more complex problem. Of the devices which helped to produce responsible public servants, some were clearly more anti-intellectual than others. Spartan living conditions, training corps manoeuvres, the prefectorial system, and a measure of hierarchy were in themselves quite compatible with independent thinking. Less compatible was the web of unquestioned etiquette by which the public schools induced group behaviour and communal loyalties.

It may well be argued, of course, that etiquette was inseparable from the prefectorial system of self-government. Comparison with other education systems suggests that, wherever schoolboys are left to run their own world, there is a strong tendency to the rule of custom and a tyranny of group opinion. In their own discreet way, however, housemasters and headmasters could have loosened the fetters of etiquette. Greater provisions for individual privacy, and for contact between the school community and the world outside, might have engendered a more discriminating loyalty to school institutions. Nor should we forget the housemaster's potential, behind-the-scenes influence on schoolboy attitudes—through talks with individual boys and through the lever of prefectorial appointments.

It must be admitted, however, that public school etiquette was an important factor in the maintenance of a responsible, dedicated public servant *élite*. If that etiquette had been reduced, something else would have had to be put in its place in order to maintain the same political motivation. The healthiest substitute would have been a more rational form of indoctrination. And that brings us back to the curriculum.

Without losing academic integrity, the curriculum itself could have inspired interest in government and a sense of public service. It could have done this, what is more, within a classical framework. Instead of concentrating so predominantly on Latin translation, the classical syllabus might have explained the history, institutions, and ideas of Greece and Rome. Such an approach might have been introduced well before the Sixth Form; it could have been primarily political and yet not incomprehensible to a secondary school age-group. In fact, the approach would have fulfilled the arguments of those public school champions who harked back to an eighteenth-century ideal of the classics—to a view which saw classical culture not as mere language-instruction but as a bond with an entire civilization, a moral and intellectual heritage.

This was very much the approach taken in Confucian China by the education system, which taught history as a political and social science exercise, although its veneration of the Chinese Empire's past was admittedly uncritical. Chinese examinations also set political essays which were largely a test of close reasoning power. Herein lies another lesson for the public schools. The best way to teach logic is not through translation exercises in an ancient language but in fields directly related to problems the student will encounter as an adult. Thus, one might well devise a kind of classroom game, in which various problems and arguments—taken from everyday life or from current, political events—were presented with different types of logical flaw. Such an innovation however, would be too daring for most British schools today, let alone the public schools of 1900.

No one can tell whether the Victorian public schools could successfully have introduced a more rational substitute, or part-substitute, for the mysticism and etiquette which helped to produce public servants. The point was that they never really tried. Seldom, if at all, did headmasters and housemasters seem to realize how oppressively far the countless, unquestioned 'do's' and 'dont's' of school tradition had been carried.

And yet, for all their blindnesses, the educators of public school England somehow produced intelligent leaders, men of balanced judgement and eminent common sense.[1] It was only when the harshness of rapid change challenged their ability to imagine bold schemes, to project themselves into realms of theory beyond their own experience—it was only then that their leadership broke down. It was then that one could wonder, 'Were all their boyhood sacrifices worth it?'

[1] For those public schoolboys who went on to Oxford or Cambridge, the freedom of university life offered a certain intellectual counter-experience to the restrictions of the public school community. Unlike the public school system, the university did something to encourage self-education, the pursuit of individual lines of inquiry. On the other hand, the compulsory undergraduate curriculum was even narrower than the curriculum of the public school.

Part Four

COMPARISONS AND IMPLICATIONS

Chapter 12

Manners and Classics in Confucian China

The winds blow as they list . . . Wisdom cannot create materials; they are the gifts of nature or of chance; her pride is in the use.[1]

So wrote Edmund Burke about the seemingly haphazard growth of a nation's institutions. To the British, such growth has often been a matter of patriotic pride, an assurance that their institutions were basically inimitable. A system like the English public schools and its archetype, the English Gentleman, could surely have no foreign parallel for the very reason that their development seemed so peculiarly and haphazardly British. 'The gifts of nature or of chance' to a particular environment, how could they be anything other than unique?

Yet they were not unique. During the late eighteen-hundreds, the public school system grew remarkably akin to an educational pattern that had dominated China during at least four dynasties: the Tang (618–907 A.D.), the Sung (960–1279), the Ming (1368–1662) and the Ching, the Empire's last dynasty, lasting from 1662 to 1912.[2]

Like the public schools, Confucian education instilled gentle-manly attitudes which in turn helped to perpetuate a public servant *élite*. Both systems taught morals by teaching manners: both moulded behaviour through etiquette, through aesthetic appeals to 'good form'. Similarly, both systems pursued an amateur ideal, the notion that manners (signifying virtue) and classical

[1] Edmund Burke, *Reflections on the Revolution in France*, 182.
[2] The Tang and Sung Dynasties were separated by a chaotic fifty-three years, a period of short-lived dynasties and, especially in the south, an era of vying régimes. This interlude was aptly named 'The Ten Kingdoms and Five Dynasties'.
The dates given for the Sung Dynasty include the last, 'Southern Sung' period, when the dynasty held only South China against the Mongols from the north. This, too, finally fell in 1279 to Ghengis Khan's grandson, Khubilai, who founded the Yuan Dynasty, the era of Mongol rule preceding the Ming.

culture (signifying a well-tuned mind) were better credentials for leadership than any amount of expert, practical training. In China, no less than in Britain, this faith in the amateur was reflected by Civil Service examinations which placed greatest emphasis on a classical, non-technical syllabus.

Confucian education, even more than the public school, was essentially the expression of a 'country gentleman' class. '*Shen-shih*', the name given to the select company who won degrees at the government-controlled examinations, is often translated as 'gentry'. The translation is loose, but it is quite justified by the degree-holder *élite's* social composition. One study of the Ching Dynasty's *élite* has ascribed 46 per cent. of its income to official, professional, and 'gentry' services (including teaching and local magistracy), 32 per cent. to land rents, and only 22 per cent. to commercial profit-making.[1]

Compared with the English gentry, it is true, the Chinese equivalent was subject to considerable 'ups' and 'downs' in a family's social status; and the latter depended largely on degree-holding and kinship with officials. When, therefore, I write of gentry in the Chinese case, I mean those families enjoying social prestige, a distinctive style, and a respected standard of culture. They were not necessarily large landowners, but their values were essentially *landed* and anti-commercial, and it is in this aspect that they bear dramatic resemblance to the gentry of England.

Why, despite the words of Edmund Burke, two societies so far apart in cultural origins should have produced so similar a pattern of education is a problem best left to the end of the chapter. Whatever the factors of historical cause, however, the comparison between Confucian China and public school England is also valuable as anthropology. In other words, when we consider the Chinese experience, features of gentlemanly power and gentlemanly education that might have seemed peculiar to the British will acquire a more universal dimension. The comparison will throw light on human society as a whole, and this in turn will help us to understand more about how the British system really

[1] Robert Marsh, *The Mandarins: The Circulation of Élites in China*, 65, reporting an estimate by Chang Chung-li.

worked. The extraordinary nature of Chinese society, moreover, the mixture of traditional privilege and rationalized bureaucracy, of intelligence and superstition, provides the anthropologist with curious and unsuspected insights into contemporary Western life.

Take, for example, the central place in China of the examination system, a rigorous hierarchy of degree-examinations with the *chin-shih*, or Ph.D. degree, at its summit. As the principal method of selecting Imperial bureaucrats, the Chinese examination system was forerunner to that current American obsession, the exaltation of Ph.D. training as a prerequisite not only for university appointments but, increasingly, for jobs in business and government. In the way it combined *élitism* with democracy, the Chinese system also resembled the modern tendency of certain business occupations—advertising and public relations in Britain are one example—to seek the dignity of a 'Profession' by setting formal examinations for recruits.[1]

All three phenomena—the Chinese examination system, American Ph.D. training, and examinations in business—sprang in part from an equalitarian impulse, the wish to select candidates fairly according to individual merit. Chinese experience, indeed, suggests that whenever there are a large number of candidates to be processed, increased reliance may be placed on impersonal examinations as a way of guaranteeing impartial selection. But Chinese experience also suggests that, however democratic its rationale, heavy reliance on examinations will generate its own form of *élitism*. A separate breed of men may spring up, talking the special language and thinking the special thought-processes of their examinations. As I suggested in Chapter 2, in the case of the Victorian professions, examinations can easily acquire the aura of an initiation rite, the key to a select membership and a secret body of knowledge. Whenever this happens, there is danger that the select membership—the profession or the Civil Service—and its body of knowledge will become so venerated that their worth

---

[1] cf. Paul Donham, 'Is Management a Profession?', *Harvard Business Review*, October 1962. The author's verdict is no, though American industry is trying its hardest.

It is interesting to note in England that one or two public relations firms have acquired the dignity of the subtitle 'Practitioners in Public Relations'.

will seldom be questioned. Such was the experience of China, and in it lies a principle of modern society: that impulses to create equal opportunity may produce partly opposite effects. The selection of leadership by formal examination, however much it is designed to reward merit fairly, can become so stereotyped that it may actually penalize the brilliant and most deserving candidate.

The Production of Public Servants

Despite its valuable perspectives, the comparison between East and West should obviously not be pressed too far. In the case of the public schools and Confucian education, two major differences should be noted right away. First, the Chinese system taught a relatively passive ethic of self-perfection rather than 'muscular Christianity'; it awarded low prestige to soldiering; and it *professed*, at any rate, that good scholarship was indispensable to good government. In the second place, Confucian education was essentially local and family-directed: there was no dominant system of national boarding schools, and classroom instruction was closely linked with the moral teaching of family etiquette and certain clan rules. Although primary and secondary schools existed, e.g. the private schools in Hangchow where upper-class children went from the age of seven to thirteen,[1] much of the schooling for children and adolescents was conducted in the home. Even here, however, some comparison can be made with the public school system: the Chinese family, no less than the English boarding school, was venerated as an historic community and it possessed a strong sense of co-operation and hierarchy.

The main academies of learning, some privately supported, some public, some both, were at university level, and for this reason our study of Confucian China must include higher education as well as secondary. Compared, of course, with the British system, Confucian education was far more expressly linked with the recruitment needs of government. Political interest in education was well established very early on. According to the classical *Book of History*, the ancient sovereign Shun allotted no less than three of his nine administrative departments to educational

[1] Jacques Gernet, *Daily Life in China on the Eve of the Mongol Invasion*, 1250–1276, 153.

128

purposes: a directorate of music, a ministry of education, and a ministry of religion.[1]

The classical curriculum of Confucian education demonstrated an official belief that study itself could instil a morality containing a sense of public service. In the *Great Learning* classic, the acquisition of knowledge is justified because it is expected to cultivate the person, thence regulate the family, thence create a 'rightly governed' State and so make the whole empire 'tranquil and happy'.[2] The trinemetrical Classic introduced quatrains on the Three Bonds (sovereign-subject, father-child, and husband-wife) right in the middle of a dissertation on natural science,[3] and the very poetry of the Book of Odes was supposed to carry a political message.

Above all, both family teaching and the curriculum persistently sought to instil a spirit of social service by emphasizing *li*. *Li* was a more elaborate equivalent of public school manners and etiquette. Unlike the latter, it was largely written, but it depended on custom and on appeals to aesthetic taste (propriety) in very much the same fashion as public school etiquette. Originally the word *li* referred to rules of religious worship, and it was not surprising, therefore, that ceremonial *li* should govern Imperial court ritual as well as ancestor-veneration and other ceremonies exalting the clan. With the passing of time, *li* came also to include an intricate set of courtesies and privileges; at one end it merged with and supported the sumptuary laws which awarded colourful status-symbols to scholar-officials. The scope of *li* was immense. It told the individual how to address other ranks; it instructed him how to behave with decorum in another man's house; it harmonized personal relations, instilled deference to rank, and its symbolic message was essentially political: that the individual should serve his community, be it the family or the nation, whose historic continuity denoted a group immortality.

The political orientation of *li* was echoed by the education

1 Ping Wen Kuo, *The Chinese System of Public Education*, 8.

2 *Great Learning*, Text 4, quoted by Chungil Rhoe in *The True Function of Education in Social Adjustment* (a comparison of Confucianism and the educational philosophy of John Dewey).

3 S. W. Green, *Education as a National Unifying Agency in China*, 30.

system as a whole. During all four dynasties, preparation for government consumed the main energies of China's schools and tutors. By the seventeenth century, the State-supported schools at the capital could declare one aim: to prepare men who had passed district examinations for degree-exams that would qualify them for government office. Some private academies did survive where learning was pursued for its own sake, but virtually all higher education performed a supply function for government office.[1]

In fact, the function was over-performed. There were three main degree-levels—*chin-shih*, *chu-jen*, and *kung-shen*, roughly approximating to doctorates, M.A.s and B.A.s—but frequently there were not even enough government places for every doctorate. To make things worse, at the *chu-jen* (M.A.) level, the examiners failed over 99 per cent. of the candidates.[2] Yet so high was the status of government office that multitudes of degree-holders eked out a living as tutors and kept their sights fixed on obtaining an official post rather than turning to commerce. (As we shall see shortly, they would have been officially disqualified from seeking public posts had they gone into business.) This in itself tended to maintain a political bias in education, since a large nucleus of scholars and teachers were aspirant—or *pretending* to be aspirant[3]—office-seekers.

Behind this 'self-confirming' pattern lay economic and social factors which compelled schools and private tutors to tailor their subject-matter to examination requirements. Government monopolies in iron and salt had existed from before the Han Dynasties; neither merchant nor farmer ever acquired enough power to attain the official's social prestige. Although Imperial government was far from being an all-pervasive dictatorship, an official's very position gave him and his family security against the arbitrary whims of an irresponsible Emperor.[4] Under these conditions it was inevitable that government officials should enjoy more social prestige than any other class, and that scholarship should come to

---

[1] W. T. De Bary, 'Chinese Despotism and the Confucian Ideal in the 17th Century', in J. K. Fairbank, *Chinese Thought and Institutions*, 179.
[2] J. K. Fairbank and Edwin Reischauer, *East Asia: The Great Tradition*, 305.
[3] Gernet, op. cit., 7.
[4] Hsiao-tung Fei, *China's Gentry*, 30. See page 104n.

be viewed primarily as the prerequisite for holding public office.

Some scholars there were, of course, who despised the careerism of their fellows. One of these was the Ching writer, P'u Sung-ling. Despite his literary brilliance, P'u failed the Imperial examinations, and he is worth mentioning here for his satiric short story, *The Bookworm*.[1] The tale tells of a serious young man who prized above all else a text entitled *Invitation to Learning*, composed by a past Emperor. The text informs its reader that in books he will find mansions and rich harvests of corn, liveried servants and carriages, wealth and fame. Idealistic, reclusive, and believing that an Emperor could tell no falsehood, the young man takes the Imperial text at face value. He becomes a fanatic bibliophile, little realizing the more worldly import of the Emperor's words: that through scholarship one could enter the ruling class and so win honour and fortune.

The story is developed in a delightfully whimsical way which should not be spoiled by paraphrase; but several ingredients of our present study are there. Confucian education stimulated both idealism and opportunism: it inspired men to seek Imperial service for its own sake, but by exalting family ties it also legitimized the pursuit of public power for the prestige and security it conferred on the individual's clan. The same ambivalence between idealism and careerism applied to scholarship itself. By the late Ming Dynasty, well before P'u Sung-ling wrote, the relation between scholarship and office-seeking had acquired a curious twist. Rather than looking on culture as a simple means of obtaining office, men now desired office as a symbol of culture. So important a symbol was it, however, that this new twist did nothing to impair the scholar's wish to obtain office.[2] Far from it, the men who desired learning for its own sake now found it harder than ever to separate learning from office-seeking.

There was much in Confucian doctrine to support this close relationship between scholar and governor. The wisdom of Confucius and the neo-Confucian sages was largely concerned with how to secure *tao*, good and selfless government. According

[1] Lin Yutang, *Famous Chinese Short Stories*, 243.
[2] J. R. Levenson, 'The Amateur Ideal (late Ming-Ching)' in Fairbank, op. cit., 321.

to the classics, good government depended primarily on obtaining good men as rulers. And this in turn depended on scholarship: 'no virtues can remain untainted without learning', decreed the *Book of Rituals*. Thus it was that, in the very educational thought of Confucian China, scholarship, the requirements of good government, and the gentleman ideal were all bound up together. Like the English word 'gentleman', the nearest Chinese equivalent *'juin-tze'* carried an overtone of moral superiority; quite literally it could be translated as 'superior man'. Government needed superior men and to this purpose scholarship was its handmaiden.

At this point, we might pause to make comparisons with Victorian England. In both societies, a classical education carried social prestige as the mark of a gentleman—or *juin-tze*. And in both, as we shall see, the place given to the classics in Civil Service examinations helped maintain the social position and political power of an *élite* which could afford the time required for learning Latin or the Confucian classics.

We have found also that, in China as in Britain, the education system reflected the supremacy of government service over other careers. Here, of course, there were differences. Under the Chinese Empire the government controlled degree-examinations—since they were really the same as Civil Service exams—and classical curricula exerted moral pressure on the student to seek government office. By comparison, the relation between British education and the needs of Her Majesty's Government was not so clear-cut. In Britain, public service never enjoyed the *complete* supremacy of status that it did in China. Governmental influence on educational content existed in both societies, but in Victorian England it was less direct and more tacit. The schools induced government-orientation by social weapons of indoctrination— 'Notions', games, and the prefectorial system—rather than by academic means. Chinese education, on the other hand, emphasized both, for *li* and clan rules were largely expressed in writing and hence formed part of the academic curriculum.

Like the Victorian public schools, Chinese education and the examination system provided a national pool of candidates for government office. To accomplish this there had to be a nationally unified culture; and here again, even more than in public school England, the education system played its part. It has several times been claimed that China was unified culturally well before it was unified politically, that the ideology of 'one China' arose before the first Emperor of the Chin Dynasty built his Great Wall and forged the Chinese Empire. In subsequent centuries, throughout foreign invasions and civil strife, there persisted the idea that culturally there could only be one China.[1] The idea clearly depended on education which guarded and promoted, for all its localism, a common heritage of custom and thought. Potent enough to make over the turbulent, nomadic Manchus into Chinese, the education system 'gave a uniform stamp to the stamp under every variety of physical condition'.[2]

Just as the public school accent and manner cut across regional differences, so Chinese education upheld a single upper-class style against immense variations of geography. Below the *shen-shih* élite there existed a wide range of regional dialects and mannerisms; by contrast the *shen-shih* themselves exhibited a like bearing, observed common courtesies (*li*), and could speak the same 'mandarin' dialect. All of these features facilitated government recruitment on a nationwide scale, but the most important feature of the élite style was the ability to write—and write elegantly. The Imperial examinations, for their part, maintained the unifying influence of Chinese writing and calligraphy by drawing candidates from all over the Empire. If and when he became an official, the Confucian scholar was expected to be able to write government memorials in a beautiful style that betrayed no trace of his regional origins.

The coupling of national education to government examinations was partly stimulated by an Imperial wish to achieve regional balance among Civil Service candidates. In A.D. 655, during the Tang Dynasty, the Empress Wu Tse-tien began to expand recruitment by examination, largely in order to bring in officials from the south-east, thereby weakening a strong

[1] S. W. Green, *Education as a National Unifying Agency in China*, op. cit., Introduction.
[2] W. A. Martin, *Lore of Cathay*, 282–3, quoted by S. W. Green, op. cit. Dr. Martin was the first president of China's first modern university, the Tung Wen Kuan.

bureaucratic clique of men from the capital region.[1] Much later, rulers of the Yuan and Ming Dynasties showed a similar desire for group balance when they reorganized recruitment on a basis of regional quotas.[2]

If Chinese education helped create a pool of government candidates by its role of national unification, it expanded that pool by its contribution to social mobility. In theory at least, the system had become democratic. Like the British Civil Service, Chinese bureaucracy evolved examination by 'limited competition' first. Under the former Han Dynasty, the examinations merely classified candidates already recommended by senior officials. 'Open competition' did not come till the Sui period, the régime preceding the Tang. 'Protection'—string-pulling by relatives and friends of the highly-placed—and 'transfer'—entrance to the Civil Service from clerical and military ranks—always co-existed with the examination system, but by 1050 degree-holders in the bureaucracy outnumbered the officials recruited by the other two means.[3] Furthermore, doctoral degree-holders frequently rose faster than the others; and one Sung historian reports that during the eleventh century only doctorate-holders could fill the government post of Censor.[4]

With the establishment of 'open competition', senior government posts were opened to promotion by merit, and this meant that public employment could confer a gentleman's social prestige upon the poor but talented individual. Frequently a clan would unite to finance the education of one of its more promising youth. There was no group of 'public schools' offering a special syllabus to people of a certain social rank and above.

On the other hand, scarcity of economic resources limited educational democracy. The details of Chinese writing and the Confucian classics demanded long hours of memory work, and this favoured the family with money, leisure, a library, and a cultural heritage. The State seemed unable to provide substantial education for everyone and at the same time subsidize schools preparing candidates for higher degrees. Even if the government

[1] E. A. Kracke, 'The Chinese Examination System', in Fairbank, op. cit., 253.
[2] Ibid., 263-4.
[3] E. A. Kracke, *Civil Service in Early Sung China*, 58.   [4] Ibid., 60.

could have provided universal free education, sheer poverty would have driven the vast majority of peasants to keep their children at toil on the land.

Figures for the examinations of 1148 show that descendants of the Sung Dynasty founder—men who were given a separate, probably easier examination—supplied 16 of 288 doctoral graduates. In 1256 they supplied 76 out of 484. 'New Men'—people unrelated on their paternal side to officials for the past three generations—supplied 56 per cent. of the graduates in 1148, and 58 per cent. in 1256.[1] Most of these, however, were relatively well off financially and/or had family backgrounds of some culture.[2]

Social studies of the Ming and Ching Dynasties confirm this pattern of privilege. Throughout both periods, successful examination candidates from the *shen-shih élite*—that is, from the families of degree-holders and officials—considerably outnumbered those from the non-*élite*.[3] On the other hand, there is some evidence that social mobility over *several generations* was more pronounced than it was in eighteenth- and nineteenth-century England. From 1600 to 1900 (late Ming-Ching), few families produced more than two generations in office;[4] and we must remember that, in the long run especially, the income, security, and prestige afforded by government office in China was an important guarantee of gentry status.

In general, however, Confucian education did resemble the British system in the way it accommodated social mobility within a class structure. To some extent, Confucius himself had condoned the co-existence of hereditary *li* (privileges) with promotion by merit: hence his criticism of Kuan Chung, the prime minister to a duke, for adopting the princely prerogative of screening his gate and placing a stand beneath inverted teacups![5] From the standpoint of making government service attractive, toleration of some hereditary privilege in government had the

[1] E. A. Kracke, 'The Chinese Examination System' in Fairbank, op. cit., 258–62.
[2] E. A. Kracke, *Civil Service in Early Sung China*, 69.
[3] Marsh, op. cit., Chapter 4.
[4] Ibid., Chapter 4.
[5] *Analects*, Book III, Chapter 22, 162–3, quoted by Lorraine Creel, *The Concept of Social Order in Early Confucianism*.

effect of clothing merit-won positions with the reflected aura of aristocracy. In Victorian England, likewise, an hereditary nobility co-existed with an hierarchy of earned honours; the two in fact merged with one another. From knighthoods to O.B.E.s, conferred titles and honours have gone out largely to distinguished men in public service—an adult counterpart to the splendid train of colours conferred by a public school on the games hero who brought glory home to his House.

The Chinese compromise between hereditary privilege and the reward of merit extended to the curriculum itself. Imperial examiners placed great weight on memory work in the classics and on style: on calligraphy and elegant composition, each judged by formalistic standards. As we have pointed out, examinations with this sort of content inevitably favoured the culture and well-heeled leisure of a gentry home. Yet—and here is the irony—when critics attacked the examiners' preoccupation with formal style, the defence was made partly on democratic grounds. Without strong rules of form, argued the authorities, it would be difficult to find objective standards for assessing candidates according to individual merit.[1]

Even when the lowborn scholar did win through, he inevitably became a gentleman first, stamped with gentlemanly manners and gentlemanly attitudes by the whole bias of his training. It was the same principle of 'synthetic gentility' that we observed in the public school case, and like the British variety, Chinese gentility made class-consciousness a trenchant advertisement for government service. Confucian doctrine posed the existence of a four-class social scale. At the top of the scale stood scholars—first officials, then non-officials—and below these, in descending order of status, came farmers, artisans, and merchants. In two respects, the Confucian scale bore a strong resemblance to public school notions about careers and social classes. First, its values were clearly the values of landed gentry: it exalted public service; it respected the life of the land; it discriminated against urban pursuits in general and trade in particular.

Secondly, the Confucian scale echoed the way in which

[1] J. Liu, 'An Early Sung Reformer', in Fairbank, op. cit., 115.

Western feudal terminology—'gentleborn', 'baseborn', 'noble', and so forth—identified social status with virtue. The teaching of Confucius morally downgraded any occupation that smacked of *lī*, a quality which should not be confused with *li* and which might roughly be defined as selfish greed.[1] It was largely for this reason that the merchant stood fourth on the Confucian scale: private profit-making was traditionally identified with *lī*. One might also argue that the businessman was penalized because his rationalism was hostile to the gentry's fondness for tradition and aesthetic style. It should be further added that the spirit behind the Confucian scale was an ideal which seldom corresponded exactly to reality. Wealthy merchants fraternized with officials and married into their families; at certain times they were even able to take on privileges of dress and household life which *li* and the sumptuary laws officially reserved for civil servants. The latter, for their part, were not always above sending into trade sons who had failed the government examinations.[2] Similarly, the more well-to-do gentry were not averse to becoming absentee landlords and acquiring mansions amid the comforts of the city.

Despite these variations on the Confucian theme, the moral message of the ideal four-class scale did have effect. The 'mean people'—an occupation group including actors, runners, and prostitutes—were rated below the four classes, and they were correspondingly debarred from Imperial examinations. Merchants and their sons were likewise excluded, although now and again the examiners' strictness lapsed.

In general, the ethic behind the four-class scale did seem to influence career motivations—and influence them in favour of government service. The Chinese connexion between social status and moral considerations bore a strong similarity to Victorian upper-class contempt for 'Trade'. Behind the moral disapproval, possibly, lay fear of the rising commercial classes and their potential power; but the moral disapproval existed none the less. In Confucian China, as in gentry England, prestige went to community leadership rather than to wealth. However rich he might be, the Chinese merchant only obtained high social

[1] Pronounced more like the French vowel sound, *lu*.   [2] Gernet, op. cit., 86.

prestige when he performed local leadership functions which were historically the charge of the gentry: service as magistrate, officiating at ceremonies, fund-raising for irrigation projects, and so forth.[1] It is significant also that, among the merchants possessing highest status, were usually those involved with the *public* salt and iron monopolies.[2]

The high status which public office enjoyed in China stemmed partly from the gentleman ideal, promoted so faithfully by Confucian education. Like the English public schools, the Chinese education system sought to create a special link between privilege and social duty. Again like the public schools, Chinese education depended on more than altruism to promote that duty. By posing community leadership as a moral status-symbol, the gentleman ideal played on egoism as well as on selflessness. Such a mechanism, of course, could only work in an appropriate social climate, a milieu where virtue was largely seen as *civic* virtue. If Confucian China lacked the Evangelical thirst for Good Works that characterized Victorian England, it did make political leadership inseparable from moral leadership. A strong theme of classical thought always persisted that, by 'self-cultivation' alone, the ruler could morally influence his subjects.

This brings us to another component of the gentleman ideal which we noticed in the case of Victorian England—the property of magic. Magic, it will be remembered, was defined as that mysterious-seeming aura which dignifies and distinguishes certain leaders.

> He had a black gauze cap and green silk gown,
> A jasper ring on his cap and a purple belt;
> His socks were white as snow,
> His shoes like rosy clouds;
> He'd a lordly look and natural dignity.
> A man like that, if not a god,
> Must at least be a high official or a ruler of men.[3]

Thus a story teller wrote in the Tang Dynasty. In fact, the

[1] Marsh, op. cit., 37–38. [2] Ibid. 2, 4.
[3] 'The Foxes' Revenge', a story in *The Courtesan's Jewel Box: Chinese Stories of the 10th–17th Centuries*, 96, quoted by Marsh, op. cit., 2.

education system supplemented the 'natural dignity' of officials by teaching *li*. Not only did *li* include rules of political decorum, but it supported the sumptuary laws which in turn awarded the scholar-official a colourful array of privileges. As we shall see later, many of these privileges were *aesthetic* privileges, ranging from emblems of clothing to styles of address.

How did the Chinese concern with magic, exhibited by Imperial government and developed by the education system, attract recruits into public office? In the first place there is the answer given by Joseph Schumpeter: that governments have simply had more need of magic than have private companies. (As a modern footnote to Schumpeter's thesis, it could be said that not until the rise of advertising and public relations have business firms rivalled government ceremonial in their *systematic* attempts to influence men by magic display of a group image.)

Schumpeter's argument, however, supplies only part of the answer. In the case of China there was another factor which made magic a specially potent appeal for government service. Like the ancient Greek notion of *arête*, or excellence, Confucian doctrine made little ultimate distinction between beauty and goodness. As a result, Chinese education went even further than the English public schools in making manners and ritual symbolic of virtue. Since manners and ritual—including Imperial court ceremonies— were a large part of the Chinese government's magic display, it followed that the magic of government was inseparable from the high moral status of public service. The bureaucracy of China, in short, could offer its servants much more than bread and security. It offered glamour, and morally respectable glamour at that.

As a final comment upon the way in which magic impelled men to seek public office, it should be emphasized that *li* itself fostered political orientation. Like public school etiquette, *li* was essentially a magical device, for it played on aesthetic emotion and invoked a mysticism of tradition. We will go into the working of *li* more thoroughly on later pages, but one prime difference with public school etiquette should here be noted. Unlike the public school ethos, Confucian education did not de-emphasize family life as a possible distraction to public service. Chinese womenfolk, it was true, were much downtrodden, but the moral teaching embodied in *li* posed Imperial loyalty as a natural extension of family loyalty. Confucian education constantly applied family analogies to politics: thus, government officials were known as *fu ma kuan*, or 'parent officials'. In like spirit, the *wu lun*, a classical list of 'Five Cardinal Relationships', stressed the sovereign-minister relation as second only to that between father and son.[1]

This is not to say that in fact 'filial piety' and loyalty to the State never conflicted: again and again, clash of interest clearly prevented the realization of *tao*, selfless devotion to good government. It did nothing, however, to deter men from seeking public office itself. On the contrary, a sense of family obligation provided an added spur to office-seeking. Not only did public position provide a comfortable income but, as we have already suggested, it promised a measure of security from Imperial power. In this respect, the ascetic tendency of gentlemanly education served a slightly different political purpose to the one it did in Britain. Although Confucian doctrine included an ethic of frugality, Chinese bureaucracy allowed its personnel greater material rewards—relative to the offerings of private business—than did its British counterpart. In these circumstances, the Confucian ethic of frugality was needed less to attract men into public office in the first place than to counter venality and corruption once they got in. By contrast, public school hardship was needed to influence the individual in his initial choice of a career, inoculating him against the relative discomforts of public life.

In our description of the gentleman ideal and the way it served Imperial recruitment, there remains to be mentioned one more component—the concept of leisure. For the Chinese *shin-shih*, as for the English gentry, leisure was a status-symbol, a sign that its possessor could pursue noble things. A far cry this concept was from the professionalism of today, when the leader who works long hours can, by so doing, demonstrate that he has a responsible and exacting job. In China it was different. With leisure, a

[1] C. K. Yang, *The Chinese Family in the Communist Revolution*, 5–6.

man could pursue art and learning; with leisure he could linger in the tea-houses and there develop a 'cultured eloquence' and a 'mellowed and humorous outlook on life'.[1] Such opportunities the life of the official afforded well: unlike nearly everyone else, including merchants, he usually had both time and inclination to paint, write essays, play chess, or go on outings.[2] Leisure, in short, was closely associated in men's minds with culture, and its very real connexion with public office made the latter all the more attractive.

It would be wrong, however, to suggest that as a political force the concept of leisure worked in China exactly as it did in England. Unlike the Imperial bureaucracy, British public office did not *promise* leisure. Instead, certain public functions—the voluntary services of the J.P., for example, and to a lesser extent the low-paid office of M.P.—*depended* on the leisure that private means could support. Even here, however, there was a parallel with China, where, on a very local level, some 'gentry services' were entirely unremunerated. In these instances, public service rested on an alliance between the gentleman's fondness for leisure activity and the confidence of the amateur. Imperial China, even more than Victorian England, was largely run in local units, administered by squirely clan-elders who claimed a general education but no specific training for the various duties they assumed.

Ethical Restraint

Despite immense differences between Chinese and British society, it is not surprising that the features of gentlemanly education common to both cultures carried through to government itself. Many of the same broad categories under which we described British parliamentary government hold, no less, for Imperial bureaucracy.[3]

The first category on our list is the dependence of responsible government on human character rather than on institutions,

[1] Hsiao-tung Fei, 'Peasantry and Gentry', *American Journal of Sociology*, Vol. III, No. 1, 1946, p. 7.
[2] Gernet, op. cit., 183.
[3] For obvious reasons the category of 'democracy' does not apply, nor does the one of 'imperialism'. I do include the category of 'change', but I do not mean this to imply that the Chinese had the same concept of change as the British.

on ethical codes rather than on formal law. Just as British Cabinets deferred to constitutional custom, just as public school prefects were constrained by etiquette, so Chinese authority—clan elder and bureaucrat alike—paid close attention to *li*.

Now it is true that the dictates of *li* existed largely in writing. It is also true that some of *li*, especially the *li* governing privileges, came to be backed by Imperial law. But *li* and law were not the same thing, and when we perceive the difference between the two we may understand better the uses and limitations of law in our modern societies.

From the standpoint of traditional Confucian thought, law (*ta*) was essentially negative. It made fear of penalty rather than joy of inner perfection the incentive for good behaviour, and for this reason it was considered potentially subversive to moral teaching. By contrast, *li* was held to represent positive ideals. As a code of manners it not only *symbolized* those virtues desired by society, but it was supposed actually to *induce* them. There was a strong assumption underlying Chinese thought that outer actions could stimulate inner morality. This brings us back to the gentlemanly connexion between beauty and goodness. The Chinese saw a direct moral value in observing aesthetic details of style and dress.[1]

In fact, of course, the forces behind law and *li* overlapped to a far greater extent than Confucian teaching would have us believe. As the experience of ancient Greece suggests, laws can do other things besides threatening wrongdoers. When the youth of Athens and Sparta learned the laws of the *polis*, they learned them as ideal codes of behaviour. Law, in this case, was counted an educative agent.[2]

Conversely, it would be wrong to say that *li*, any more than British custom and etiquette, depended purely on ethics. Quite obviously, it too threatened transgressors with penalty—the penalty of shame. *Li*, in other words, enjoyed external, as well as internalized, sanctions. People obeyed *li* not only because they felt they *ought to*—not only, that is, because *li* represented internal conscience—but because they feared public disapproval of disobedience.

[1] Gernet, op. cit., 128.   [2] H. D. F. Kitto, *The Greeks*, 94.

The way in which the qualities of *li* and law overlap, merely indicate that the difference between the two is relative, a matter of relative emphasis, rather than absolute. To the extent that sanctions defending civil order threaten penalties, particularly penalties levied by such *institutional* means as law courts and judges, they are legal sanctions. To the extent that they depend on internalized feelings of moral obligation they are ethical sanctions. The distinction, as I have said, is largely one of emphasis. In public school society, for example, prefectorial authority was ready to punish persistent breaches of school etiquette. So seldom, however, did breaches occur that school etiquette rarely had to fall back on punishment for its defence. The public schoolboy was too well indoctrinated, too well steeped in the ethical sanctions of etiquette, to wonder for long what would happen if he defied them. This is not to say that public school society was non-coercive: prefects in most schools certainly exercised their powers of corporal punishment. But boys were beaten, not so much for breaking rules of social behaviour set by tradition and the whole student body, as for disobeying more administrative rules—e.g., school boundary laws—promulgated by masters and senior prefects. Consequently, corporal punishment seldom seemed to inflict shame—a point easily forgotten by outside critics of the public school system.[1]

In Confucian China, law was much less developed than *li*. Against a traditional environment, clan and government could strongly influence individual motivations through custom, and hence through the education system which maintained custom. The Imperial government, furthermore, officially considered that one of its prime functions was to afford a moral example to its subjects. By their very beauty, court rituals and court memorials were thought to inspire both subjects and officials to virtue.

This faith in the power of moral example was reflected and propagated by education. Teachers frequently taught their pupils by rote and imitation; and Confucian doctrine stated that anyone, especially a ruler, could influence his fellows by self-perfection alone.

[1] At my own school, Winchester, being beaten was counted an honourable and manly experience: 'You're not a *real* Wykehamist till you've been beaten.' How far and how strongly this applied to other schools and to the Victorian-Edwardian era, I do not know.

Belief in moral example, however, was not the only means by which education encouraged responsible government. Like public school etiquette, Chinese *li* placed an aesthetic premium on moderation and emotional self-restraint. Just as public school etiquette appealed to 'good taste', so the rules of *li* appealed to 'propriety'. 'Respectfulness, without the rules of propriety, becomes laborious bustle', said the Confucian classic, the *Lun Yu*; '. . . carefulness (becomes) timidity: straightforwardness (becomes) rudeness'.[1] As we suggested in the case of the public schools, gentlemanly moderation was inseparable from an aesthetic ideal of harmony. On the personal plane, the ideal is best summed up by the classical remark I have just quoted—the notion that virtues themselves must be moderated and balanced against each other. On the social level, the ideal of harmony inveighed against the jarring force of egoism; it taught gentleness; and it posed a clearly defined social hierarchy as part of a natural, cosmic order. Small wonder that the Chinese, like the ancient Greeks, taught music for its *moral* benefit. 'The *kung* note is a prince; *shang* a minister; *chio* the people; *chih* affairs and *yu* things', stated an old passage from the classics. 'If all five are out of due order, then ruin must follow.'[2] Implicit in the phrase 'due order' was not only the idea of aesthetic harmony but the absolutist notion that there could be only one proper social system.

A great danger, of course, in looking at government through the window of education is that one can easily mistake the ideal for the real. The danger is particularly pronounced in the case of Confucian education where the ideals were so well defined in writing. On three scores the Chinese civil servants and gentry can be said to have fallen beneath the ideals of gentlemanly education. First, their rule was bribe-ridden and corrupt. Secondly, few landlords demonstrated personal *noblesse oblige* to their impoverished tenants; far more likely were they to ignore the peasant's lot and levy extortionate rents. Thirdly, when an irresponsible Emperor, clearly opposed to Confucian precepts of good govern-

[1] Quoted by Lorraine Creel, *Concept of Social Order in Early Confucianism*, Ph.D. thesis, Chapter 1.
[2] Vincent Cronin's account of Matteo Ricci, the great Jesuit visitor to Ching China. Vincent Cronin, *The Wise Man from the West*, 181.

ment, sat on the throne, most senior officials grovelled in their subservience to him.

In considering these three counts, we must remember that gentlemanly education faced a very different environment in China from the one it faced in Britain. Take, for example, the first charge: that Chinese officials were corrupt. It is quite true that, by contrast, British civil servants have been famously un-corrupt—an attribute promoted by the public school ethos. British education, however, did not have to carry the full burden of promoting honest government; in this aspect public school ideals were supported by laws circumscribing the bureaucrat. In China, on the other hand, there was little law to support Confucian ideals of honest government.[1] Furthermore, during the Ching Dynasty at least, officials were paid low salaries and it was gener-ally assumed that they would pad their incomes illicitly. The few civil servants who kept to their official salaries ran a risk of im-poverishment when they retired.[2] Under such conditions, the wonder is not that Confucian ideals permitted corruption, but that they induced so many officials to limit their corruption and to show as much benevolence as possible into the bargain.[3]

With regard to the second count, the argument that Chinese landlords were calloused towards their tenants, the economic context must again be remembered. The privileged few grew up accustomed to seeing immense poverty on all sides. Those who might have wished to effect wide-scale improvement could only have felt a sense of helplessness,[4] a sense to be drugged by harden-ing the heart. In some ways, it must be admitted, Confucian education indulged such callousness by stressing the relatively passive ideal of self-cultivation and setting a moral example to others. On the other hand, the education system did promote altruism, and it awarded the private philanthropist with prestige above that of the mere fortune-builder. Jacques Gernet's account of Hangchow life in the thirteenth century tells how merchants

---

[1] Admittedly, the Civil Service enjoyed a censorship system which looked into an official's record and tended to favour honest men for promotion. The strength and scope of this discrimination, however, varied between eras.

[2] Mu Fu-sheng, *The Wilting of the Hundred Flowers*, 64.

[3] Ibid., 65.   [4] Ibid., 125.

'made up for being excessively wealthy' by distributing largesse to suffering families, and how officials, on being appointed or promoted, sought prestige with similar acts of philanthropy.[1]

All in all, it must be said that the education system instilled public duty more in terms of maintaining self-restraint and civil order than of feeding hungry children. Yet even here the system performed an ameliorating function for the masses. By inspiring the gentry to local leadership, Confucian education supported a decentralized pattern of government which, by and large, the peasantry seemed to prefer. However extortionate his rent-collection might be, the landlord usually governed in a predictable way. As a result his rule was seen by the peasants as a shield against the press-gangs and decrees of an arbitrary Emperor.[2]

With regard to the third argument against the Chinese political system, that it produced opportunist bureaucrats who placed subservience to the Emperor above *tao*, the answer lies partly beyond the realm of education. Given the fact of Imperial power unbridled by constitutional machinery, one can hardly wonder that few officials directly opposed that power. As it was, a minority who persistently tried to put *tao* first nearly always remained in office. Back in the former Han Dynasty, the idealist minority even tried to make itself a priestly Supreme Court, threatening with heavenly wrath the Emperor who opposed their interpretation of classical precepts. This attempt was firmly scotched by a Han Emperor who rewarded Tung Chung-shu, a scholar-official and would-be high priest, with imprisonment.[3]

Despite this setback to the idealists, the classics themselves, gradually acquiring semi-divine status, could not be destroyed as a source of moral suasion, though opportunists could often get around them by ignoring their true spirit. The fact remained that

[1] Gernet, op. cit., 90–91, 100–1. Note that the merchant was not 'making up for being wealthy' in terms of acquiring credit in a life hereafter. Religious notions of individual immortality were not sufficiently developed in China for such heavenly incentives.

[2] Hsiao-tung Fei, 'Peasantry and Gentry', op. cit., 7–8. In *The Good Earth*, Pearl Buck paints the frightening experience of a poor peasant who moves to the city and is nearly seized from his dependants by a general's press-gang. He hides successfully, however, and eventually returns to the safety of his land.

[3] Hsiao-tung Fei, *China's Gentry*, 55–56. It should not be thought, however, that the Emperor always took the side of 'opportunists' in faction-disputes. Sometimes a new Emperor would come along who supported the more responsible officials against an entrenched faction of less highly motivated bureaucrats.

all scholar-officials derived moral prestige from their position as classical interpreters, and thereby, from the ultimate relevance of moral doctrines. Even the payment of mere lip-service to these doctrines created a climate of opinion which gave them some constraining force.

Behind the emphasis on ethical rules lay the factor of unity. Ruling a country less unified administratively and economically than it was culturally, Imperial government relied extensively on the clan to maintain order. This enhanced the ethical emphasis in two ways. First, rigid laws were not suited to the personal relationship of clan life. Secondly, administrative reliance on the clan enabled Imperial government to restrict its own administrative and legal activities and, ideally, to focus on the function of setting a moral example.[1] Confucian and neo-Confucian writings endorsed a 'wu-wei'—minimum government policy—and exalted tranquillity as a state of goodness, both within the individual and throughout the population at large.[2] The education system, however, did encourage an active policy in such fields as flood control and famine relief. Linking as it did moral absolutes with principles of natural science,[3] it contributed to the religious belief that natural disaster represented a heavenly visitation upon the government for transgressing classical precepts of morality. It was significant that when such disaster did occur the idealist minority often gained in power.[4]

Despite its support for some government activity, the education system possibly helped delay the elaboration of a national body of law. Unlike the Victorian public schools, Confucian education did not pose respect for law and respect for an ethical and aesthetic code as perfectly compatible attitudes, sharing the same time-hallowed traditions. Because cultural unity, cemented by one written language, preceded a very great degree of economic and administrative unity, China developed a national set of strongly articulated values before a unified and detailed body of law could

[1] Maintenance of the moral tradition is the main task in government', wrote the Ming commentator, Lu Shu-chien. Quoted by C. K. Yang, 'Chinese Bureaucratic Behaviour', in S. Nivison and A. F. Wright, *Confucianism in Action*, 141.
[2] Ibid., 137.
[3] S. W. Green, op. cit., 30–32.
[4] Max Weber, *Essays in Sociology*, 442–4.

emerge.[1] In this phenomenon Confucian education played its part. Not only did it help crystallize ethical values but it elaborated them into a network of internalized rules centred on the clan. Herein lay both the strengths and weaknesses of Imperial China. On the one hand, reliance on ethical, rather than merely legal, rules, imparted flexibility to the administration of justice. As we have already mentioned in strengthened local government: like the public school J.P., the local leader was imbued with a strong sense of obligation to his group, and clan rules helped make tax payment and crime prevention a matter of collective responsibility. On the other hand, the ethical emphasis possibly obstructed the development of formal laws which bureaucratic efficiency and, later, a cross-regional pattern of trade required.[2] Furthermore, by focusing the individual's loyalties on the clan, Confucian education weakened his interest in the Empire as a whole and heightened inter-clan tension.[3]

Loyalty and the Historic Community

Both Confucian education and the Victorian public school used the small, hierarchic community to inculcate deference to rank and loyalty to the group. As stated before, the community upon which Chinese education mainly focused was the family. Another educational unit was the Imperial college, in Sung times the National University, the Military Academy, and the Imperial Academy. All three colleges exalted loyalty to the school community. Over each stood an imposing array of semi-deities, sages, and heroes from the past, and the student ceremonies honouring these figures seem to have formed an important part of the discipline. In like spirit, when students from the same college went into town, they all had to wear the same uniform[4]—just as public schoolboys wore prescribed school clothing and distinctive house colours.

[1] Even the legalism of the short-lived Chin Dynasty came after the Chou philosopher. And Fairbank and Reischauer argue as late as the Ming Dynasty, Chinese national self-confidence was largely cultural, by comparison with modern nationalisms. Fairbank and Reischauer, op. cit., 292.
[2] R. Bendix, Max Weber, 132–3.
[3] Hui-chen Liu, 'Clan Rules', in Nivison and Wright, op. cit.
[4] Gernet, op. cit., 155.

The Chinese family, even more than the Imperial college, fanned communal loyalties by presenting itself as an historic and immortal entity, a community much greater than the sum of present members. This was particularly true of the gentry clan which, unlike socially inferior families, tended to gather cousins and grandchildren together and live as one group.[1] Not surprisingly, gentry families enjoyed the greatest elaboration of clan *li*; and *li*, for its part, promoted group loyalty in two main ways.

First, it conferred dignity on those who headed the clan. By much the same process that public school etiquette awarded privilege and prestige to prefects, *li* marked out family elders— including any clan members who held official posts—for special acts of deference. 'Filial piety', a prime ethic in Chinese education, exalted the power of the clan patriarch, but it did so without really elevating one individual far above the community. Key decisions frequently sprang from a consensus of senior men's opinions, arrived at after talk in the teashops.[2] Against the dissension that close-knit living conditions could easily cause, clan etiquette placed a premium on mutual compromise, co-operation and—from the women especially, alas—self-sacrifice.[3]

The second way in which *li* promoted clan loyalty was to support the great ceremonies which marked the human life cycle. At birth, at marriage, at death, and at times of ancestor-veneration, the family would join together in festive ritual. From the standpoint of loyalty-indoctrination, the honouring of ancestors was a particularly important ceremony, stressing as it did the historic dimension of the clan. Like public school reverence for school tradition, the Chinese gentry family inspired loyalty by invoking a mysticism of the past.

So successfully did the clan provide a focal point of interest, so powerfully did it control and channel individual drives that, in the eyes of its junior members, it seemed a whole world. To this very fact, indeed, has been ascribed the suicides of Chinese women.[4] Taught that the family was noble and an end in itself,

[1] Fei, 'Peasantry and Gentry', op. cit. Extended-family living was not *always* prevalent in a region, but it remained the ideal, and a practised one.   [2] Ibid.
[3] C. K. Yang, *The Chinese Family in the Communist Revolution*, 168.   [4] Ibid., 7–8.

yet downtrodden by family demands, women could escape from their family—escape both physically and emotionally—only through death.

It is significant that, of the Five Cardinal Relationships emphasized by Chinese education, three were relationships of the family: father-son (solidarity and affection), husband-wife (attention to separate functions), and old-young (proper order).[1] It is also interesting that when a new pupil was introduced to his teacher, he was explicitly instructed to view the teacher-student bond as a parallel of the father-son bond.[2] Education and the family were inextricably linked.

Unlike the public school community, however, the Chinese clan community was much more than education; it was a continuing way of life, binding for adults hardly less than for youth. In this lay its drawback as a political training ground. Whereas the old public schoolboy could to some extent 'put aside childish things', could transfer once and for all his loyalty from his boyhood group to the State, the Chinese official could never do this. He always remained a prominent member of his clan: in fact, the higher he rose in government circles, the more his family expected of him. Scholarship, moreover, did little to prepare him for clash of interest between the small community and the national one. When conflict did occur, classical authority could be quoted on both sides of the dilemma. According to legend, the son who concealed his father's theft of a sheep received full endorsement from Confucius: 'With us the father screens the son, and the son screens the father; that is real uprightness.'[3] Such a sentiment was hardly in keeping with the neo-Confucian precept of *tao*.

Nobody can say, of course, that old public schoolboys never fell prey to conflict of interest, that 'good connexions' have not speeded promotion in the top echelons of British government. Conversely, it is also true that the bureaucratic appointment system under the Chinese Empire sometimes made influential connexions a promotional liability to the official. But unlike the

[1] The other two bonds were sovereign-minister (righteousness) and friends (fidelity).
[2] C. K. Yang, *The Chinese Family in the Communist Revolution*, 6.
[3] Quoted by H. A. Giles, *The Civilization of China*, 45.

public schools which isolated the student from family life, Confucian education treated professional loyalty and discipline as a mere extension of family bonds. The exaltation of personal friendship always threatened the bureaucracy's standards of impartiality, the predictability of its behaviour, and the continuity of its policy.

Unlike his British counterpart the Chinese civil servant also faced potential conflict between *tao* and loyalty to his political chief, the Emperor. There was no democratic machinery to replace the Emperor who got out of line with *tao*, who ignored the community interest, or who flouted a majority opinion interpreting that interest. And, despite its ethical teaching, Confucian education gave some support to the official who tailored his concept of *tao* to fit his subservience to a selfish Emperor. According to the classical writings, after all, loyalty to the sovereign was an expression and projection of filial piety.

At the same time, the great emphasis which Chinese political education placed on personal morality contributed to faction-fighting within the bureaucracy. Originally, the historical classics mentioned the capacity for effective leadership among the ideal attributes an official should have. By the Sung Dynasty, however, most educational writings ceased to mention functional qualifications, including the practical ability to get on with people, as an ideal.[1] The moral categories themselves, furthermore, became increasingly over-simplified[2]—an inevitable tendency, it seems, given the educational attempt to express all values in writing and given the existence of a language unsuited to precise, psychological definition. One effect of the moral categories on the bureaucracy was to exacerbate conflict between different interest-groups. The obscuring of effective leadership as a norm meant that the compromising necessary for such leadership was morally down-graded. Similarly, the emphasis on simplified moral categories in assessing bureaucratic behaviour added to the emotional bitterness of policy debates.[3] It was not uncommon in Chinese bureaucracy to find two official factions, whose original disagreement sprang largely

[1] J. Liu, 'Classifications of Bureaucrats', in Nivison and Wright, op. cit., 170.
[2] Ibid., 167.   [3] Fairbank and Reischauer, op. cit., 341-2.

from mere policy problems but which quickly became an exchange of moral charges. On such occasions one side, at least, was often quick to label the other side 'opportunists'.

In general, it seems that Confucian education did less than the Victorian public schools to facilitate political co-operation. The oral or, more often, tacit nature of public school indoctrination gave the values it instilled a flexible and realistic quality: vain man is more likely to include an emphasis on 'will-it-work' among his values if he does not have to face it in stark writing.

It would be unfair, however, to mention only the disruptive effects of Confucian education on government operations. Outside educational writings proper, the government encyclopaedias of the Sung and Ming Dynasties did give written endorsement to political skills along with personal morality. This indicates that, in practice, Chinese bureaucracy made some effort to temper ethical perfectionism with the requirements of practical action. More important, the outlook and manners taught by Confucian education, extending as it did to all classes, facilitated communication between public servants with widely contrasting regional and economic backgrounds. By comparison, the unifying task faced by the Victorian public schools amid a relatively homogenous population, did not pose much difficulty.

Confucian education also contributed to political co-operation by the way it subordinated the individual to the group. Its teaching strove to impress upon the student that only through social contribution could he achieve the fullest inner development; he should view himself as part of an historical stream of thought and action promoting service to others. Unlike the anti-individualism of public school life—a countervailing value to Western liberalism—the Confucian subordination of the individual reflected a central value of the society.

Admittedly, Chinese education did not match the public school's success at converting its suppression of individualism into the capacity for political co-operation. As we have already observed, dedication to rigid altruistic principles, whether sincere or merely professed, could disrupt co-operation as effectively as the overt egoism it replaced. On the other hand, the absence of militance in Confucian moralism reduced the anarchic effect of moral disagreements within the bureaucracy. Although the Confucian idealist put moral rectitude before effective government, he did believe in moral suasion rather than violence. Where loyalty to the emperor and the requirements of *tao* conflicted, he would frequently resign from government rather than obstruct government policy from within. Motives of personal security from imperial power often dictated such actions, but it was also encouraged by his education. Faith in the power of moral example raised the idealist's hopes that protest resignations and external advice could influence policy.[1]

In the case of idealist and opportunist alike—to use the official black-and-white categories—Confucian manners helped to harmonize personal relations. The requirements of propriety, embodied in *Li*, moderated emotional expression and invested political proceedings with a veil of official courtesy. (The superior man, Confucius is supposed to have said, was 'moderate in his words, but ardent in his actions'.)[2] Whatever dissensions occurred beneath the veil, *li* did assist the cause of co-operation by providing a uniform method of communication and a symbol of selflessness. Even moralistic mud-slinging was conducted with some decorum.

Dignified Government

When the victorious rebel commander, Liu Pang, founded by force of arms the former Han Dynasty, he wasted little time before he had spun a web of elaborate court etiquette.[3] This tactic placed the throne, and the man who occupied it, at a dignified and safe distance from former intimates who had helped him win power. It was the same tactic that the Victorian public school performed when it differentiated the living habits of the newly promoted prefect from those of his one-time contemporaries. Familiarity may not create contempt for government, but neither does it lead easily to political magic.

[1] Buddhism and Taoism helped to create such political passivity, sanctioning as they did the contemplative in man.
[2] Lun Yu, Part XIV, Chapter 29.
[3] Latourette, *The Chinese—Their History and Culture*, 101.

The problem of how to secure political magic—or rather, of how to secure it without losing political efficiency—is still with us today. We need dignified government as much as ever, not simply because government must inspire its subjects but because government must attract recruits. And, without a special glamour and dignity of its own, government is not likely to attract high-calibre recruits under conditions of political democracy.

As Joseph Schumpeter pointed out, the vulgar tendencies of democratic politics may well deter the intellectually discriminating from seeking public office.[1] There is also a good deal of historical evidence to suggest that an hereditary ruling class can more easily accrue a magical aura than can a democratic system relying solely on merit to select its leaders. This argument is borne out even by the political experience of American cities. In *Who Governs?*, a study of New Haven, Connecticut, and its power structure, Robert Dahl describes how political control passed from the 'patricians'—well-established New England families—to the *nouveaux riches* and thence to the 'ex-plebes'. Under patrician rule, political power and high social status were linked; to be a high New Haven official was to enjoy honour and prestige. But when new self-made leaders appeared, observes Dahl, 'dignity was undone by the horse-laugh' and patrician rule was in decline.[2] Today in America, especially among the older cities, high municipal office is by no means a certificate of the highest social prestige.

Why does an hereditary ruling class enjoy magical advantage?

[1] cf. my discussion of Schumpeter's argument in Chapter 2 and Chapter 8. In modern industrial democracy—especially American democracy—upper-class attitudes towards politics as a career carry faint echoes of gentry attitudes towards 'Trade'. Politics is referred to as a 'dirty business', rendered morally unattractive by the alleged insincerity and shallowness that electoral *competition* breeds. Strictly this is applied to electoral office and not appointed posts in the bureaucracy. In America, however, some Civil Service posts are elective; and anyway it is not easy for all government to escape a general 'dirty business' stigma. In New Haven, Connecticut, Robert Dahl has noticed that practically none of what he calls the 'Social' and 'Economic Notables' go in for public office any more; and we have already reported Vance Packard's estimate that less than 1 per cent. of the graduates from seventeen leading U.S. private schools have gone into government ('The Select Seventeen', *Esquire*, November, 1960).

[2] Robert Dahl, *Who Governs?*, 29. Although this is the study of one city, New Haven, it has been suggested, by other political scientists as well as Dahl himself, that the book reveals important characteristics of many U.S. cities.

The factor of dignity, of course, is only one factor in the decline of patrician power as Dahl describes it. Dahl is also careful to point out that the term 'patrician' is relative—the New Haven 'patricians' came from no higher than middle-class English families.

One answer can be found in Lucy Mair's analysis of African kingship and ritual. The authority of African kings frequently stemmed from a popular belief that their ancestors were supernatural, or that they, the kings, had supernatural powers, such as the ability to make rain. In many instances, too, royal lineage signified a unique relationship with the community and its land. The king thus symbolized the total polity.[1] Mair also notes that hereditary officials, or the king himself, were often the only ones able to undertake those rituals which exalted the king's position.[2]

From Lucy Mair's description of African kingship it can be seen that the person who claims he is *born* to rule bases his claim on a far more mysterious process than the person who claims that he has tangibly and rationally proven himself worthy to rule. Government selected purely according to merit must base its leadership qualifications on an aggregate of individuals still alive, on the character they have shown, the efforts they have made, and the training they have received during their own lifetimes. By contrast, an aristocracy can attribute its leadership qualities to a long line of ancestors, including famous men whose glory is intimately linked with that of the historic community.

Biologically, of course, the above is nonsense. There is little evidence to suppose that leadership qualities can be largely inherited. When men say that the aristocrat or king is born to rule, they really mean that he is *brought up* to rule. Family traditions and home influence are just another form of education—as the Chinese experience declared.

This does not alter the fact that a political *élite* based on hereditary privilege can attain a glamour that democratic governments will find it hard to equal. Mythical as the basis of that glamour may be, it will none the less exist in the eyes of *élite* and non-*élite* alike, provided social values are not actively hostile to the notion of hereditary privilege. Nor is it purely a matter of myth. Upbringing in a family accustomed to dominate does seem to create a relaxed assurance, a presence well suited to dignified government. This is not to say that, in many instances, self-made leaders too—Napoleon as much as the patrician Caesar—have displayed

[1] Lucy Mair, *Primitive Government*, 214–16.   [2] Ibid., 140.

magical qualities which inspire and attract. But we are talking here of a general, social tendency and not of individual cases. Although, for example, the Chinese gentry family subordinated its members in relation to the historic clan itself, it also strengthened them, granting them poise in their dealings with outsiders. In this process the inheritance of *land* became a fortying agent, an immutable part of the clan that declared the latter's immortality. It was not for economic reasons alone that a Chinese gentry family often held its property in common.[1] Like Chekhov's landowners—like, perhaps, all landed families—the gentry of China drew spiritual strength from the mystique of *The Cherry Orchard*.[2]

The magical advantage enjoyed by inheritors of privilege places us in a quandary. On the one hand, government needs glamour and dignity to attract able men into public service. On the other hand, glamour and dignity are most easily secured by governments which select men according to birth rather than ability. The quandary is a very real one for the modern democratic State: if electoral politics tend to reward the candidate with glamour, it is more the glamour of the film star, or the charm of the salesman, than the deeper dignity which will imbue office itself with prestige.

To a lesser extent Confucian China faced the same quandary, the problem of how to secure political magic and yet reward merit. China's tacit solution of the problem was broadly that of Victorian England—to compromise. As we have already seen, the Imperial examination system represented a rational attempt to reward individual talent, yet the classical content of the examinations, added to string-pulling by the influential, favoured certain families. As a result, the Chinese political *élite* did something to acquire new blood and still preserve an aristocratic aura. This aura

[1] cf. Hsiao-tung Fei, 'Peasantry and Gentry', op. cit. The interpretation as to *why* the gentry family held property in common is mine.

[2] In *The Good Earth*, Pearl Buck attributes somewhat the same mystique to the peasant hero, driven by natural disasters to work in the city, but fighting to return to his land. It will be remembered that in the end he prospers and becomes a landlord.

was enhanced by an elaborate system of magical devices which government and education together developed.

Like the manners and ceremony of British government, Chinese magic performed three political functions. First, it inspired popular deference to the ruler by differentiating his way of life. Some of the privileges awarded degree-holders and officials had utilitarian value—e.g. the exemption from *corvée* labour duties and from corporal punishment. Even these privileges, however, might be claimed to have a mystical dimension. Just as African kingship rituals, according to Lucy Mair, were 'largely a matter of preserving [the kings'] bodies from defiling substances',[1] so the *shen-shih élite* felt itself above wordly squalor and defiling work. At one end this outlook shaded into the amateur ideal which induced contempt for technical specialization. The idea that a gentleman should not 'dirty his hands' was a prevalent notion among scholars, and by keeping the scientific thinker out of practical experimentation, it was an attitude that in the long run penalized Chinese technology.

Superiority to technical specialization was echoed by superiority to regional parochialism, in style if not always in outlook. We noticed the same phenomenon in Victorian England. Like the public schools, Chinese education supported a national *élite* style which stood out above regional differences. Against a profusion of dialects and a background of mass illiteracy, the ability to speak Mandarin and to write fluently carried a cosmopolitan flavour. The advantage was also aesthetic, since education gave both bureaucrat and Emperor the ability to dignify State memorials with exquisite language and calligraphy.

Many of the aesthetic distinctions claimed by Chinese government revolved around privileges of dress. Just as public school etiquette reserved certain styles and emblems for student leaders, so the Imperial sumptuary laws conferred on degree-holders the right to wear a special gown. Rules about dress were probably most binding in Tang times. Under the Tang and early Sung, each of the nine bureaucratic grades boasted its own colours: turquoise robes for the ninth grade, green for the seventh,

---

[1] Mair, op. cit., 225. The author refers here to the *personal* ritual of kings.

vermilion for the sixth, and so on.[1] Over time these distinctions *within* the government became blurred; it is also true that the grander merchants frequently took on official privileges of dress —and got away with it. Nevertheless, the ideal remained that degree-holders and officials should be distinguished by their dress. If others usurped official privileges, they did so as individuals, rather than as a challenging group.

The distinctiveness of the political *élite* was by no means confined to material symbols and accoutrements. The requirements of *li* dictated that leaders should display a formal, reserved dignity, and among the *shen-shih* prevailing notions of beauty contained a strong element of graceful ease.

Puns, euphemisms, allusions to classical quotations, and a refined and purely literary intellectuality were considered the conversational ideal of the genteel man. All politics of the day were excluded from such conversation.[2]

The last sentence of this description by Max Weber suggests that preoccupation with graceful ease, a posture which betokens mastery of life's struggles, may encourage the ruler to avoid those struggles in the first place. Like Sir William Gilbert's aristocracy, Imperial government itself frequently sought magical advantage in a *wu-wei* policy, in doing little and doing it 'very well'.[3] Graceful ease, like harmony, was an aesthetic ideal best suited to a relatively static and, from the bureaucracy's viewpoint, automatically self-regulating society. For here, order and tranquillity carried no stigma of backwardness or stagnation; prosperity was not dramatically accompanied by bustling change.

In addition to differentiating the ruler's way of life, magic performed for the Imperial government its other two political functions: it channelled emotions into communal and harmless means of expression, and it symbolized morality. Partly due to the educational emphasis on ritual, these last two functions were

---

[1] Gernet, op. cit., 128.
[2] Weber, op. cit., 437. cf. H. A. Giles, op. cit., 160.   [3] cf. Chapter 5.

subtly intertwined. Certain clan rules, for example, decreed that only major contributors—often officials—to clan prestige or welfare might attend ancestral rites.[1] On the one hand, the latter represented formal and collective demonstrations of feeling; on the other, they symbolized the ruler's obligation to an historic community hallowed by ancestor worship. Again, the State ritual learned by Civil Service examinees absorbed the energies of the ruler and the interest of the ruled in aesthetic form rather than substantive action; here the same ritual was also supposed to teach ideal conduct to governor and governed alike.

There remains one more observation to make on the myriad methods by which Chinese political magic wrought its effect. The very possession of an advanced classical education itself embued the scholar-official with dignity.[2] In the first place, he derived moral prestige from the widespread, Confucian notion that study was a prerequisite for superior virtue. The large artistic and poetic content of the curriculum, furthermore, played on the Chinese propensity to see beauty as a sign of morality. In the second place, classical scholarship conveyed what might be called a synthetic aura of heredity. With the development of 'open competition' Civil Service examinations, Chinese government might have been expected to have lost some of its hereditary aura. Some remained, of course, due to the presence of the Emperor, to special entrance examinations for Imperial clan members, and to the advantage that the examinations themselves conferred on gentry families. As a supplement to whatever hereditary character remained, classical scholarship gave the bureaucracy a special kinship with the origins and continuum of Chinese culture and the semi-deified sages of the past.

At this point an objection may be raised. Classical learning in China, it can be argued, was not the sole preserve of degree-holders and officials, and therefore any talk about them having a synthetic hereditary aura is nonsense. Logical as this argument is, it ignores the Chinese fondness for the symbolic. The magical property that men acquired through learning depended largely

[1] Hui-chen Liu, 'Clan Rules' in Nivison and Wright, op. cit., 82.
[2] Weber, op. cit., 434.

on *symbols* of cultural status: degrees,[1] and public office itself.

In the same way that certain *li*-ordained privileges seemed to convey magic by their very lack of practical utility, so the whole body of classical education dignified the scholar by its non-technical nature. With the passing of time, the examination system and individual scholars alike showed an increasing tendency to stress the classics' aesthetic form at the expense of the political messages that lay beneath.[2] By the Ming Dynasty, artistic amateurism and literary versatility were consciously valued more because they conferred prestige than because they gave the best mental training for government office.[3]

The Amateur Ideal

Somewhat like the British Civil Service, Chinese bureaucracy was run by an 'Administrative Class' of generalists. Only at 'the rank operatives and clerical workers' did it regularly employ men with specialized training.[4] The scholar-official shared Liddell Hart's belief that the general supervisor should have a general education. Whatever specialized knowledge he needed he could acquire on the job and, anyway, he should be able to relate the essence of the classics to practical situations.[5] In China, even more than in Victorian England, a non-technical training—whose very syllabus included lessons in manners—was supposed to help the ruler to harmonize different interest-groups. As well as providing a common background to officials with differing functions, Chinese education made style in handling men one of its prime concerns. On several occasions Confucius himself seemed to identify knowledge *per se* with knowing men.[6] This preoccupation formed part of the Confucian concept of government—namely, that the ability to select the right men for office was a better guarantee of efficient and ethical administration than any amount of institutional engineering.

Educational generalism was also well suited to a *wu-wei*

[1] Weber, op. cit., 434.
[2] J. R. Levenson, 'The Amateur Ideal (late Ming-Ching)', in Fairbank, op. cit., 323.
[3] Ibid, 322–3.
[4] C. K. Yang, 'Chinese Bureaucratic Behaviour', in Nivison and Wright, op. cit., 137.
[5] Ibid., 141–2.
[6] *Analects*, Book III, Chapter 14, p. 152, quoted by Lorraine Creel, op. cit., 42–43.

government policy. Imperial reliance on local self-government, coupled with the simplicity of the legal system, enabled magistrates to discharge their duties without specialized training in law and finance. Trust in general education, furthermore, supported the Imperial practice of limiting senior posts' tenure to as little as three years. Likewise it accommodated the policy of rotating Imperial officials assigned to the provinces. This last policy had mixed benefits. On the one hand, it broke the continuity of policy, and sometimes it exalted the power of junior clerks in the provincial offices, men who possessed more local expertise but less training in political ethics than their superiors. On the other hand, the rotation policy did reduce corruption among senior officials themselves, for it gave them a limited time in which to build local empires of graft.

Apart from its emphasis on men and morals, in what sense could Confucian education be called general? In subject matter, the Chinese scholar received a more rounded literary training than the Victorian public schoolboy and the Oxford and Cambridge undergraduate. During the early Sung, for example, the doctorate degree in letters, a field which gradually eclipsed the others, required knowledge of ritual, cosmology, and the *Analects* of Confucius, analytical compositions on given texts, poetry, and dialogue. Under the Tangs, the examination for the bachelor's degree in classics set a political essay on a subject related to current events, as well as demanding interpretation of classical passages. Later, under the Ming, there emerged the famous 'eight-legged' essay, a paper written under eight main headings, following set forms of thesis and antithesis, and discussing such classical quotations as 'scrupulous in his own conduct and lenient only in his dealings with the people'.[1] Mathematics, by comparison, fared hardly. The Tang schools taught it, and there was, during the Tang, a mathematics degree, but the subject was only stressed as a universal examination requirement for a brief period in the Ming Dynasty.

As general training of the mind, Confucian education did more for the memory and less for the imagination than a superficial

[1] Fairbank and Reischauer, op. cit., 306. A quotation from the *Analects*.

description of the examinations might suggest. Even the interpretative essays and poetry, constructed by rigid rules of form and the examiners' deference to the ancients, gradually became mere tests of elegant imitativeness.[1] We have already seen that one reason for the growing obsession with a standardized form—both in style and calligraphy—lay in the examiners' wish to find an objective marking standard.[2] Just as strong rules of propriety provided in Chinese eyes a convenient standard for social behaviour, so rules of aesthetic form became a measure of academic achievement.

Limitation of classical forms was also concomitant with the deference to seniors, the worship of ancestors, and the veneration of deceased Emperors that Chinese education supported. When the early Sung reformer, Fan Ching-Yen, pressed for greater examination emphasis on classical content, his opponents successfully used the argument that reform would insult past degree-holders and emperors. The fact that Fan wanted more attention paid to Confucian principles of politics made no difference. Given the Chinese fondness for the symbolic, the close link between aesthetic appearance and moral worth, it is not surprising that imitation of a golden age led to preoccupation with its style.

The great premium placed by the examinations on memory-work did not only stem, however, from the narrowing influence of stylistic formalism. It also represented the logical outcome of a certain attitude towards knowledge. During the dynasties under review, or at least until the Ming pragmatist school of Wang Yang Ming, absolutist concepts of knowledge predominated. That is to say, most scholars believed that there was a body of absolute truths, a body which combined moral principles with cosmological laws.[3] The essence of this knowledge, so the scholars believed, had already been understood and set down in writing by the Confucian sages. It followed, therefore, in Burkian vein, that there were no new and basic principles to be learned about

---

[1] W. T. De Bary, 'Chinese Despotism and the Confucian Ideal in the Seventeenth Century', in Fairbank, op. cit., 184.
[2] J. Liu, 'An Early Sung Reformer', in Fairbank, ibid., 115.
[3] S. W. Green, op. cit., 30. cf. R. Chungil Rhoe, op. cit., 22–23, 32.

society or politics or life in general.[1] As a consequence of this belief, Chinese education ceased to equate imaginative ability with the formulation of fresh ideas. By the late Ming, originality was so little praised that the 'Southern' School of painting, 'patently derivative' and traditional though it was, could call itself intuitional and spontaneous.[2] What its 'spontaneity' meant was imitation of those ancients who were thought to be *really* spontaneous.

Scholastically, the belief in a body of absolute truths, already perceived by past interpreters, fostered erudition—great devotions of energy towards mastering classical writings and standard interpretations—rather than independent thinking.[3] Like public school Latin, however, some examination compositions demanded a capacity for abstract logic and the application of general set rules to a particular situation or problem. In this sense, and as a trainer of memory, Confucian education did afford a general training of the mind.

In terms of intellectual approach, on the other hand, the system did not give the scholar much freedom. To conclude with the words of Ping Wen Kuo:

The high veneration for Confucius and the principles represented by him had an important bearing upon the subsequent history of Chinese education, for from the Han Dynasty on Chinese education became less liberal than it was, and the content became narrowly confined to the Confucian classics.

. . . The over-emphasis upon the teachings of one school of thought to the exclusion of other systems originating during preceding dynasties must be regarded as being extremely unfortunate for the progress of Chinese civilization, for the study of Confucian classics became a habit of the student class who . . . were afraid to advance new thoughts of their own. . . . As a result the thoughts of the scholar class continued to run in the beaten paths of the ancients, and no longer enjoyed the freedom necessary for all true advancement in civilization.[4]

[1] Edmund Burke, op. cit., 97.
[2] J. R. Levenson, 'The Amateur Ideal', in Fairbank, op. cit., 329.
[3] Admittedly a new set of interpretations emerged in the Sung Dynasty but these quickly became standard for pupils. cf. Kuo, op. cit., 48–49; W. T. De Bary, 'Chinese Despotism and the Confucian Ideal in the Seventeenth Century', in Fairbank, op. cit., 183.
[4] Kuo, op. cit., 34–35.

'The natives of this city', said Marco Polo when he visited Hangchow in the thirteenth century, 'are men of peaceful character. . . .'

They know nothing of handling arms, and keep none in their houses. You hear of no feuds or noisy quarrels and dissensions of any kind among them . . . and there is such a degree of good will and neighbourly attachment among men and women that you would take the people who live in the same street to be all one family.[1]

For centuries at a time, China remained stable and united. The Tang and Ming Dynasties each lasted nearly 300 years, the Sung 150; the last Imperial dynasty, the Ching, lived for 250 years. That this could be so, that a vast empire could remain one and at peace for so long, was partly to the credit of education, which supported the flexibility of local self-government and yet nourished a central bureaucracy. Although the training of leaders was a prime educational concern, the ethic of self-restraint which the schools promoted affected the smallest unit of Chinese society.

Despite these achievements, each one of the four dynasties ended in bloodshed and rebellion, and each one died already weakened by mounting political and economic difficulties. Against these difficulties, central government could do little more than delay the collapse of dynastic power. Reformers who might have saved the empire—men like Wang An-shih of the Sung—were either followed half-heartedly, or discredited by conservatives.

One reason for the failure was the absence of any real concept of progress. Few people were imbued with the notion that major change was inevitable and that one must exploit it early to prevent it hurting one later. This Chinese attitude, or lack of attitude, towards change was reflected and reinforced by Confucian education in three ways.

First, scholars were apt to glorify the past as a social ideal and cultural ideal alike: 'they made no attempt to supersede the civilization of early antiquity, and all they wished was not to fall

[1] Henry Yule (ed. and transl.), *The Book of Ser Marco Polo Concerning the Kingdoms and Marvels of the East*, 204, quoted by Gernet, op. cit., 152.

too far away from it'.[1] Belief in the potency of moral example encouraged educators to whitewash historical biographies, and to venerate classical teachings until they could not be denied by word *or* deed. The administrative and economic reformer, who wanted to win official support for his programme, usually had to justify it as a restoration of classical standards.[2] Since the practical applicability of these standards could be interpreted in varying ways, their effect was to strengthen the forces of factionalism and inertia. Major reform proposals frequently created controversy, less about practical needs, than about the more inflammatory issue of loyalty to the past and respect for hallowed principles.[3]

This brings us to the second way in which education reflected and reinforced the Chinese attitude toward change. The education system was essentially hostile to inductive thinking. Convinced that classical wisdom was absolute, and constantly stressing its applicability to practical situations, the educator did not encourage his pupil to ask whether, in turn, practice should develop wisdom. In politics and technology alike, there was little cross-feeding between theory and experience. We have already seen what happens politically when ideals of political behaviour were insulated from the requirements of reality. Technologically, the education system had a doubly obstructive effect on innovation. It stymied experimentation not only by discouraging inductive thought but by making non-utilitarian pursuits into a gentleman's fetish.[4]

Lack of inductive thinking, one must observe, characterized the public school curriculum as well as the Confucian. Latin and mathematics were essentially deductive; history and Divinity tested little else but memory; scientific experimenting—'Stinks' —was barely stressed until well into the twentieth century. Despite these features, however, the academic side to public

[1] Kuo, op. cit., 35.
[2] cf. Fairbank and Reischauer, op. cit., 207, 342.   [3] Ibid.
[4] Giles, op. cit., 117–20; Hsiao-tung Fei, *China's Gentry*, 73–74. cf. Edwin Land, 'Patents and New Enterprises', *Harvard Business Review*, September–October, 1959. Land, the inventor-chairman of Polaroid and a pioneer in education, argues not only that easy cross-feeding is vital between applied and 'pure' science, but that sometimes it is difficult to tell whether a basic new idea emerged with the applied scientist or the 'pure' one.

school life did not match Confucian education in its unfriendliness to innovation and change. The rigid principles governing Latin and mathematics were not aggressively applied to real-life situations, nor did the moral absolutism of Divinity invade other subjects. Above all, the whole curriculum was slowly changing in response to its critics. Amid the rationalism and flux of the industrial revolution, public school traditionalism was a countervailing force. By contrast, the Confucian attitude to change reflected perfectly, too perfectly, the seemingly static conditions of Chinese society. It was the lot of China that change should be enough a part of the society to bring about the downfall of dynasties, but not clearly enough a part of the society to be recognized by education and the value-system. Muted when times were peaceful and the country secure, changing conditions were associated in men's minds not with good things but with chaos.

The third way in which Confucian education reflected the Chinese attitude toward change again makes a significant point of comparison with the public schools. Both education systems stifled imagination and individualism—sources of creative innovation—with a web of custom and etiquette. But the Confucian web was especially stultifying because it was largely elaborated in writing. Whereas the part oral, part tacit, nature of public school custom permitted gradual modification and some flexibility, the written nature of *li* made for greater rigidity. The same difference between the two systems reappeared in politics. However flexible over personal matters the non-legalist Chinese bureaucrat might be, he was less ready than his British counterpart to view change as a prerequisite for institutional stability.[1] This applied particularly to matters of organization and method. Even more than the public school ethos, the Confucian outlook saw the solution to political problems as one of getting good men, not of perfecting systems.

In several respects, the writing system itself tended to preclude sympathy for innovation. Mastering the language required such efforts of memory that the student may have had little interest or

[1] cf. Weber, op. cit., 432–3. Characteristics of Chinese bureaucrats described by Weber include decorum-consciousness, and dislike of innovation, of forensic speech, and of speculative problems.

energy left over for speculating on his own account.[1] Furthermore, the great emphasis on writing as a gentleman's means of expression dampened spontaneity: 'phantasy and ardor fled from the formalistic intellectualism of the spoken word into the quiet beauty of the written symbols'.[2] An undeveloped state of oratory, combined with clan rules discouraging political conversation, slowed the turnover of serious ideas by the same token that they removed sources of social friction.[3]

Given China's diversity and size, educational emphasis on the writing system was perhaps necessary for national unity. The sinologists Edwin Reischauer and John K. Fairbank in fact argue that if the Chinese

had had a phonetic system of writing, they might have broken up into separate national groups, as did the Italians, French, Spanish and Portuguese. The stature of China as the largest national grouping in the world is to be explained at least in part by the writing system. It may also explain the extraordinary cultural cohesiveness of the Chinese abroad.[4]

When we remember the great unifying task that Confucian education achieved, we should not be surprised at its failure to teach adaptability to change. In the absence of a strong legal network, the main brunt of achieving national unity fell on education, the instrument for instilling ethical restraints and cementing cultural bonds. To meet these goals it was inevitable, perhaps, that education should take a form unfriendly to imaginative development and intellectual freedom: that it would make the student conform unquestioningly to group customs and spend long hours memorizing the details of a cultural heritage.

The difficulty of attaining national unity heightened the dilemma that any government runs into when it controls education. Ultimately, the Chinese State considered independent

[1] Fairbank and Reischauer, op. cit., 42.   [2] Weber, op. cit., 430.
[3] This point may seem to contradict my thesis that Confucian education was essentially political. One must remember, however, that the education was not *vocational*: it taught classical principles of politics and when it set exercises applying those principles to contemporary problems, it did so under examination controls.
[4] Fairbanks and Reischauer, op. cit., 43–44.

thought subversive to the cultural unity on which its very existence was based. When, towards the end of the Ching Dynasty, the Empress Dowager opposed the dissemination of newspapers throughout the country, she voiced a traditional fear that political discussion might subvert respect for ancient theories and institutions of government. Yet—and here lay the dilemma—without permitting a measure of independent thought, the government could not hope to find the imaginative policy-makers so necessary for its survival. As the cyclic appearance of Chinese history perhaps indicates, the dilemma was never resolved. Through the examination system, the government enhanced the supremacy of the official school of thought, Confucianism. This undoubtedly strengthened cultural unity. But in the long run it also reduced the imaginative capacity of the nation's leadership. For one thing, the weakening of the non-Confucian schools rendered meaningless any strong notion of intellectual progress through dialectical conflict. Even reform proposals for extending academic freedom did not stress diversity of opinion for its own sake.[1] In the second place government domination of education deprived the State of constructive criticism. Intense, academic preoccupation with examinations, and with the prestige that degrees conferred, did not easily accommodate true academic curiosity.

Furthermore, the very success that Confucian education enjoyed in directing students towards the Civil Service deprived the non-governmental professions of able men. Even teaching and the military carried far less social prestige than the bureaucracy. As a result, the education system failed to nourish with talent a diversity of occupation and, thereby, a diversity of critical opinion. This was especially true in the case of the commercial professions. If the Confucian stigma on *li* encouraged able men to choose public office rather than private profit-making, it also prevented merchants from contributing their calculative abilities to the service of the State.

Under Confucian influence, China failed to strike the balance between the call of business and the call of government that was

---

[1] cf. W. T. De Bary, 'Chinese Despotism and the Confucian Ideal' in Fairbank, op. cit., 178.

obtained in post-Meiji Japan. The comparison is interesting because in Japan, as in China, government service held high status and the Civil Service attracted far more candidates than it could accommodate. Yet Japanese education, despite its concern with traditional loyalties, seemed to produce ample tycoons and entrepreneurs who incurred no stigma when they went into trade. The recognition that the Japanese accorded business cannot be fully explained by the government's close involvement in heavy industry: Chinese government, after all, was similarly involved in the great salt and iron monopolies.

Even within the public professions themselves, Confucian education helped to produce one-sided effects. The failure of the system to orientate educated youth towards military service may itself have been a factor in dynastic downfalls, so often characterized by rebellion and invasion. Notably, one element in the Tang decline was the low morale of professional soldiery and the rift between central bureaucrats and regional commanders, many of whom were foreign-born.[1] With its opposition to coercive legalism, Confucian education was essentially pacifist in values. To the extent that it directed scholars away from the military, it deprived the latter of talented personnel and weakened the potential bond between Army and civilian officials. By contrast, the public schools conferred high prestige on military service and at the same time imbued officers with some deference to national authority.

Conservatism

If the essence of conservatism is to *conserve* traditional ways and institutions, the Confucian scholar's attitude to change was, of course, conservative. It is interesting, therefore, to compare his political outlook with McCloskey's more elaborate definition of Western Conservatism (see Chapter 10) and ask how universal a concept the latter is.

McCloskey's first category of conservatism—the notion that men are mainly irrational and doomed to imperfection—did not jibe completely with the scholar-official's view of human nature.

---

[1] Fairbank and Reischauer, op. cit., 189-91.

Granted, the education system did instil ethical restraints by playing on the emotions: aesthetic feeling, sense of shame, desire to
identify with the group, desire for self-perfection, sympathy and
so on. But the moral bias of the curriculum proclaimed the Confucian belief that men could perfect themselves by intellectual
effort. The fact that reason was not greatly appreciated for its
innovative powers did not mean that it was devalued altogether.
The disdain, moreover, that Imperial government and the clans
held for legalism reflected a strong optimism about man's potential sociability.[1] It also revealed the Chinese confidence in education, and the ruler's educative function of personal example, as a
means of regulating social behaviour.

We find more identity between Western conservatism and the
political outlook of the Chinese scholar when we turn to Mc-
Closkey's second category. If the word 'religion' is used in a
broad sense, the Confucian education system can be said to have
taught a religious concept of society. It was not simply that education infused political authority with a mystical aura. More than
this, education posed the historic continuum of society as a spiritual entity engulfing the individual. Reverence for this entity
joined present and past: it demanded filial piety and ancestor
veneration, loyalty to the community and respect for ancient
learning.

With his religious outlook on society, the scholar-official shared
the Western conservative's love of tradition, his suspicion of
major change and his regard for authority and stability (Mc-
Closkey's third, fourth, fifth and seventh categories). Unlike the
Western conservative, admittedly, the Chinese official framed
traditional wisdom in theoretical form; Confucian education paid
more attention to general principles as a policy guide than did the
Victorian public schools. But both systems seemed to breed
similar doubts about *new* theoretical schemes, especially those
entailing social change. Like the British civil servant of H. E.
Dale's description, the Chinese bureaucrat sensed the destructive
effects that major innovation might have on stability. As the

[1] Confucius saw men as a mixture of good and evil, but perfectable by religion and
education; Mencius, the most famous neo-Confucian philosopher, believed more in
natural good—cf. Lorraine Creel, op. cit., Chapter 5.

reader will remember, according to Dale the British civil servant was highly aware of industrial society's complexities and he felt that extensive reform must bring unpredictable consequences. The Chinese official, for his part, was apt to regard his own, more agrarian society as a largely self-regulating mechanism: public welfare depended less on feats of administration than on personal morality and good husbandry.[1] In a context like this, the bureaucracy's outlook showed how a conservative concern for tradition and stability can foster the desire for minimum government. 'What is needed in administration at the present time', wrote a typical commentator of the Ming Dynasty, 'is to keep troublesome business at a minimum, not to add to it; to preserve the rules, not to change them; to bring about tranquillity in all situations, not stir them up. . . .'[2]

Concerned as he was with social 'tranquillity', the scholar-official fitted fairly well into McCloskey's sixth and seventh categories of conservatism—the belief that social inequality is natural and good, and the emphasis on duty rather than individual rights. With regard to the sixth category, Confucian education endorsed class distinction and underpinned with customary privileges the prestige of a ruling group. It is true, however, that towards the idea of natural inequality the trend of Confucian thought was ambiguous. On the one hand, Confucian doctrine taught that the individual of low social station could attain moral perfection. On the other hand, the dominant Confucian tradition during our period, the Chu Hsi school, held a somewhat Thomistic view, a concept of natural hierarchy in society and universe alike. Both Confucius and Mencius defended privileges of birth, yet they also demanded merit qualifications for public office. The examination system met the ambiguity by creating a 'meritocracy' at the same time that it favoured the gentry, with their educational advantages.

With regard to the seventh conservative category, Chinese

[1] Creel, op. cit., Chapters 2 and 4; Weber, op. cit., 441.
[2] C. K. Yang, 'Chinese Bureaucratic Behaviour', in Nivison and Wright, op. cit., 141; cf. Fairbank and Reischauer, op. cit., 207. At times the Chinese bureaucracy could be very 'meddlesome' in country affairs, but not to the point of demanding major change in the bureaucracy's own structure. The idea that social mechanism was sensitive and easily upset by change was applied to government itself.

education consistently stressed the importance of social duty, and it made no mention of individual, natural rights. It defined the family not as a sphere of freedom for the individual so much as a stabilizing institution, disciplining and socializing each member. It is true that the Confucian ideal of 'self-cultivation' posed individual development as an end. Such development, however, could only be achieved by contribution to the social group, particularly the family.[1] If men sometimes interpreted 'self-cultivation' in more individual fashion, this was due largely to the influence of Taoism and Buddhism.

Behind the conservatism of the Chinese lay a pride which can be more stubborn than any nationalism—cultural pride. In the Chinese case, cultural pride was especially obdurate because it concealed its emotionalism in a veil of seeming intellectualism. Although classical doctrine was little questioned, the Chinese system did profess reverence for scholarship and learning. As a result, the Chinese bureaucracy was able to phrase in deceptively —self-deceptively—intellectual terms what was basically a love of tradition *per se* and veneration of an absolutist dogma. As Mu Fu-sheng points out in *The Wilting of the Hundred Flowers*, when the empire was foundering under Western influences and pressures, opposition to radical reform was offered partly on intellectual grounds:

that Chinese craftsmanship was superior to machines, that it was impossible to overtake western material progress and hence futile to try, that materialistic civilization was beneath the Chinese who sought 'higher purposes', that the labour-saving machines would create unemployment and other labour problems, and that the natural resources in the mines would be exhausted.

The last reason, offered by Yu Yueh, indicated the obstinacy of a static view of the world in which to exhaust anything in nature was sacrilegious. It was also feared that westernization would corrupt the mind of the people and that reliance should be placed on men and moral principles to save China rather than on machines and technique.[2]

[1] Robert Lifton, *Thought Reform and the Psycholology of Totalism*, 366.
[2] Mu Fu-sheng, op. cit., 85–86.

Today we are accustomed to finding social theorists on the side of 'liberals', reformers, and progressive planners. By contrast, self-styled conservatives have, since Edmund Burke at any rate, emphasized experience and common sense above abstract schemes. Such men may oppose sudden change, but over smaller proposals they will often be flexible and realistic. It is when they make an *ideology* of *status quo*, building conservatism into scientism, that their position promises to become rigid. That is one lesson for us today in the history of Chinese conservatism.

Conclusions about Confucian Education

Compared with the Victorian public schools, Chinese education seemed to show two major weaknesses as a political force. It made little real provision against conflicts of loyalty, and practically none for the requirements of change. Both weaknesses, however, stemmed from environmental factors that were altogether lacking in Britain. Both could perhaps have been mitigated—as we will shortly explain—had China enjoyed Britain's combination of ethical reliance with a strong legal tradition. Whether Chinese education *might* have supported such a combination, whether the education system continued to oppose legalism after China possessed the sociological and military conditions to make detailed law effective—these are 'if' questions of history which I am unqualified to meet. What can be said is that, given the absence of a strong legal tradition, the weaknesses of the education system brought their own advantages. The loyalty conflicts exacerbated by Confucian education, for instance, provided two safeguards against government oppression of the people. First, the civil servant's family loyalties enhanced the tradition of limited bureaucratic interference with clan authority. Secondly, the conflict between 'idealists' and 'opportunists' checked the *effective* power of the latter and of the Emperor. In the absence of a legal constitution, the idealist minority could not make workability and compromise the norms that they were in parliamentary England. Unlike the British civil servant, the Confucian official was unable to assume that attention to workable government and smooth co-operation was compatible with *tao*, for there was no legal machinery binding the Emperor to the community interest. However much he endorsed the harmonious *manner*, the idealist had to exhibit fairly rigid moral principles over substantive policy if he wanted the latter to serve the whole community. In short, Confucian education itself functioned indirectly as a constitutional check. Contributing a moral note to factionalism and providing classical support for the idealists' position, it promoted government responsibility. Even when it failed in this function, even when government *was* irresponsible, the education system at least tended to limit despotic power.

To account for the system's second weakness—its failure to foster an imaginative response to change—we have already pointed out factors in the Chinese environment that were unknown to Britain: relatively static conditions, and the task of maintaining cultural unity in a great and varied land. Unaccompanied by strong law, the education system was vital to the unity which made central government possible, let alone durable. If the Victorian public schools were better able to provide adaptable rulers, Confucian education achieved a great task in making national government feasible at all. This comparison is merely another way of expressing the dilemmas of political education stated at the beginning of this book. The more directly and heavily a government relies on an education system for its very existence, the more likely it is to destroy the intellectual sources of its long-run survival.

The Timing of History

We have seen how two societies, totally removed in cultural origins, far apart in geography, produced a remarkably similar social institution performing a remarkably similar social function. We must now ask the historical question that we deferred in the early stages of this chapter: what convergence of conditions could the vast Middle Kingdom and a small northern island have had in common to evolve such an identical pattern, the system of gentlemanly education? The reasons suggested here are offered only as speculations, and they surely do not comprise the whole answer.

The first point to notice about both societies is that they possessed a heritage of local gentry power. Certain conditions, moreover, encouraged gentry power to rely on etiquette and custom,
as much as on law, to obtain social harmony and make social
obligations binding. In the first place, the leisure of the landlord
may have produced an ethic of leisure*liness*, hence an aesthetic
predilection for graceful manners. In the second place, both
societies enjoyed enough stability to place relatively little strain
on the regulating power of manners and custom. Both countries,
it must be remembered, were geographically cushioned from the
disruptive force of foreign ideas and onslaughts—Britain by the
sea; China by the sea, mountains, and desert. Manners and custom, little shaken by the gradual seep of new ideas, became
educational devices not only for regulating society as a whole but
for directing the gentry to community leadership.

The second factor to notice is the unusual relationship that
existed between gentry and bureaucracy. Imperial responsibilities,
trade growth, and a rising population helped create the need for a
central bureaucracy, characterized by formal methods of recruitment and promotion, methods stressing merit as much as birth.
Before the rise of a commercial middle class could evolve active
threats to their political power, the gentry were given time to
stake out special claims on this new bureaucracy. (Hence the
attention given classics in Civil Service examinations.) The
traditional gentleman ideal of public duty and personal obligation
was pressed into service with the new *rationalist* organization: it
produced candidates for bureaucracy and it supported the bureaucracy's moral code.

In this process the gentry's education system played its part.
Linked to Civil Service—and in the British case, military—
recruitment, Confucian education and the public schools alike
defended the gentry's social position, political power, and aesthetic
and traditional values from the rising commercial group and its
rationalist individualism. At the same time, social mobility
allowed the gentry and aristocracy to admit talented members
from other classes and to indoctrinate them as one of their
own.

175

Inextricably linked with these factors were certain national assumptions: that a people could achieve strong moral agreement; that a boy's upbringing could inhibit selfish impulses and encourage voluntary service; and hence that education itself was a potent political force.

Chapter 13

A Question of Freedom I:
Manipulation and Free Choice

In 1962 *The Guardian* reported an interview with the headmistress of a leading and very famous girls' public school. One of the questions raised by the interviewer was the problem of student conformity. Did a public school, it was asked, 'suppress individuality'? The headmistress replied that she did not think this was true of her establishment. 'In a girls' school', she explained, 'you can't enforce anything except by consent—you can't beat them like boys.'[1]

Now, at the interview the headmistress may have said other things which were not reported and which confirmed, indeed, that her girls were not conformists. It should also be pointed out that she added to her first remark about 'consent' a cursory explanation based on human nature. Girls, she was reported to have said, 'are more realistic, more practical than boys'.

As published, however, her statements abetted an old-fashioned fallacy about freedom: the assumption that coercion and formal rules comprise the main constraints which authority can put upon individual liberties; that he who acts of his own consent invariably acts with free choice.

A vivid exposure of this fallacy occurred in my own school experience. At Winchester it was frequently said—by boys as well as masters—that membership in the Combined Cadet Force was 'non-compulsory'. This belief was firmly, and I am sure sincerely, echoed by the master commanding the Winchester 'Corps' in his recruiting address (at which attendance *was* compulsory). One part of the address went approximately as follows:

[1] Strahan Soames, 'Headmistress', *The Guardian*, 21 February 1962.

'I do want to impress upon you that the Corps is *not* compulsory. You are quite at liberty not to join. If you do not join, I don't honestly know what we'd do with you . . . ' (pause for thought) 'it's so seldom happened. But I'm sure we would find something . . . digging potatoes or something.'

At first sight a statement of this sort may sound blatantly coercive, threatening the individual with punishment-work in a potato patch if he did not conform. It must be realized, however, that agricultural labour appeared no less uncomfortable than polishing boots and mounting drill parades—exercises which, on a superficial plane, were the target of constant grumbling. In fact, the pressure applied by the Corps Commander's recruiting address was more subtle than mere coercion. Quite simply it stated that there was no traditionally sanctioned, socially respected alternative to service in the Corps. The argument was effective because it was not operating in a vacuum. New members of the school had quickly learned, from the regular testimony of house-masters and prefects, that the Corps was a school 'Institution' and that it was a 'bad notion'—i.e. 'bad form'—not to join. In reality, it was more than a 'bad notion'; it was virtually unthinkable.[1] With the exception of the medically unfit, everyone in my house, and probably everyone in the whole school, joined the Corps while I was there.

I am sure that many, perhaps most, recruits felt they had joined the Corps voluntarily. And in a sense they had. No formal steps had been taken to conscript them; in many instances they had signed up because they felt they *ought to*, because service with the Corps seemed the only decent and respectable course.

Their choice might be called voluntary, but could it be called free? If an organization or society so controls the very desires— the consent—of men that they all *want* to do the same thing, such manipulation clearly represents a human constraint on free will.

[1] True, senior boys were often heard to defend the Corps on the grounds that it would improve one's performance as a National Serviceman at Officer training school. But this argument may have been a mere rationalization: I never heard it rigorously tested by inquiries, say, into the National Service fortunes of well-educated youth who had not had C.C.F. experience—or by discussions as to whether the discomforts of the Corps were a reasonable exchange for whatever future advantages they might bring. When National Service was abolished, the Corps continued to be as 'compulsory' as before, although the drill parade was emphasized less.

To an extent, of course, this kind of constraint will always be with us. Every community, in varying degree, regulates the individual by irrational pressures to conform.

It must also be recognized that manipulation of the emotions cannot easily be separated from rational persuasion. Appeals can be addressed to the individual simultaneously on different levels, some more intellectual than others. To what extent, and in what sense, some brands of rational persuasion themselves comprise a constraint on freedom is a philosophical question beyond the scope of this discussion. The reason that I focus on irrational pressure, on the manipulation of emotions, is that such pressure may operate subliminally, influencing the individual's actions without his realizing it.[1] By contrast, rational persuasion—to the extent that it *is* rational—is 'in the open': ideally the individual can oppose it with counter-arguments, and the net result may even be to widen the range of choice which the individual considers.

With the development of technology, the threat to human freedom presented by irrational manipulation has clearly increased. Not only have mass media become more powerful, adding television and radio to the voice of the Press, but its appeals have become psychologically more subtle. This trend has not gone unrecognized by thinking men; indeed, phrases like George Orwell's 'Big Brother' and Vance Packard's 'Hidden Persuaders' have become good cocktail party usage.

In modern Western society, the issue of irrational manipulation versus freedom has been fought out largely in debates about advertising. John Kenneth Galbraith, for example, has accused American advertising of making a mockery of free consumer choice. A central thesis of his book, *The Affluent Society*, is the principle of 'social balance'.[2] In its private sector, argues Galbraith, the American nation has done itself proud, but in its public sector —the sector of schools and roads and urban renewal—the nation is relatively poor. Consumers invest heavily in cars, television

[1] Public awareness that authority's constraints cannot be so effectively circumscribed when they are secret constraints helped cause the popular British outcry against 'Q'Cars —police cars disguised as ordinary vehicles. The same concern is also reflected in the careful signposting of electrical and radar 'speed traps' for motorists, both in American states and in Britain.

[2] J. K. Galbraith, *The Affluent Society*, Chapter 18, especially pp. 202-3.

sets, and washing machines, but they refuse to do likewise in taxes for better schools.

Now comes the part of Galbraith's argument that has infuriated defenders of Madison Avenue. When the American people, declares Galbraith, plump for private goods rather than for public goods, they are acting with less freedom than they imagine. One reason for this is the factor of advertising which shrills at the customer to buy more and more consumer goods but does relatively little to tout better social services. Under these conditions, Galbraith claims, the customer is not making his choice in a fair market; the situation resembles more a bazaar with two vendors, one of whom possesses a megaphone while the other can scarcely be seen or heard.[1] The buyer in this situation has less autonomy, less freedom in which to make up his own mind, than if both vendors had megaphones, thereby presenting him with genuine choice.

Against the Galbraithian viewpoint, there is the defence, commonly put up by motivational researchers, that advertising cannot create new wants. It can only play on existing wants, and in view of this fact it cannot be said to manipulate human desire. The question that remains to be answered, however, is whether advertising changes the *priorities* of human desires, (1) by *indulging* some to the virtual exclusion of others, (2) by morally *legitimizing* motives which the individual might otherwise contain within limits as unworthy and even ultimately destructive—greed, exhibitionism, and so on. The very experience, for example, of seeing in print appeals to status-seeking may indulge and legitimize vanity. Even Martin Mayer, a student and defender of the advertising industry, admits that advertising can magnify certain motivations, though basically it cannot create them. Thus, toothpaste manufacturers who 'force people to worry about mouth odours' are stimulating an anxiety[2]—stimulating it in order to sell its remedy. One might add that to deny the influence of advertising on men's motivations is to deny the emotional influence of any kind of education, which advertising essentially is.

Martin Mayer's findings about advertising are extremely

[1] Simile mine.   [2] Martin Mayer, *Madison Avenue, U.S.A.*, 326 (Penguin ed.).

relevant to our discussion of freedom, because he reveals a key principle of irrational manipulation. The principle is connected with Mayer's 'added value' concept of advertising.[1] According to this concept, advertising itself contributes to the total satisfaction provided by the product it is selling. The particular satisfaction— or value—which advertising supplies is a psychological satisfaction, a value over and above the intrinsic function which the product performs. To take one of Mayer's own examples—

... Two identical lipsticks marketed under different brand names may have very different values for a teen-age girl. Wearing one of them, she feels her ordinary self; wearing the other, which has been successfully advertised as the highroad to romance, she feels a beauty—and perhaps she is.[2]

In similar vein, Mayer argues that the advertising campaign which builds up a certain model of car as a status-symbol thereby increases the product's value to its owner. 'The admiring eyes that follow the car ... are satisfactions not likely to be missed by the consumer.'[3]

Now there is an important inference to be drawn from the added value concept of advertising. In its ferreting out of psychological needs to fulfil, advertising may increasingly draw upon the social environment as a whole.[4] 'Be Sociable, Have a Pepsi' is perhaps the most clear-cut recent example of an advertisement using a product (Pepsi-Cola) as a catalyst of social pressures and corresponding social needs.[5] In this case, the advertisement both

[1] Martin Mayer, op. cit., 320.　　[2] Ibid., 320.　　[3] Ibid., 324.

[4] This is not an *inevitable* outcome of the added value concept. As Mayer himself points out, two schools of motivational researchers can be identified—the 'psychoanalysts' concentrating on childhood factors in personality, and the 'sociologists' who stress contemporary social influences on the individual. Both schools could be said to seek added psychological satisfactions of a product. Today's trend, however, is in favour of the sociologist group. cf. Mayer, op. cit., 231–2.

[5] Advertisements playing on the individual's sensitivity to group opinions will probably be pronounced in a society where the individual is responsive to the opinions of his peers ('other-directed') as opposed to holding more fixed values, internalized in childhood ('inner-directed'). cf. Sanford Dornbusch and Lauren Hickman, 'Other-Directedness in Consumer-Goods Advertising: A Test of Riesman's Historical Theory', *Social Forces*, December 1959: a study of the shift in advertising appeals during 67 years of *Ladies Home Journal* publication.

But advertising, like formal education, helps to *induce* such vulnerability to social pressures. And there are other social forces, fitting other societies, besides the consensus of peer-group opinion—for example, appeals to nationalism and patriotism.

reinforces and appeals to what David Riesman, in his well-titled book, *The Lonely Crowd*, called the 'other-directed' tendency of American social character. Advertisements emphasizing status-seeking and status-symbols represent a similar attempt to use central phenomena of the whole society as a lever on the individual consumer. Gone, or rapidly passing, are the days when most products are sold purely for their own direct functions and intrinsic properties—for their taste, or their comfort, or their sturdiness.[1]

Advertising, in short, has reached the age of the 'wholistic approach'.[2] This phrase, coined by Ernest Dichter, the pioneer of motivational research, is itself significant. In *The Strategy of Desire*, Dichter explains the phrase with a diagram consisting of five concentric circles. The inner circle is the product itself; the outer circle 'the philosophy surrounding our contemporary world', including the inheritance of past cultures.[3] Between these, from the outside in, Dichter puts the 'national culture', the 'sociological frame of reference'—the social role the product plays between people—and 'the soul of the product'—what the product means psychologically to its owner. The successful advertising man, says Dichter, practises 'cultural anthropology more than anything else': to sell his product effectively he should understand the feelings it arouses on all levels.[4]

The world of Pepsi-Cola and motivational research may seem far from that of a public school cadet force. Yet, in their own unsystematic way, the authorities of the public school have practised elements of Dichter, unconscious as that practice may have been. Service in the Corps was not 'sold' purely on its intrinsic merits as an educational experience: it was not, in other words, sold only as a product. It was also given a mystique: it was sold as a symbol. In its symbolic function it represented school 'Institutions',

[1] Ernest Dichter (see below) claims to have used mainly irrational and symbolic appeals in selling such severely practical items as engineering equipment.

[2] Ernest Dichter, *The Strategy of Desire*, 145.

[3] Dichter gives a colourful account of the associations, some mystical and emotional, which even so lowly a product as soup has aroused, as he contends, through the ages, p. 147.   [4] Ibid., 148.

'Tradition', and 'good taste'. The emotions it triggered were, therefore, complex, a mixture of nationalism (a desire to identify with the community), mysticism (here, a veneration of unbroken tradition), and aesthetic feeling (a wish to conform to 'good taste').

Whether it was so intended or not, the recruitment appeal of the Winchester Corps derived special strength by making itself an integral part of a great whole—as Dichter would say, the 'wholistic approach'. In other words, the Corps and Corps service stood for 'Winchester', for all the emotions and satisfaction that the word 'Winchester' represented. From this, its symbolic function, it followed that the Corps could not be by-passed in one's allegiance to the school community. Such was the widespread assumption, and it was not always a merely tacit assumption. On one or two occasions when I heard it said that the Corps was 'non-compulsory', a rider was added to the statement: 'if you don't want to join, you shouldn't have come here'. But, as it has already been suggested, people seemed to *want* to join.

The comparison between a public school experience and the nature of modern advertising has been pursued partly because it casts a perspective on totalitarian power. We have observed that when advertising sells a product, as when the public school promoted an activity, it has tended to arraign the whole weight of social values and attitudes against the individual. It plays on the social, conformist side of the individual's personality; even the advertising campaign which promotes its product as a mark of distinction usually applies narrow but well-established social standards of what in fact comprises distinction. Above all, advertising, like public school authority, has posed its product as an integral part of a whole social milieu. It is this point, as much as any other, that is crucial to totalitarian power in general, and Communist indoctrination in particular.

Now I am not suggesting that Dichter's wholistic approach is merely an embryo of what experts on Chinese 'brain-washing' call the totalist ideology. Both psychologically and philosophically, ideological totalism has ingredients that have not appeared along Madison Avenue; and its attempt to explain all of life in one great theoretical scheme is far from the public school mentality.[1] Nevertheless, the tendency to base a specific emotional appeal on a whole social system characterizes the wholistic approach as well as totalism. This fact, in turn, suggests that totalitarian attempts to manipulate individual volition include at least one important element that can be exploited in many different societies.

Before we go any farther, we should define what is meant by a 'totalist ideology'. Basically the term refers to any doctrine which attempts a complete, unified explanation of world and society, and whose moral prescriptions and emotional demands seek to embrace all of the individual's energies.[2] Such doctrines offer not only a sense of purpose to the individual but a sense of belonging and certainty. As such they have great appeal in times of social flux and the uprooting of traditional values—conditions which characterized modern China before the Communist Revolution and which mark many new nations today.

These reflections add a foreign policy dimension to the problem of manipulation and free choice. Imagine two hostile world powers, Power A and Power B. Let us imagine, further, that both powers have sworn to brand as aggression and to resist by arms any attempt by the other to gain control forcibly of a third country. But suppose also that of the two world powers Power A enjoys clearly better techniques of persuasion and manipulation. And suppose that, one day, a third country, C, *invites* occupation by the forces of A. If ideological influence by Power A was well established, could this be called a constraint upon C? The question

[1] Psychologically, it depends on *individual* totalism which Robert Lifton, in his case-study analysis of Communist 'thought-reform', defines as extremism, one element of which is a 'tendency towards all-or-nothing emotional alignments'. Robert Lifton, *Thought Reform and the Psychology of Totalism*, 8, 129.

This, in itself, is a far cry from the public school emphasis on moderation and a balance of ideals.

It is interesting, however, that Lifton himself admits the possibility of there being 'a continuity between [thought-reform] and many less extreme activities' in Western nations. The misgivings of those who have seen ' "brainwashing" in American advertising, in large corporation training programmes, in private preparatory schools and in Congressional investigations . . . are not always without basis'. Ibid., 4, 6.

[2] It is possible, of course, to say that some systems are more totalist than others. In this sense, certain all-inclusive theories of science or of history might be called relatively 'totalist' even if they do not extend to moral prescription.

would be all the more complicated if A's influence contained both rational argument—persuasion—and emotional sloganing—manipulation, not to speak of economic assistance.

I have no solution, either practical or philosophical, to the quandary, but I would like to put forward some observations, placing the problem in historical perspective. First, the problem is not altogether a new one. In the sixteenth century, Hideyoshi, Civil Dictator of Japan, crucified a number of Jesuit fathers. He did so largely through fear: to Japanese officials, the Jesuits' highly successful Christianization campaign smacked of political subversion, and a report had spread that the priests were the vanguard of Spanish *conquistadors*.[1] (As a footnote with a contemporary ring, it is interesting to record that, on at least one occasion in the preceding régime, the Jesuits converted a lord by offering him trade in firearms.)[2] It will also be remembered that in seventeenth-century England, Puritan hatred of Rome was inflamed by fear of another Armada, as well as of political infiltration by Jesuit 'Fifth Columnists'. Whether or not these fears were realistic, the parallel with current Western anxieties—especially American anxieties—concerning Communism is plain.

This leads us to two observations which should be made about Communist indoctrination. Both apply to China, and to our study of Confucian education. The first is that the Chinese Communists' dramatic use of education as a political weapon rests partly on foundations laid in the Empire. The second observation is more speculative, but it follows from the first. I am going to argue that the society which, to establish order, relies on ethics much more heavily than on law has a special tendency to devalue social freedom in *any* form—freedom from coercion as well as from manipulation. To understand why this might be so, we must first return to the preceding observation, about the links between Confucian education and Chinese Communism.[3]

---

[1] Rene Fülöp-Miller, *The Power and Secret of the Jesuits*, 233–5. Edwin Reischauer, *Japan, Past and Present*, 88–89.

[2] Fülöp-Miller, op., cit., 232.

[3] The account that follows does not pretend to cover the full complex range of similarities and differences between the two Chinas. I have relied heavily on *The Wilting of the Hundred Flowers* by Fu Mu-sheng, and even more heavily on Robert Lifton, op. cit., who spent two years in Hong Kong on a psychiatric investigation of both Chinese and Western thought-reform 'patients'.

Both Imperial China and the Communist government have placed immense reliance on education as a political instrument. We have already described the political role of Confucian education and the way in which it was harnessed to State needs through the examination system. Turning to Communist China, we find that the 1960 national budget allocated more funds to education than it did to military defence. A majority of schools, furthermore, were not covered by the budget but run by local communities, communes, and factories.[1]

In both Chinas, too, emphasis on political education reflected a 'national genius' for personal relations.[2] Robert Lifton, indeed, suggests that the Chinese Communist skill at political indoctrination is due partly to this very fact.

No other civilization has paid so much attention to the conduct of human relationships. . . . The Chinese family, with its characteristically complicated inner manœuvring, has been an excellent psychological training ground: in order to be 'proper', Chinese children have had to learn to be aware of the emotional currents in their milieu. And this personal emphasis has extended from the family into the rest of Chinese life: whether performing official duties or seeking personal influence upon the people involved—and there is only a fine line between influence and manipulation. These human-centred skills have been nurtured over centuries, and emphasized at the expense of technical achievements. . . .[3]

This does not imply that the spirit of Confucian education was identical with that of Chinese Communist 'thought-reform'. Far from it: as Lifton points out, Confucian tradition embodied a self-preserving moderation and a 'cult of restraint', whereas thought-reform fosters a rapturous 'cult of enthusiasm' and a 'demand for total self-surrender'.[4] On other levels, too, vast differences lie between the two societies in their use of education. Yet in a strange way, much of the new contains seeds of the old.

---

[1] Felix Greene, 'China: Tomorrow's Giant', *Observer*, 22 October 1961. cf. Gerald Clark, *Impatient Giant: Red China Today*, Chapters 4, 7.

In the pages that follow, I discuss the thought-reform of adult intellectuals and potential 'deviants' rather than the education received by most students. In terms of ideology, however, both systems have much in common.

[2] Lifton, op. cit., 397.   [3] Ibid., 396–7.   [4] Ibid., 397.

The relation between the two societies is, in short, ambivalent; some of it can even be explained by using a form dear to the Communist mind—the dialectic.[1] Under the old régime, the family represented the prime vehicle of political education. Family training provided candidates for Civil Service examinations, and it taught loyalty to the sovereign as an extension, an analogy, of 'filial piety'. At the same time the family, through its strict discipline and tight organization, helped to keep local order.

Now comes the antithesis part of the dialectic. During the nineteenth and twentieth centuries, the impact of the West—notions of liberal individualism; commercialism; science and questioning; and other factors—eroded the traditional values which supported the family's command over the individual.[2] As a political unit the family was finally destroyed by the Communist Revolution. The family was now 'dead', but some of its political essence survived to join what the dialecticians would call a higher synthesis. Thus, the Communists retained and developed the principle of political indoctrination in local units—the street committee, the Young Pioneers and, so it was hoped, the commune. Likewise, 'filial piety' became filial respect for Party authority.[3] The Communists could tap traditional sources of loyalty and deference, once they had removed the conflict in that loyalty, the division of allegiance between family and State. The new political units which replaced the family were and are unequivocally servants of the national government.

Under the Communist régime, of course, grass-roots loyalty indoctrination is firmly wedded to a mass education campaign, including an onslaught on general illiteracy. In many respects this is a far cry from the old system which favoured gentry families and whose Mandarin culture has been replaced by a

[1] This is not to suggest that the Communists' own dialectical interpretation of history would follow suit.
[2] For a fuller account of the weakening of the Chinese family unit, see C. K. Yang, *The Chinese Family in the Communist Revolution.*
[3] Lifton, op. cit., 379, 386. Other Confucian echoes include the Communist use of the word 'sincerity'. In modern parlance, the term means total commitment to Communism; traditionally, the 'sincere man' was he who genuinely desired with his whole inner being what was right. (Ibid., 382, 391–2.) Likewise, Communist leaders have actually quoted Confucian passages on 'self-cultivation'. Ibid., 390–1.

technically oriented proletarian culture.[1] Even here, however, there is a vestige of continuity between old and new. Confucian education thought held that the meritorious youth, be he rich or poor, should be promoted to high office; one expression of this belief, however imperfect an expression, was the examination system itself. The Communist nation-builders, for their part, have found that educational *élitism* has a stubborn ally in the economics of scarce resources. Secondary education is not yet universal and only a small minority of youth go on to college. It must be said, however, that universal education is the government's goal.

On the level of ideology, can we again find links between Confucianism and Chinese Communism? In its early stages particularly, Confucian doctrine was more a 'genial orthodoxy', to use Whitehead's phrase, than a totalist ideology.[2] Confucius himself hesitated to postulate absolute, watertight laws,[3] and a prime classical precept was the Doctrine of the Mean, or 'nothing too much'.[4] Nevertheless, as Confucian teaching gained a monopoly of the State schools and examination system, and as the State apparatus, in turn, came to dominate Chinese education, the Confucian classics ascended to the position of an absolutist ideology. The seeds of totalism became apparent. Like Communism, classical doctrine mixed moral precepts and social theory with laws of science and the universe. Its wisdom was declared absolute and unquestionable.

Unlike Christianity, moreover, Confucian doctrine contained no developed concept of personal immortality in a life hereafter. Instead, it offered the individual a collective immortality, the joy of contributing to the historic community—the family and, less vividly, the Empire. In other words, it offered a certain mysticism of society, restrained, it is true, by the reclusive filament of Chinese Buddhism and Taoism.

Communism, too, offers its mysticism of society. Communism also entwines that mysticism with the intellectual pretensions of scientism: it claims to base its moral philosophy on a science of

[1] cf. C. T. Hu, 'Communist Education: Theory and Practice' and Theodore Chen, 'Elementary Education in China', *China Quarterly*, London, April–June, 1962.
[2] Lifton, op. cit., 455.　　　[3] Mu Fu-sheng, op. cit., 296.
[4] From the *Great Learning*, cited by Vincent Cronin in *Wise Man from the West*, 103.

society and history,[1] just as the classics based their philosophy on cosmological laws of 'due order'. There is, of course, a difference between the scientism of Communism and the scientism of classical doctrine. Whereas the first involves a theory of social change progressing towards an ideal future condition, the latter invisaged the maintenance of a society emulating as perfectly as possible a past Golden Age. Despite this important difference, it can be argued that Confucian ideology, fusing emotional loyalty indoctrination with attempts to satisfy the intellect, paved the way for the more all-out efforts of Chinese thought-reform.

About thought-reform itself, there is only one point, specially relevant to our study of freedom, that can be made here. The emotional manipulation involved in thought-reform includes the element of coercion.[2] It is only one component in the complex process of 'brain-washing', and often it exists only as a vague threat, but it is an important element none the less. What this means is that coercion and manipulation are not necessarily two quite separate constraints. As Robert Lifton and Mu Fu-sheng reveal in their accounts of thought-reform, the Chinese have used the threat of coercion, along with other messages, so subtly that the individual's innermost resistance collapses and he *wants* to conform.[3] Under certain conditions and pressures, the individual who faces only one safe choice—choice of behaviour, or of allegiance—can be induced to make himself enjoy that choice, to greet it as if spontaneously.

To what extent, and how deeply, these effects are in practice achieved is very difficult to say. Most Chinese intellectuals, it has been suggested, are adapters rather than zealots, accepting the régime, partly approving its programme, and seeing in it both good and bad.[4] This in itself may signify a measure of loyalty.

---

[1] Lifton, op. cit., 422, 428. cf. Mu Fu-sheng. op., cit., 216–18.
[2] This is not so easily the case when political indoctrination is applied abroad as a part of foreign policy.
[3] Mu Fu-sheng, op. cit., 218–20, 226. Lifton, op. cit., 438–9.
Besides the threat of coercion ('become what we tell you—or else'), Lifton enumerates the *exhortative* message ('you ought morally to become what we tell you'), the *therapeutic* message ('you are sick, but can be cured if you do what we tell you') and the message of *realization* ('you can express more fully your potential if you challenge your ways with our new concepts'). Of the four messages, Lifton says, coercion and exhortation are the most important.   [4] Ibid., 401.

On the other hand, when Mao Tzc-tung, in his 'Let a Hundred Flowers Bloom' speech of 1956, invited constructive criticism of the régime, the Party leadership underwent a torrent of bitter attacks from the intellectuals. The criticisms continued until the newly-given freedom was sharply withdrawn.

From the standpoint of our problem, however, too much should not be read into the 'Hundred Flowers' episode. To cite Lifton again—

. . . Thought-reform is able to promote an emotional contagion—of resentment as well as enthusiasm. These emotions are closely related and easily changed from one to the other. Individual feelings of hostility and resentment toward reform may exist consciously, or may be deeply repressed, but when encouraged by external conditions, they can emerge suddenly and unexpectedly.[1]

Under such conditions, reversals of loyalty when free choice is extended do not, by themselves, refute the possibility that loyalty may enjoy a certain voluntary element when freedom is not extended. It should be remembered, furthermore, that the episode occurred when the Communist national government was less than a decade old. One wonders what would happen if the 'Hundred Flowers' invitation were to be repeated in ten or twenty years time, when more of the intellectuals had been exposed to indoctrination from their earliest schooldays. A repeat of the experiment would tell us much about the resilience of the human mind.

Our last observation about manipulation and free choice is an inference from what has gone before. Reliance on ethical restraints far above that on legal restraints will, over the long run, make a society liable to devalue freedom from *any* social constraint, coercion as well as manipulation.[2] This statement is very much an 'other things being equal' contention: obviously there are numer-

---

[1] Ibid., 411. Many students of Peking University joined in the criticism; although 90 per cent. of them were Communist Party members and in many respects continued to identify with the régime. Ibid., 408.

[2] For a concise description of the ethical tradition *vis-à-vis* the legal tradition in government, see Frederick Watkins, *The Political Tradition of the West*, Introduction, x.

ous contingencies, social, economic and historical, which go to making totalitarianism. It is also probable that there are several, quite different paths to totalitarianism and that one such path lies in a certain type of *legalism*. Finally, it must be pointed out that the statement in no sense implies a belittlement of the role of ethics in liberal society. We have only to recall the Prohibition era in the United States, the era of bootlegging and Al Capone, to see what can happen when a law does not enjoy strong moral support. To secure peace and order with the maximum amount of personal freedom there must clearly be balance—an alliance between legal restraints and ethical restraints.

Having made these qualifications, I think it can be said that great attention to ethical restraints rather than to legal restraints breeds totalitarian *tendencies*. The case is borne out not only by the Chinese experience but by England. As we have tried to indicate, the public school community was itself essentially totalitarian—a characteristic that could never be applied to British society as a whole. A major difference between the school community and the nation was that the latter enjoyed a strong legal system in the Western liberal tradition. Law existed not only to ensure social harmony but to guarantee an area of free choice for each individual.[1] It is true that common law, like the Constitution, sprang from custom and precedent, but it has come to be viewed as a body wholly separate from the more informal restraints involved when one invokes tradition *per se*. In the public school community by contrast, social harmony depended much more heavily on ethical restraints—custom and etiquette—than on official rules and regulations. Yet, behind the etiquette lay covert coercion: as we suggested in the last chapter, the prefect's cane was ready to punish the rare offender who persistently breached the ethical norm.[2]

To understand why social dependence on ethical restraints contains within it the seeds of totalitarianism, we must look more

[1] To some extent, it is true, public school etiquette awarded certain freedoms and immunities to the middle-aged groups, but they were still strongly subject to restrictions of 'good form'. And junior boys enjoyed far less freedom.

[2] cf. Chapter 12, p. 143. Also Cyril Connolly's account of beatings for the offence of 'generality' at Eton, Chapter 4, p. 42. The worst punishments for general noncon- formity, slovenliness, etc., possibly occurred at Marlborough where a public spectacle was sometimes made of the 'deviant'.

generally at the concept of freedom and its relation to the two kinds of restraints. Both legal and ethical restraints restrict the individual's freedom *to do* certain things and thereby confer upon the individual freedom from the aggressions of others. Both legal and ethical restraints limit choice. Legal restrictions, for their part, circumscribe an area of freedom within which the individual can make varied choices. Ethical restraints, on the other hand, tend to limit the individual's desires. If the ethical tradition—reliance on ethics rather than on law—covers a great variety of interests and potential outlooks, it is particularly unlikely to induce social cohesion solely by posing broad ethical goals and making *conscious* compromise and self-restraint into virtues. The ethical tradition will be a more effective binding force if it induces the individual to conform *unconsciously* to one standard of taste and morality, and to find uncloyed pleasure in subordination to the group interest. (Hence the importance to the ethical tradition of a disciplining education system.)

Under these conditions of ethical restraint, the individual might still be considered free, provided one defined freedom by the number of choices available to the individual *if* he wanted to make them. Or again, one might call the internally-restrained individual free by using a Pauline concept: freedom from base desires. Centuries before the birth of Christ, this concept was recognized by Confucius in a tribute to his own education: 'At seventy I could follow what my heart desired, without transgressing what was right.'[1]

If, however, freedom is defined as the relative absence of any human constraint, either by coercion or by indoctrination, then one implication of the ethical tradition is to downgrade freedom as a desirable condition. In the first place, the dependence of a political system on strong ethical restraints may seem to require the restriction of *intellectual* freedom. In the atmosphere of questioning and doubt produced by opposing schools of thought, it is not very easy to indoctrinate men with such uniform values and so strong a communal loyalty that social cohesion need not depend on law.

In the second place, however, the inculcation of ethical restraints

[1] *Analects*, Book III, Chapter IV.

may ultimately devalue even freedom from legal restrictions backed by coercion. Western liberalism has valued such freedom, *within* the boundaries of law, largely because it permits individual variation and uniqueness; because it has appeared to be a pre-requisite for voluntary choice; and, therefore, because it affords opportunity for individual self-development. The ethical tradition, by contrast, stresses the existence of absolute moral standards and an ideal social behaviour above the joys of individual variation.

The difference in this respect between the two traditions comes out sharply in Felix Greene's report of a debate he had with Han Pei-chun, secretary of the Chinese Writer's Union.[1] According to Greene, Han said that the job of a writer was not simply to write 'as one pleases', but to describe the 'reality' of the time and express the people's desire to build an equalitarian society where individuals worked for the good of all. Greene's reaction to this statement was as significant as the statement itself. In part, it is true, he criticized Han's viewpoint on the pragmatic grounds that popular approval was an unreliable criterion of a writer's worth. But he also seemed to regard as *evil in itself* 'the monolithic unanimity with which everyone talks and thinks in China today'.[2] This outlook is very much in the Western liberal tradition, which has tended to make individual variation an end *per se*, as well as a means to individual self-development and voluntary choice.[3] Han Pei-chun, on the other hand, belonged to a completely different tradition; he did not view freedom as an end; and he devalued it as a means.[4] For the Chinese Communist, the path of self-

---

[1] Felix Greene, *Awakened China*, 244.

[2] Elsewhere, Greene has defended freedom as a means as well as an end. In a debate with an administrator of Peking University, for example, he argued that a people must retain the habit of criticizing their leaders if they want those leaders to remain responsible. Greene, 'China: Tomorrow's Giant', *Observer*, 22 October 1961.

[3] The same tendency marks the report of an American educational research team that visited Russia a few years ago. In their assessment of Soviet education, they assumed that 'man's individual freedom and responsibility' were the vital factors underpinning 'the meaning and value of life and man's sense of dignity and worth'. By contrast, Soviet educators sought supreme moral development in the 'closely-knit children's collective', a state which removed selfishness and gave a sense of noble purpose. If anything, the Communist assumptions were stated in more precise terms. George Bereday *et al.*, *The Changing Soviet School*, 418-19. The authors are the members of the team.

[4] Like most of us, Han probably felt that he had more freedom than was the case. At one point in the conversation, he stated that the Chinese people were free to criticize the government within State-imposed limits, 'provided they accepted the basic concepts of our new society'. Felix Greene, *Awakened China*, 224.

development lies not in the uniqueness of the individual but in identification with the socialist community and the following of one 'correct' Way.

The same devaluation applies to freedom as a prerequisite for voluntary behaviour: moral indoctrination, so we have already suggested, can sometimes make a man *want* to take a certain course of action, regardless of how many or how few alternative courses are available to him. It is significant that when Confucius opposed the close legal regulation of behaviour, he did so because law could only present a minimum ethical standard.[1] In a sense, therefore, he attacked legalism not because it fettered freedom but because it was not so close a constraint as ethical teaching. Today, the Chinese Communists have shown how potentially compatible ethical teaching and a coercive brand of legalism really are. Behind their political indoctrination lies not only the power of technology but, at home, legal restriction and military force, the latter covert to all save the deviants and the unredeemable.

[1] Lorraine Creel, *The Concepts of Social Order in Early Confucianism*, Chapter 1.

Chapter 14

A Question of Freedom II : Loyalty and Intelligence

The ultimate question before us is a question of survival. Can a totalitarian system, a system which in its demands for total loyalty restricts individual freedom, produce a quantity of imaginative leaders? Can it do this, or must it eventually choke off the flow of ideas which nourish creative intelligence?

The question is one of survival in two senses. First, there is the survival of life itself. As one looks across to the totalitarian societies of Russia and China, one wonders what new types of statesmen will be forthcoming from Communist schools and universities. Whatever their loyalties and hatreds, how rational will they be in the furtherance of their ends? If they are not very rational, if they seek simple solutions when matters are complex, if they see one viewpoint and not many, if they possess neither flexibility nor foresight, prefer force to cunning and confuse patience with weakness—if such men become the dominant product of totalitarian education, civilization will be unlikely to avert the final war.[1]

Yet, ironically, if modern totalitarian systems *do* produce highly rational and resourceful leaders, civilization goes on trial over another kind of survival, the survival of a cultural tradition. If totalitarian society and totalitarian education can clearly show that the same system which belittles social freedom can still develop able minds, Western liberalism will be on the defensive as it has

---

[1] The question assumes that Russian and Chinese education will remain totalitarian in the indefinite future. The same question should be asked of democracy's own leaders, but here the problem is less one of fostering intelligence in the schools than of directing enough of the ability education *does* produce to public service, and of inspiring political rationality among the electorate as well as the leadership.

never been before. For it has long been an assumption of the Western liberal and the democrat that a relatively free society enjoys immense *intellectual* advantages over authoritarian society; that intellectual attainment is impossible without a wide range of social freedoms; that the political criticism and conflict of ideas which is supposed to characterize democracy will, in the long run, produce the ablest leaders.

Uncomfortably it is often conceded in the Western world that totalitarianism enjoys certain advantages over democracy, just as the narrowly-channelled vigour of Sparta enjoyed certain advantages over Athenian wealth and sophistication. In frank moments it is admitted that the leading democratic nations do not appear able to match Soviet and Chinese success at harnessing individual energies to a common State purpose. Vaguely, uneasily, we of the Western world may sometimes even wonder whether our liberties and riches have not spoiled us, whether we lack discipline and hardiness and a sense of public service, and whether such deficiencies will, after all, prove our undoing. And then we remind ourselves that, whatever their disadvantages, we believe in freedom and individualism. We believe in them not only as ends good in themselves, but as a means, as a necessary condition for creative human behaviour.

It is our task here to question this last belief, to ask whether a totalitarian system can, in certain circumstances, produce creative intelligence as effectively—or nearly as effectively—as any other system. That it cannot easily do so we have already seen from our study of the Victorian public schools and Confucian education. We must now ask if the feat can *ever* be accomplished.

The place to begin is with our findings from gentlemanly education. Any school system geared to the output of political leaders and public servants must obviously make a prime ethic of loyalty. In the first place, the spirit of public service is most easily inculcated if it includes moral obligation, a loyalty to the sovereign, the State, the people, a group of people, or an ideology. In the second place, strong loyalty, like any commitment, can breed belief in oneself by breeding belief in one's purpose. The result is self-assurance, a vital prerequisite for the decisiveness and personal authority which the political leader must possess. As countless old public schoolboys have shown, deference to social authority may under certain circumstances increase rather than decrease one's self-esteem.

In the final analysis, both the public schools and Confucian education taught loyalty as a faith. That is to say, they taught it as a value beyond reason and instilled through the emotions. Reason might temper loyalty—in the Chinese case, intellectual learning actually helped to promote loyalty by showing its 'noble' consequences—but it was never really relied upon to prove loyalty's worth. For the public schoolboy, as for the Mandarin, the chief bastions of loyalty were manners and mysticism.

This is not to suggest that only *political* education relies on irrational indoctrination to instil values. On the contrary, it is difficult to think of any education system which has lasted over time, has based morals mainly on reason and enquiry, and done it effectively.[1] Moral education, in other words, is largely a matter of developing faith. The enlightened liberal educator will, it is true, seek to broaden the choice offered by his moral principles; he will suggest to his students that faith can be served by different courses of action and that reason can help to select the course taken. But this is a far cry from saying that reason itself can establish the basic ethical assumptions by which man acts. In fact, once reason is accepted as the arbiter of faith, it will be more likely to destroy than to affirm. The philosopher may indeed be able to build abiding moral precepts on the wings of his intellect—but few of us are philosophers.[2]

[1] One exception to this *might* be Athenian secondary education when the *polis* itself was still an educative influence, when youth learned public service partly by hearing their elders debate public affairs in the gymnasium. cf. E. B. Castle, *Ancient Education and Today*, 43–48; James Drever, *Greek Education*, 24–25. I do not count isolated schools such as may have existed in the Renaissance and Enlightenment.

[2] This problem, of course, represents one of the eternal dilemmas of the Trial and Death of Socrates. Although he was as aware as anyone of the need for moral discipline, Socrates might be said to have had a subversive influence by placing immense trust in reason as the way to perceiving virtue.

This is not to say that even the most basic moral values should not be exposed to philosophical questioning. My own solution would be to place the burden of instilling a moral faith firmly on the schools and free the university for unlimited speculation about values.

These observations hold whether or not one maintains that there is an absolute and eternal morality. The moral consensus needed for the cohesion of every society cannot come about if it depends on differing individual judgments about what morality is. Nor, in times of stress, will moral assumptions stick if they are not given an irrational sanctity and bedded firmly in the emotions. As Athens found in the heyday of the Sophists and philosophic schools, when men are told that their beliefs are a matter of reason, they will find it easier to ridicule the emotional basis of old values than to establish new ones. Reason, in such instances, does not readily move beyond the role of scepticism and doubt.

Furthermore, once reason is allowed to attack basic loyalties and beliefs, the self-assurance fostered by those beliefs may be jeopardized. Perhaps this helps to explain the psychological difference between the 'man of action' and 'the thinker'. The anthropologist Paul Radin suggests that these two psychological types can be identified even in some primitive communities, where one of the thinker's distinctive attributes is that he is 'impelled by his whole nature to spend a considerable time analysing his subjective states'.[1] Although Radin does not say so,[2] the rational introversion of the thinker, laying bare his secret fears and innermost assumptions, may lead, in more modern societies at least, to the plight of a Hamlet—'the native hue of resolution . . . sicklied o'er with the pale cast of thought'.[3]

The difference between the thinker and the man of action should not be exaggerated. As Radin himself found in the tribes he studied, the two psychological types were not mutually exclusive; many people were a bit of both. Today, it might well be argued that educators have a responsibility for making the two

It must be remembered, however, that those academics who say the humanities should include values in their province often refer merely to the application and reformulation of existing values rather than a quest for new ones.

[1] Paul Radin, *The World of Primitive Man*, 38.

[2] Radin's thinker, unlike the pragmatic man of action, sought a unified explanation of the world, giving a greater meaning to the objects round him. The achievement of such a synthesis might be said to increase the thinker's self-assurance—but in later societies, as the world grows more complex, that kind of unity has been harder to build purely on thought alone.

[3] *Hamlet*, Act III, Scene I.

come together as much as possible. In the words of the Chinese proverb, the pupil should be inspired to 'think as a man of action; act as a man of thought'. But the very wording of the proverb recognizes the two categories and, implicitly, recognizes the contrast between them. If there was no contrast, there would be less punch to the proverb.

It is in the case of totalitarian education that the tension between the thinker and the man of action becomes most apparent. Whether it is designed to train leaders, educate the masses, or do both, the totalitarian school will find it *relatively* easy to produce the man of action, spurred to enthusiastic deeds by an unquestioned moral commitment.[1] By the same token, because the moral commitment *is* unquestioned, the totalitarian school is liable to thwart the profound thinker who is by definition a questioner. Totalitarian education faces greater difficulties in this regard than do other systems of moral education because it places greater emphasis on loyalty and tends to sanctify a political authority. Furthermore, it relies to an unusual extent on social discipline and the curtailment of liberty. For the essence of totalitarianism is the demand that the individual dedicate his very being to the health and ambitions of the whole.[2]

The true totalitarian, of course, would not agree with the true individualist about what to call such dedication: whereas the latter would call it self-sacrifice, the former would see it as enriching participation in a higher order, the order of the collective. Whatever we call it, however, the fact is that totalitarian schools instil the principle of selfless dedication by levying social restrictions and pressures against the individual. It does not matter in this context whether the individual is first made to conform or made to *want* to conform: his choice of alternative conduct is severely limited, by coercion, by manipulation, or by both. In this respect totalitarian education differs sharply from other more liberal systems of moral education which try to instil basic values

[1] Please note the 'relatively'. I do not suggest that *most* graduates from Communist education systems are zealots.
[2] Some 'political behaviourists' will immediately attack me for implying that a social whole, a group or community, can have ambitions. Pedantically speaking, of course, they are right: only persons have ambitions. 'Ambitions of the whole' refer to those ambitions declared by those who purport to speak for the whole.

and yet give individual judgment some power of choice over living habits and the details of social behaviour. By contrast, totalitarian education tends to rely heavily on social discipline itself for the transmission of values. The narrow, set pattern of life ordained by school discipline symbolizes principles of totalitarian morality—loyalty, comradeship and so on.

In these circumstances, the circumstances of totalitarian discipline, can a school *ever* attain much success at producing creative minds? If it can be done, I would like to suggest two methods by which such a school may achieve it. Although the suggestion springs from our study of gentlemanly education, it is very hypothetical. To prove its validity, more research must be done on the psychology of how men think in seemingly restrictive conditions. Furthermore, one cannot gauge precisely the intellectual output of an authoritarian school, of any school for that matter, without scrutinizing closely the raw material—the calibre of students at the point of intake. It is this kind of information that we lacked in the case of the Victorian public school and which we sorely need for an exact appraisal of Communist education. Unless we have it, we cannot ascertain with complete certainty the changes, for better or for worse, that a given school brings about in its students.[1]

Having made these qualifications, we can now state the hypothesis. The first method by which a school may combine intensive loyalty-indoctrination with creative intelligence is one that we might call 'academic schizophrenia'. In mild form it was implemented by the Victorian public school which kept loyalty-indoctrination and scholarship in two, quite different, spheres of school life. Despite the Samuel Smiles-like notion that unpleasant classroom work was good for 'character', moral education was largely confined to the extracurricular sphere, to house life and the playing field. The latter was ruled by etiquette; the classroom by reason. As we have already suggested (in Chapter II), the public school classroom might have done much more for individual imagination without infringing upon the ethos of the social

[1] In the United States student development studies beginning at the intake point have been under way for some years—e.g., the studies at the University of California, Berkeley, and at Stanford University.

side. There was a place for reason and a separate place for loyal emotion.[1]

The second totalitarian method of combining loyalty with intelligence may, at a cursory glance, seem a contradiction of the first. In fact it need not be, though it can easily become so. According to the second method, the student should be encouraged as far as possible to associate loyalty-indoctrination and moral education with reason, however unquestioned and irrational the basis of his loyalty remains. A totalitarian system may block questioning beyond a certain point, but it need not—though it often tends to —induce scorn of reason itself. In other words, the *attitude* that a student holds towards reason is as important as the amount of actual exercise which the school provides. The two are obviously very much bound up together, but they are not quite the same thing. At least one study of creativity has suggested that the more intellectual scope an individual *believes* he has, the more likely he is to show creative energy.[2]

How can this kind of harmony between reason and irrational sentiment be achieved? One way is through dogma. On a relatively crude level, Confucian education essayed just such an approach, teaching political loyalty partly through political philosophy. Another way is to give, as much as possible, a rationale for social discipline, an explanation, even if the fundamental tenets of the discipline are emotional and unquestioned. Certain Russian educators, it seems, are very aware of this point, of the need to tell the child *why* in terms of Communist values he must obey the rules.[3] The Victorian public school, by contrast, did virtually nothing to provide a rationale for social discipline. Overtly, the myriad conventions of school life were each justified for their own sake as a matter of good taste. Their logical connexion with the values they represented—loyalty, co-operation,

[1] Lessons were prepared in the House of course, but here the House mainly acted as a mere physical facility for the classroom. The only real overlap between the two was in the case of Divinity lessons, a classroom subject.

[2] I am indebted here to Roxanne Harvey for information based on her Undergraduate Honours Thesis on creativity presented to the Harvard Department of Social Relations in 1962.

[3] George Bereday *et al.*, *The Changing Soviet School*, 415. Also 'Ethical Conversations' in the schools—438. Loyalty-indoctrination is also carried by more emotional devices, however, such as wall-slogans.

responsibility, and so forth—was largely implicit. Only in Chapel and in Divinity lessons did ethical teaching become explicit, and for all Thomas Arnold's endeavours, neither Chapel nor 'Divinity' were ever the main vehicles of moral education in the public school system as a whole.

This is not to say that intensive loyalty-indoctrination can be carried by reason alone; the necessarily irrational core of totalitarian discipline has already been pointed out. Without loyalty-symbols and rituals that played on the emotions, it is unlikely that the Victorian public school could have produced the *esprit de corps* it did. But moral indoctrination can be directed at the individual on different levels, rational as well as irrational. Nor need the rational element subvert the discipline by stimulating questioning. In the hands of learned and psychologically adept educators, men like the Jesuits whom we shall consider shortly, reason can be used to *explain* rather than question school discipline, while freer inquiry is channelled into academic subjects. This, obviously, can only be done when the first hypothetical method I have described operates—when social discipline and academic enterprise are kept firmly apart in the student's mind.

Undeniably the very harnessing of rational devices to loyalty-indoctrination can incur intellectual liabilities. It need not do so, but it easily may. Once the realm of the intellect is accepted as pertinent to the building of loyalty, loyalty-indoctrination may invade the curriculum and stifle free inquiry. Thus, in Confucian China, where men hailed learning as a threshold to civic virtue, history and the classics were taught for the moral object-lessons that they provided. As a result, historical biographies were whitewashed and the student was not encouraged to criticize orthodox interpretations of China's past. The curriculum, it is true, continued to exercise the student's intellect, but it did so mainly in the areas of memory-work and close reasoning following set rules. In authoritarian systems, deductive thinking is counted less likely to subvert loyalty and morals than is imaginative, *inductive* thinking, which by definition does not begin with absolute premises. We shall see some evidence of this attitude towards thought when we look at Japanese and Jesuit education.

Another liability incurred by the association of loyalty-indoctrination with reason is that the reason employed may be a sham. When loyalty is promoted by a dogma of inferior and distorted logic—e.g., a grotesque scientism—the individual may confuse what he thinks is rationalism with what in fact is emotionalism disguised by rational-sounding words. It has already been suggested that a system of loyalty and discipline can explain its prescriptions, though not its basic premises, rationally. It does not follow, however, that totalitarian education should make the student believe he is being rational when he is not. Such an outcome can only damage the student's whole intellectual apparatus, his ability to discern logic from non-logic. Here again, habits of mind bred by loyalty-indoctrination may invade and corrupt the academic side of school life.

Whether modern totalitarian education can avoid these liabilities, whether it can emphasize both intensive loyalty-indoctrination and highly developed reason is very much an open question. Hypothetically we have suggested that totalitarian education will harmoniously achieve both aims to the extent (1) that the area of rigorous social discipline is clearly separated from an area of free academic enquiry, (2) that reason is given some relevance to the imposition of discipline and the building of loyalties. If these requirements can be met, the very discipline may carry intellectual advantage as well as disadvantage. Certainly this is true when the discipline becomes internalized. Rigorous thinking, as much as any other work, depends on moral qualities of persistence and fortitude[1] and self-dedication. In 1961, a journalist asked the headmaster of Culver Military Academy, an American secondary school with fairly high academic standards, why he bothered being military at all. 'Discipline is essential to the learning situation,' was the reported answer. 'Without it there would be no stable path to intellectual growth and eventual maturity.'[2]

[1] In an enterprising article on creativity, Gerhard Wiebe suggests that the *courage* to leave the security and ego identifications afforded by old ideas is one characteristic of the creative innovator. Other equally intelligent men may unconsciously suppress, or more consciously not follow up, their imaginative associations. —*Public Opinion Quarterly*, Fall 1962, Princeton.

[2] *Time*, 5 January, 1962. Interview with Delmar Spivey.

To see whether totalitarian education can ever find the right conditions for producing imaginative leaders let us look briefly at two unusual systems—Japanese national education as it developed from the eighteen-seventies to the Second World War; and the Jesuit schools of Western Europe during the first three centuries after St. Ignatius Loyola founded the Society of Jesus in 1534. I have chosen both systems, not only because they felt obliged to produce men of unshakable loyalty and faith—and to do so partly through a somewhat restrictive social discipline —but because circumstances clearly demanded that they turn out intelligent leaders who could understand and exploit change.

In 1868 the old Tokugawa régime of Japan, already crumbling, fell with surprising swiftness. The new Meiji government, an oligarchy of bright young *samurai*,[1] immediately embarked Japan on the dramatic modernization programme that transformed a 'backward' nation into a world power within half a century. A major component of the modernization programme was education, whose importance as a capital asset Japan's young rulers never doubted. In 1872 the Educational Code authorized the plan for a network of public universities, 'middle schools', and primary schools. The system was essentially meritocratic. On the primary level it was designed to provide universal public education—only two years after Britain's similarly-designed Elementary Education Act of 1870. From the primary schools the most talented pupils were selected for the middle school in each prefecture, and from the middle schools a minority[2] went on to five national 'higher schools'. These latter were special institutions preparing entrants for Tokyo Imperial University, the pinnacle of the educational hierarchy. In time four other Imperial universities were added, and there also sprang up public universities at prefectural and city level. But right up until 1939, Tokyo Imperial graduates provided at

[1] Knightly retainers from the old feudal fiefs such as Satsuma and Choshu.

[2] The proportion was 56 per cent. in 1896, but it fell thereafter to 21 per cent. in 1916 , 17 per cent. in 1950.—Ronald Dore, 'Education and Politics in Japan, 1870-1960', p. 14. (Paper given to the Seminar on the Political Modernization of Japan and Turkey, Gould House, New York, September 1962.)

least five-sixths of those who passed the civil service examinations.[1]

By the turn of the century, government control over the main-stream of Japanese education was well established. Despite the quality of a private university like Waseda, private education never attained the prestige of the Imperial universities and their attendant high schools. Public authority, for its part, had no doubts about what education was for. 'In the administration of all schools', said Arinori Mori, Japan's first Minister of Education (1885–89), 'it must be kept in mind, what is done is not for the sake of the pupils but for the sake of the country.'[2] On the academic side, perhaps the best statement of Japanese purpose in education was to be found in the article of Tokyo Imperial University's charter:

to have as its object to teach and to explore the innermost secrets of those branches of scholarship, technology and the arts which can meet the needs of the State.[3]

Note the inclusion of the word 'technology' and remember that this was the charter of the land's highest educational institution. Unlike the public school ethos, the Meiji concept of public service awarded an important place to technology and industry. Science instruction began in primary school, and the middle schools not only paid great attention to science but gave courses in economics and commerce.[4] At Tokyo Imperial University itself, science and engineering were heavily enrolled, although the largest faculty in 1900 was the government-oriented Faculty of Law, which included the Politics Department.[5]

On the moral side of education, the same pattern of government direction and nationalist purpose could be identified. Even the Western-educated Arinori Mori, who once proposed for mainly practical reasons that English replace the Japanese language,[6]

---

[1] Dore, ibid., 14. Graduates of all Imperial universities enjoyed considerable advantages in gaining any sort of job, both in government and industry.
During the years of party government, many Cabinet ministers were ex-bureaucrats.
[2] Sir George Sansom, *The Western World and Japan*, 459.   [3] Dore, op. cit., 12.
[4] Hugh Keenleyside and A. F. Thomas, *History of Japanese Education and Present Educational System*, 106, 181–2. Separate technical and commercial schools were also set up.
[5] Dore, op. cit., 12–13.
[6] Keenleyside, op. cit., 92–93. Mori argued that the Japanese language would prove a frail vehicle for the dissemination of Western ideas and scientific methods, and that complete mastery of English was vital for foreign trade. Furthermore, 'the laws of the State can never be preserved in the language of Japan'. His proposal was not popular.

attached considerable importance to developing 'our national spirit and morale . . . so that it can stand hardships and carry out the heavy responsibility in the future.'[1] Mori believed that military discipline taught virtues conducive to patriotism, and he made much of this belief in the teacher-training system he established. Barrack room living, uniforms, dormitory inspections, minute gradations of rank, petty regulations enforced by senior students, route marches, and even a spy system wherein picked students reported on the characters of the rest—such devices were incorporated in Tokyo Higher Normal School which pioneered teacher training.[2] Military exercises also formed a part of middle school discipline, especially after 1925 when regular army officers were appointed to school staffs. Students received five hours of military training a week, besides lectures calculated to stimulate martial patriotism.[3] In like spirit, students were periodically sent on visits to national Shinto shrines, and their participation was enlisted in patriotic ceremonies and festivals.[4]

Finally, the government used the curriculum itself, through the central control of textbooks, to instil patriotic virtues. Not only did the middle school syllabus allocate a few hours a week to 'Morals' and 'Civics' but according to official regulations for primary schools 'the essential aim of teaching Japanese history [was] to make children comprehend the fundamental character of the Empire and to foster in them the national spirit'.[5] A guide issued to primary school teachers in 1891 stipulated that:

In education the greatest attention should be paid to moral culture. Hence, whatever is found in any course of study relating to moral or national education should be taught with care and assiduity. All teaching should be based upon matters essential to life; lessons should be so taught that they may all be turned to practical uses.[6]

[1] Tatsuo Morito, 'Prospect and Retrospect of Japanese Education', *Ide*, 1961, 17. Although he wanted to borrow much from the West, Mori shared the fear of influential contemporaries that Western ideas were threatening to errode traditional Japanese values without replacing them. This contributed to his conservative stand on moral education.
[2] Dore, op. cit., 38. Keenleyside, op. cit., 87, 243, 254.
[3] Ibid., 117–18, 199–201.
[4] Japanese National Commission for U.N.E.S.C.O., *The Development of a Modern System of Education in Japan*, 77. Keenleyside, op. cit., 254. cf. Kinnosuke Natsume, *Botchan* (a novel about a Japanese middle school), 230–4.
[5] Regulations quoted by Keenleyside, op. cit., 179.
[6] Quoted by Sansom, op. cit., 467.

The three-way connexion made here between moral education, service to the State, and *practical* training pre-echoes Soviet and Chinese Communist education today; for all Japan's feudal heritage and attachment to tradition—'The National Essence' as conservatives called it—the emphasis was far from the amateur, non-technical ideal of gentry England. One factor, and only one, behind this difference was that public school patriotism was mainly the patriotism of the *guardian*, whereas Japanese patriotism included the spirit of the *nation-builder*. For the men who moulded Japanese education, patriotism meant both reverence for national tradition, the source of spiritual strength, and respect for techno-logical prowess, the *sine qua non* of national development. The nation-building brand of loyalty, in other words, carried a built-in appreciation of change, especially technological change.

Admittedly, the original and most creative architects of Japan's modernization were those leaders who had grown up before the education system hardened into its nationalist pattern.[1] Many of Meiji Japan's first rulers had been educated abroad; and as Edwin Reischauer points out, Meiji's *samurai* élite had learned under the old régime 'a capacity for adjustment to new situations in the confused politics of their individual *daimyo* realms, and in the intrigues and counter-intrigues of the Kyoto court'.[2] For the first few years after the Meiji 'Restoration', moreover, educa-tion enjoyed a period of intellectual ferment: the presence of Western teachers was not yet frowned upon, and student life hummed with political questioning and debate. After this first generation of Meiji education, the academic schools produced fewer dynamic leaders, but rather what Ronald Dore calls the new society's 'maintenance men'.[3] (The military academies pro-duced a very different product, and we will come to this later.)

In things economic and technological, however, Japanese administration continued to show resourcefulness and foresight. This applied both to the big industrialists, the *zaibatsu*, and to their opposite numbers in the ministries of Commerce and Finance, men who had frequently come from the same school

[1] Dore, op. cit., 17.
[2] Edwin Reischauer, *Japan Past and Present*, 117. Daimyo were the feudal lords.
[3] Dore, op. cit., 17–18.

background. Industry's rapid development in organization and techniques, especially between 1927 and 1931; the government's credit-assistance to key industries, and her bold 'pump-priming' policy during the nineteen-thirties; her moves in the Depression to strengthen the small businessman; the readiness for large-scale planning that lay behind the Industrial Rationalization Bureau[1]— none of these phenomena, taking place in a society where tradition was still greatly revered, could be called the product of narrow administrative minds. From the educator's standpoint, moreover, it is interesting that Elizabeth Schumpeter, the economic analyst of Japanese industrialization, cites as a major factor in the nation's post-Depression recovery 'the co-operation between business, labour and government for a common purpose'.[2] This co-operation the education system supported by fostering a sense of national enterprise and unity, and by exposing different social classes to the same core of teaching.[3]

Nor was intelligent adjustment to change wholly confined to the technological and industrial front. The introduction of party government in 1918, and the extension of the suffrage in 1919 and 1925 could be described as further political innovations made in response to changing social pressures.[4] Yet we all know how it ended. By the time party government had collapsed in 1932, control over national policies was swinging into the hands of extreme militarists. In their resort to assassination and the 'smear' campaign as devices for getting power, and in their fanatical and narrow definition of patriotism, the Army and Navy's extremist element injected a growing irrationality into Japanese politics. I say 'irrationality' because the policy of military aggression upon

[1] Elizabeth Schumpeter (ed. and principal author), *The Industrialization of Japan and Manchukuo*, especially pp. 18, 678, 728–32, 746–8. The Industrial Rationalization Bureau did not fulfil its grand designs, but the tendency to countenance large-scale planning was there.

[2] Ibid. It is true that during the nineteen-twenties, labour strikes were common. But, seen against the recent emergence of Japan from feudalism, government and industry's toleration of these strikes represented a certain political progressivism. And so in the case of student rebellions (see text below) the strike weapon could co-exist with a general inter-strike pattern of co-operation.

[3] Sansom, op. cit., 467. Dore, op. cit., 53–55.

[4] It might be argued here, however, that in 1925 the last of the more freely educated politicians were still in power. The education system became more restrictive after 1890, and one must allow a time-lag of twenty to thirty years between the time an individual left university and the time he attained the upper reaches of public service.

which Japan now embarked did not, in the long run, serve even the nationalist goal of increasing Japan's power. A major characteristic distinguishing highly irrational leaders from the more rational is that the former often select over-simplified, direct-approach solutions to problems, solutions which prove ultimately self-defeating. The prime example of such thinking—or non-thinking—is the *initiation* of war when the outcome is likely to yield no more than Pyrrhic victory at best. In the early nineteen-twenties Japanese businessmen had perceived that economic expansion overseas was a less costly way of nation-building than military aggression. They accordingly threw their weight against colonial expansion, and Japanese troops were withdrawn from Siberia.[1] By contrast, when Japan invaded Manchuria in the nineteen-thirties, economic interests were less able, and less willing perhaps, to prevent a policy of violence.[2]

This is not to deny that many leading bureaucrats and politicians were moderates who distrusted military adventurism. But to the extent that they thought they could ride and rein the tiger of Japanese militarism,[3] they did not show great political insight. Furthermore, the mainstream of public opinion, 'reverting to the feudal tradition of rule by military men, accepted the claims of military extremists at their face value . . .'[4] Although as late as 1936 the electorate endorsed relatively liberal candidates for parliament, army officers continued to increase their political influence by resort to assassination.[5] This leads us back to the political role of the education system, whose military values and discipline the civil government itself had shaped.[6]

[1] Reischauer, op. cit., 149. Another factor was the internationalist sentiment of the years following the First World War.
[2] Ibid., 179–80. And when, in 1941, the Western powers threatened to starve Japan economically if she did not withdraw from China, the militarists chose the face-saving course of war against the West, rather than conceding and sitting back 'to profit economically from the new war in Europe as she had done . . . during the First World War'—ibid., 191. [3] Ibid., 181.
[4] Ibid., 183. Japanese susceptibility to martial appeals also attested by Keenleyside and Thomas, op. cit., 200.
[5] Reischauer, 183–4. The Army's reaction to the 1936 election was to assassinate several leading moderate statesmen, including their own General Watanabe. Aided by assassination, the Army had secured the replacement of party Cabinets with a 'Nationalist' coalition in 1936.
[6] I do not, of course, suggest that education was the only moulder of the climate that favoured the militarists' ascension to power. The special place of the armed services in the

Japanese education supported the trend to irrational militarism in two ways. First, it exacerbated the difference in outlook and the difficulty of communication between the military officer and the bureaucrat. Instead of going to middle school, the would-be army officer went to a military academy at the age of twelve or thirteen years. His secondary education thus consisted of specialized training in war, a training which included an intensive loyalty-indoctrination little tempered by liberal arts learning. As a result the military academy fostered excessive trust in force, in the direct and drastic solution to complex social problems. At certain points fanatical ideals of military honour and loyalty to the 'National Essence' even threatened the Army's technological development. Thus, Colonel Kobayashi repeatedly warned that too great a reliance on 'material goods' would corrupt the Army's soul. Along with other officers of the same viewpoint, Kobayashi favoured 'mass tactics', stressing the human element above mechanization, and trusting in the spiritual power, *seishinshugi*, of Japanese culture. Despite the influence of this faction, however, the military also had men like Ugaki, Tojo, and Nagata who pressed home the advantages of modern organization and technology.[1]

The second way in which education promoted militarism applies to the main part of the system, the hierarchy of public schools and universities. I do not contend that the majority of middle school graduates were extreme militarists. On the contrary, even in the late nineteen-thirties Hugh Keenleyside and A. F. Thomas observed that Japanese students were 'as happy to evade or be excused conscription as in the average country where military service is compulsory'.[2] But the two orientalists also observed that the place of military exercises in the schools represented 'a fundamental assumption, to which very few Japanese would hesitate to subscribe, that warfare if not inevitable is at least not improbable'.[3]

Constitution; the foreign tariff restrictions which hampered the policy of peaceful trade expansion; and the *apparent* contradictions of Japanese social character, as described by Ruth Benedict, Robert Lifton, and others—these are just some of the factors that must be considered.

[1] James Crawley, 'Japanese Army Factionalism in the Early 1930's', *Journal of Asian Studies*, May 1962, Ann Arbour, Michigan.
[2] Keenleyside, op. cit., 199.   [3] Ibid., 199.

One result of linking moral and nationalist education to military exercises was to reward extreme militarism by default. The social connexion made between virtue and martial discipline granted a moral initiative to the militarist interpretation of Imperial service. This enabled bellicose officers to seize a *cultural* initiative, to hark back to the militarist traditions of feudal Japan.

It must be remembered that the Emperor himself wielded no real power, and that this power vacuum really permitted flexible interpretation as to how nation and Emperor could best be served. Had the Emperor been an arbitrary tyrant, demanding compliance with whatever he decreed, Imperial loyalty would have borne all the restrictions of an intense, personal subservience. Such restrictions did not in fact characterize Imperial loyalty, although they may have appeared to in the eyes of many people. The early Meiji politicians fully appreciated this situation: as Ronald Dore explains, they possessed the intellectual ability and will to 'manipulate the fictions of Imperial authority'. When, however, leaders of less dynamism rose to high civilian office, the initiative passed to the more decisive and energetic military.[1] One factor in the relative passivity of the new-style bureaucrat and politician[2] may have been a 'drain upon the nervous and physical energy' produced by the intensely competitive examination system.[3] At nearly all levels of the civilian school hierarchy, fact-'cramming' for examinations filled much of the student's day. The tension which examinations can create was particularly pronounced in Japan where competitive performance involved notions of shame and obligation to 'one's name'.[4] But this, of course, was only one possible factor.

As a final assessment of the political mind produced by the civil education system, let us look at the latter in terms of the two hypothetical requirements we postulated for totalitarian education. First, 'academic schizophrenia'. Did Japanese public education

[1] Dore, op. cit., 17–18.
[2] As stated in an earlier footnote, many civilian Cabinet ministers were ex-bureaucrats.
[3] Keenleyside, op. cit., 209. H. E. Dale claims that he observed the same phenomenon before the war among British senior civil servants from working-class homes. He describes it as a 'certain lack of animal spirits and of mental and nervous energy . . . as a rule, due to being over-driven in boyhood and youth'—Dale, *The Higher Civil Service*, 75.
[4] Ruth Benedict, *The Chrysanthemum and the Sword*, 126–7, 176.

provide an area of free academic enquiry, as distinct from the sphere of moral training? Only in science and technology can it be said to have done so consistently over the decades. Considering, however, the mounting restrictions placed upon the rest of the syllabus, this in itself represented a considerable achievement. As one commentary puts it,

naturally, for science education the formation of a rational attitude and creative inventiveness had to be postulated, quite out of line with the rest of the curriculum. . . .

[This led to] the phenomenon that ceremonies signifying the divinization of the Emperor were held in the same modern schools which gave rational instruction in science.[1]

The rest of the curriculum either became subservient to the requirements of moral education, as in the case of history, or else simply demanded memory work and deductive thinking (languages and law) above imaginative speculation and criticism. The pattern bears out very much contemporary observations on Communist education: that, in a totalitarian system stressing political loyalty, subjects like science which do not use the language of politics can most easily preserve academic freedom. Here and there in the schools' extracurricular life, other oases nurturing independent thought might be identified. Fencing and judo were consciously taught for their mental as well as their physical benefit[2]—but it is not yet certain how far the intelligence needed for non-linguistic games is transferable to completely different pursuits. Social discipline itself varied between schools and between decades, although the trend was to greater restriction. At the turn of the century, life in the select higher schools was characterized by 'endless philosophizing and exhibitionist oratory, and students were apparently fairly free to spurn conventions.[3] By 1910, however, restrictions were tightened, and a more adult decorum replaced student gaiety and excitement.

Another source of intellectual ferment and political debate was university life, particularly in the years following the First World War. This course too was dried up by official restriction. By the

[1] Japanese National Commission for U.N.E.S.C.O., op. cit., 75, 77.
[2] Keenleyside, op. cit., 106–7.   [3] Dore, op. cit., 15.

nineteen-thirties some college dormitories had come under direct police supervision and café life was tightly curbed.[1] The Ministry of Education even ran a Bureau of Thought Problems, designed largely to combat 'radicalism' among university students.[2]

In the middle schools, many of the teachers had been exposed to military discipline and indoctrination at the teacher training establishments. As a result, they were hardly the type to encourage free speculation and a wide range of questioning. The Japanese classroom, in fact, was marked for its absence of give-and-take discourse between teacher and pupil. By and large, there was no halfway house between passive deference to the teacher and the student strikes that broke out when boys felt shamed or wronged.[3] And it is difficult to tell whether the student rebelliousness that did manifest itself from time to time[4] provided avenues for individualism or represented just another source of conformity to the student group.[5] Rebellion as well as obedience may follow convention; certainly it need not respect intelligence.

This brings us to our second requirement for the nourishment of independent minds amid totalitarian training. Did Japanese education make reason highly relevant to loyalty-indoctrination? The answer is that some attempt was made but that it was not carried very far. The curriculum, as we have seen, taught ethics; and in 1935 the ultra-nationalist Pedagogy Reform Council elaborated a mystical theory, unifying Shinto worship, Imperial devotion, and the need for modern efficiency in serving the State.[6]

[1] Keenleyside, op. cit., 277–8.

[2] In the early nineteen-twenties, many student radicals called themselves Communists and Socialists, but by the nineteen-thirties 'radicalism' in the authorities' eyes included what Americans and Britons would have called a leftish liberalism. cf. Keenleyside, op. cit., 278–9. In another sense the militarist officers themselves were radicals: by and large they were from below the *samurai* class, and they identified themselves with peasant grievances versus the big *zaibatsu*.

[3] Keenleyside, op. cit., 142.

[4] cf. Kinnosuke, op. cit.

[5] In *The Chrysanthemum and the Sword*, Ruth Benedict suggests that the group teasing to which middle-school newcomers were exposed created resentments which were contained for later release and revenge (pp. 176–7). This was even more so in the military academy where, according to Benedict, the resentments felt against older students and unleashed at juniors prevented the establishment of a 'public school' school spirit (p. 278). Benedict also examines the extent to which the *particularist* nature of Japanese social ethics provided both spheres of binding obedience and spheres of freedom to act impulsively without guilt.

[6] Japanese National Commission for U.N.E.S.C.O., op. cit., 74.

As late as the nineteen-thirties, moreover, the official higher school curriculum included instruction in the Chinese classics.[1]

These facts notwithstanding, Imperial loyalty-indoctrination possessed no ideology of great logical rigour and sophistication.[2] On the contrary, the militarists frequently used language itself— slogan phrases like 'National Crisis', 'Japanese Spirit', and 'National Structure'—to replace thought with mystic feeling.[3] In the long run, furthermore, nationalist propaganda had a boomerang effect, damaging the Japanese leader's own capacity to make rational policy. At no time was this more true than at the time of Pearl Harbour. To quote Edwin Reischauer—

. . . The Japanese miscalculated, not so much on geographical, economic or military as on human factors. They counted heavily on their own moral superiority, the famed 'Japanese spirit', and the supposed degeneracy and pacifism of the Western democracies, particularly America, which they believed to be corrupted by too many luxuries.
. . . The Japanese showed themselves to be so blinded by their own nationalistic and militaristic propaganda that they were unable to evaluate the spirit of other peoples or to judge their reactions correctly.
. . . (They) even failed to judge correctly other Far Eastern peoples.[4]

The technological and industrial achievement that enabled Japan even to contemplate an attack on Pearl Harbour makes a sharp contrast with the 'psychological blunder' that the attack itself represented.[5] It also makes an interesting comparison with the record of the Victorian public schools. In a way, the strengths and weaknesses of public school-type leadership were the converse of the pattern produced by Japanese education. Each wrought its effects within the confines of a small island, as proud of her traditions as she was poor in material resources. One system, the British system, produced men who were sensible if not highly imaginative *politically*, who combined moderation

---

[1] Keenleyside, op. cit., 212. Ruth Benedict argues, however, that the Chinese ideal of *jen* (comradely benevolence and mutual obligation) was only peripheral to the Japanese ethical system; that it carried the conspiratorial refrain of 'honour-among-thieves' (op. cit., 117). If this is the case, it is significant that *jen* formed a part of the gentlemanly premium on political moderation.
[2] cf. Reischauer, op. cit., 165.
[3] Ibid., 174.   [4] Ibid., 194.   [5] Ibid., 195.

with vigour, who would bend to social change and then ride it. The same system did little for technology: if the Industrial Revolution began in Britain, it was not because of the public schools. By contrast, Japanese education produced leaders who had the vision to treat science and the business firm as vital public servants. Yet, in the realm of politics, the *net effect* of Japan's educational system was to contribute to disaster, to political extremism and folly.

Is this how it must always be? Can a totalitarian system never consistently produce creative intelligence *both* in technology and in human affairs? To shed further light on the question, let us turn to the Jesuits.

From its foundation in 1534, the Society of Jesus was a militant *élite* organization, dedicated to audacious missionary work and the spreading of Christian education.[1] In a sense, therefore, its outlook fully accepted the notion of change, for the man who would convert the heathen could only be an innovator.

The Jesuits made the Glory of God an enterprise to which each member could add and with which each could identify.[2] The inculcation of this 'spiritual nationalism' was reinforced by the Society's insistence on military discipline and obedience. St. Ignatius Loyola, founder of the Society, laid down that a Jesuit's obedience to his superior should be absolute: not only should he find joy in executing his superior's will, but he should seek to assume the latter's very way of thinking as his own. When he faced a clearly sinful order, the subordinate might make 'discreet remonstrance', but in all other relationships between superior and subordinate the latter should make a 'voluntary renunciation of private judgment'.[3]

[1] The story, of obscure origin, is told of three priests, a Jesuit, a Dominican, and a Franciscan who were visited by an angel, told they were about to see a vision of the Nativity, and invited to make one statement each to any of the Holy Family. The event duly came about, and it was the Dominican's turn first: 'Blessed Lady, on behalf of all Dominicans, I want to thank you for giving us the Rosary.' Then came the Franciscan's statement. 'Blessed Mother, on behalf of my Order, I do thank you for giving the world the Scapular.' When the Jesuit's turn came, he spoke to Joseph, 'Where are you going to send the Boy to school?'
[2] Rene Fülöp-Miller, *The Power and Secret of the Jesuits*, 12.
[3] Constitutions for the Society, quoted by Fülöp-Miller, ibid., 18-21.

215

The Society, in fact, was organized as a highly disciplined army. Its pyramid of ranks, crowned by the General of the Society, reflected a hierarchic view of the universe;[1] and it is not surprising that the Society went in for a certain amount of central planning. This was particularly so in the case of education during the first century: the *Ratio Studiorum* of 1586, and its subsequent revisions of 1591 and 1599, 'rationalized' the curriculum, provided guidelines for school administration, and specified some ingenious methods of teaching.[2]

Despite the Society's authoritarian structure, however, it produced a quality of intellectual leadership that seems, at first sight, an impossible companion to the ethic of absolute obedience.[3] In the field of education itself, the Jesuits were a stimulating force. 'Partly in themselves,' wrote Francis Bacon in 1603, 'and partly by the emulation and provocation of their example, the Jesuits have much quickened the state of learning.'[4]

Overseas, in India, the Far East, and the Americas, Jesuit mission leaders based their spiritual salesmanship on shrewd and flexible strategies. With considerable scholarship and sensitivity they absorbed both native cultures and the details of alien religions.[5] They were ready to defend their position on the most philosophical level, as in the grand debate before the Great Mogul Akbar of India when the Jesuits won a qualified victory over Zoroastrians, Brahmins, and Mohammedans.[6] In their bids to win local power and influence they even became technologists; the fathers who followed Matteo Ricci to China impressed the Emperor by forecasting a solar eclipse, and later gave advice on how to cast cannon.[7]

Above all, the Jesuits were resourceful *politically*. They were

[1] Fülöp-Miller, op. cit., 24.

[2] Allan Farrell, *The Jesuit Code of Liberal Education*, 230-1, 241.

[3] J. H. Kennedy gives an interesting portrayal of the Jesuit missionary in New France and the way he frequently combined dedication and discipline with versatility and curiosity—Kennedy, *Jesuit and Savage in New France*, 80–96.

[4] Bacon, *Advancement of Learning*, quoted by E. Boyd Barrett, *The Jesuit Enigma*, 166. For a similar tribute overseas, see Jerome Jacobsen, *Educational Foundations of the Jesuits in Sixteenth Century New Spain*, 229-40 (the chapter on the Jesuits' cultural legacy).

[5] H. Boehmer, *The Jesuits*, 111–112. Fülöp-Miller, op. cit., 226, 231. For the following historical survey of the Jesuit political style overseas I rely heavily on *The Power and Secret of the Jesuits*, one of the most intelligent books on the subject and one more balanced than the title may imply.   [6] Fülöp-Miller, op. cit., 229.

[7] Ibid., 237. Ricci himself had learned mathematics and astronomy under Jesuit teachers.

masters of diplomacy, of planned patience, of the indirect approach. During the seventeenth and eighteenth centuries, they actually ran their own nation state, the Jesuit Republic of Paraguay. Although the Republic paid taxes to Spain, it possessed an army and cannon foundries, and under Jesuit supervision each settlement was run by publicly-elected Indian officials.[1] Home in Europe, the Jesuits were showing another sort of political flair, the flair for court politics. Again and again they secured key positions as advisers to sovereigns, and when they were excluded by a Protestant monarch like Elizabeth, they turned to 'fifth column' activities, reaching their Catholic audiences as stowaways and impersonators.[2]

Small wonder that the Jesuits had their enemies. Their very rationality, their strange mixture of zeal and quiet cunning, their frequent possession of worldly power, their seeming to do 'everything for a purpose'[3] indicated, in the eyes of some, a feline malice. Eventually suspicion reached the Catholic monarchs themselves. When in 1773 Pope Clement XIV officially suppressed the Society, a major reason for his action lay in the complaint, received from numerous Catholic courts, that the persuasiveness and power of the Jesuits represented political subversion.[4]

Yet the Society survived. It continued to exist mainly in Russia, where Jesuit education was well appreciated; but elsewhere, too, it lived on under different names.[5] After 41 years of *de facto*

---

[1] The Republic emerged from mission activities: one way that the fathers made contact with the Indians was to play music from river boats. They were finally expelled by a Portuguese-Spanish invasion. The Republic had a largely communist system of property ownership. cf. Fülöp-Miller, op. cit., 283, 302. Robert Cunninghame, *A Lost Arcadia*.

[2] Fülöp-Miller, op. cit., 303–8.

[3] E. Boyd Barrett, *The Jesuit Enigma*, 303. cf. *The Secret Instructions of the Jesuits* (London Edition printed for John Walthoe). These enumerate tactics from how to curry favour with rich widows to the best method of poisoning authority's ear about rival orders. The Preface states that the instructions are to be denied as authentic if they fall into outsiders' hands; even if they are not authentic, they still give a picture of how the Jesuits' enemies regarded them.

[4] Fülöp-Miller, 374, 384. The actual Papal statement suppressing the Society declared the Jesuits a source of 'discord and jealousy' within the Church and *mentioned* past charges of laxity and materialism among the Society. Historians differ about the degree of truth concerning these charges. cf. Boehmer, op. cit., 187–9. Joseph McCabe, *A Candid History of the Jesuits*, 334–63. Harney, *The Jesuits in History*, 292–8.

[5] The Pope officially allowed the Russian organization to reassume the name 'Society of Jesus' in 1801.

operation it was officially reinstated and, despite expulsion by country after country—or perhaps partly because of it—the Jesuits retained their *élan*.

We have here, then, an organization surviving immense changes in fortune and doing so because it possessed *both* resourceful leadership and a strong, unifying faith. Extreme critics of the Society have argued that in fact the Jesuits survived by twisting their faith to the requirements of wordly power and by letting their ends justify any means.[1] Whether these accusations contain truth is a vexed matter to which a brief comparative study cannot do justice.[2] There is evidence, however, to suggest that the Jesuits did not bend to expedience tenets which they felt to be an integral part of their ideology. In Ming China the Jesuits refrained from telling about the Crucifixion, because the stigma attached by the Chinese to such a death would have made Christian conversion far more difficult. Likewise, they allowed Chinese Christians to perform traditional 'heathen' rites honouring the dead.[3] The justification made here was that the rites represented reverence for ancestors rather than religious worship.

In India, on the other hand, the early Jesuits steadfastly refused to play down the ethic of humility, and the doctrines of Christ's Incarnation and the Trinity. It was chiefly because of these points that they were unable to convert the Great Mogul Akbar, whom they had visions of making a second Charlemagne.[4] The Jesuits showed similar firmness on questions of sexual morality: as confessors to Louis XIV and Louis XV, they inveighed persistently, if sometimes gently, against royal practices of adultery; once, when Louis XV caught a high fever and hurriedly sent for his confessor, the Jesuit refused the king extreme unction until he had promised to send his mistress out of the city.[5]

[1] For an account of alleged chicanery, corruption, false preaching, and shallow conversions in the Far East and India, see McCabe, op. cit., 279–310.

[2] The Jesuits were also accused of corrupting Christianity, replacing Jesus with Dostoevsky's Grand Inquisitor who takes the terrible burden of free moral choice and conscience from frail man. 'The Jesuits speak and write like the Grand Inquisitor,' says Ivan in *The Brothers Karamazov*. Quoted by Fülöp-Miller, op. cit., 467, cf. 463–79. cf. Fyodor Dostoevsky, *The Brothers Karamazov*, 292–314.

[3] Fülöp-Miller, op. cit., 268. Boehmer, op. cit., 156.

[4] Fülöp-Miller, op. cit., 228–9.

[5] The king recovered and his duchess was recalled. Fülöp-Miller, op. cit., 372.

From the foregoing account of Jesuit faith and intelligence, I do not mean it to be inferred that a *majority* of Jesuit leaders salted their loyalty and discipline with imagination. As a Jesuit teacher and historian recently put it to me, the great bulk of the Society were probably 'administrators, good organization men' rather than innovators.[1] But then, the innovator is a comparatively rare bird at the best of times. The important point is that the Society seemed to produce a significantly large minority of imaginative men who had a decisive effect on the fortunes of their organization. When I say 'significantly large minority' I mean it from an educational viewpoint: the Society produced enough men of high intellectual stature for one to suspect that their education was partly responsible.

Other factors there were, of course, including the high calibre of pupil and novice accepted by Jesuit school and seminary in the first place.[2] Doubtless, the Society's very environment—the attacks upon it from many quarters; the far-flung nature of its enterprises—presented intellectual challenge and stimulus.[3] But to meet the challenge, to respond rather than be crushed, Jesuit leaders had to have a potential from which they could produce their response. And that potential, the Jesuit's capacity for resourceful leadership, had somehow to survive the long junior years of absolute obedience, the years of probation and lower-echelon priesthood. How could this be done? Let us now examine the Jesuit style of education, and consider it as a totalitarian system. The study that follows is limited to the Jesuit school at secondary level; it does not deal with higher education. The latter, however, should not be discounted as a powerful influence. When he had completed his novitiate, the Jesuit candidate spent two years reviewing the classics, followed by three years of philosophy, mathematics, and science; five years of college teaching;

[1] Though certainly not Organization Man in the sense William Wyte means it.

[2] Boehmer, op. cit., 111, 118–19.

[3] One is reminded of Macaulay's famous testimony: 'In spite of oceans and deserts, of hunger and pestilence, of spies and penal laws, of dungeons and racks, of gibbets and quartering blocks, the Jesuits were to be found under every disguise, in every country; scholars, physicians, merchants, servingman, in the hostile court of Sweden, in the old manor houses of Cheshire, among the hovels of Connaught, arguing, instructing, consoling, animating the courage of the timid, holding up the crucifix before the eyes of the dying.'

and four of theology. The sheer length of this programme must have made it a formidable intellectual factor.

Despite the Society's respect for formal learning, the Jesuit schools do not at first glance appear to have marked out a sphere of academic freedom. St Ignatius Loyola, who set much of the tone for the education system, valued learning not as an end in itself but as a means for carrying the Gospel. 'For ourselves', he once said, 'theology would do well enough with less of Cicero and Demosthenes.' He went on to say, however, that as St Paul spoke to men in terms of their own culture, so the Society 'seizes upon the spoils of Egypt to turn their use to God's honour and glory'.[1] St Ignatius also valued literature as an aid to persuasion: the Society, he said, should 'give a proper literary formation its own subjects so that they may become useful labourers for Christ. . . .'[2] Oratory, likewise, was stressed in the schools not only for its mental training—following the prescriptions of Quintillian and Cicero—but to develop persuasive self-expression.

Despite this utilitarian approach to the humanities, academic freedom was less curtailed than may be imagined. It is true that classical writers included in the syllabus were selected and treated on moral as well as intellectual criteria. It is also true that the Jesuit classroom taught virtually no inductive and experimental science, lest the latter upset orthodox views of the universe.[3] The curriculum, in fact, was heavily weighted towards the classics.

Within these restrictions, however, the system provided considerable scope and stimulated great intellectual vigour. Indeed, it honoured a broader concept of learning and a more rigorous standard of thinking than many systems which have not felt obliged to put the same moral limits on academic enquiry.[4] Take, for example, the Jesuit treatment of philosophy. E. Boyd Barrett tells of the Jesuit professor, somewhat after our period, whose career suffered because of an heretical enthusiasm for Kant.[5] Philosophical teaching, it is true, concentrated on those philosophers passed by the Society as exemplary and 'correct'; in the

<hr>

[1] Farrell, op. cit., 136. [2] Ibid., 137. [3] Fülöp-Miller, op. cit., 408.
[4] The curriculum treated modern history and geography as auxiliary subjects, but it must be remembered that these subjects were little taught elsewhere at the time in Europe.
[5] Barrett, op. cit., 176.

better Jesuit colleges other philosophers came to be taught—to indicate where they went wrong. But, at secondary school level, it was an achievement teaching philosophy at all, even if the courses, beginning at age sixteen, focused overwhelmingly on one thinker, Aristotle.[1]

Although the curriculum was ultimately designed to illustrate and implant an absolute moral ideology, the paths taken to that ideology were varied enough and indirect enough to foster some academic curiosity on the way. '. . . Professors [must] be capable of inspiring their students little by little with a love of theology', wrote Polanco, St Ignatius' secretary, to the Duke of Bavaria in 1551.[2] Theology itself was not taught as a curricular subject until university level. Instead, the school curriculum concentrated on a medley of classical writers, and in sharp contrast with the public schools it taught them for content as well as for language construction. Such writers, headed by Cicero and Virgil, were held to offer an abiding wisdom.[3] This belief, that moral truth could be found in differing forms, prevented too harsh a restriction of academic freedom; the same belief sanctioned tactics of deviousness, tolerance and moderation for the Jesuit father who found himself in an alien culture.

As totalitarian systems are wont to, Jesuit education placed greater emphasis on deductive reasoning than on spontaneous imagination.[4] Classical historians were presented largely for their style of argument; and the schools taught formal principles of oratory and logic. Yet, Jesuit education was also much concerned with inspiring student interest in the subject-matter.[5] The practice of classroom debates, greatly used by the Jesuits, did something to develop powers of questioning.[6] Some of the debate topics,

---

[1] Farrell, op. cit., 313–14, 373–4. The main courses in mathematics and science were also begun at this age.

[2] Barrett, op. cit., 170.

[3] Other important writers included Horace, Ovid, and Demosthenes, in carefully chosen selections.

[4] E. B. Castle points out the tendency for Jesuits to assume 'that the content of instruction is given'—Castle, *Moral Education in Christian Times*, 85.

[5] One method used here was the student play, dramatizing stories from classical history. This may have inculcated imaginative expression; I do not know if it generated independent thinking about classical content.

[6] The Jesuits' critics, both within and without the Roman Church, have attacked as a form of materialism the way in which the Society's educators consistently played on the

furthermore, were quite general and involved independent investigation,[1] although at the end of each contest the teacher would pronounce the 'right' answers. On occasion the class would compare two historians' interpretations of the same event; and no new author or poet was supposed to be introduced without background discussion of his life and thought[2]—without, in other words, outlining what Jerome Bruner calls the whole 'structure' of the subject.[3]

What about the social side of the Jesuit school? What part did reason play in the moral discipline? To answer this question we must go back to St Thomas Aquinas, whose thought provided the philosophic cornerstone of Jesuit faith. St Thomas, it will be remembered, saw no inevitable conflict between reason and faith. Although reason could only go a limited way in understanding God, it could perceive some truths about Him and, indeed, could supply certain proofs of His existence.[4] Reason was a 'bodyguard' to faith, defending it by showing it to be reasonable; reason could also rationalize faith, giving it systematic order.[5]

In practice, as we have already seen, the Thomist ideal of faith-reason harmony did not lead Jesuit educators to foster completely free inductive thinking. This applied particularly in the case of science: after initial warmth towards Galileo, the Society felt it had to oppose him for questioning the orthodox Christian concept of an earth-centred universe.[6] Undoubtedly, reverence for Aristotle and the cosmic pronouncements of early fathers and the Bible hampered the Jesuits' own scientific enquiries.[7]

competitive and emulative in boys. Although the influence of Quintilian cannot be denied here, it might be argued that the Society, for all its authoritarianism, displayed an element of the capitalist 'Protestant ethic'. Remember that the first century of the Jesuits was the century of the Reformation and Counter-reformation.

[1] Farrell, op. cit., 294–5. Sample debate topics put forward by the *Ratio Studiorum* of 1591 included, 'Were the kings justly expelled from Rome?' and 'Which was the greater leader, Hannibal or Scipio?'   [2] Ibid., 263, 267.

[3] Jerome Bruner, *The Process of Education*, Chapter 2.

[4] Bertrand Russell, *A History of Western Philosophy*, 452–63.

[5] M. C. D'Arcy, *St Thomas Aquinas*, 198–9.

[6] Fülöp-Miller, op. cit., 396–400. Rene Fülöp-Miller argues that, in fact, the Jesuits were more conciliatory and personally respectful towards Galileo and Kepler than were many other religious groups.

It was the same trait of moderation that they showed in China where, by contrast, the Dominicans and Franciscans were imprisoned and expelled for saying that past emperors were damned to hellfire, having died as heathen. Ibid., 267.   [7] Ibid., 303.

The same demand for unquestioning acceptance of authority characterized the schools' social discipline.[1] There tended to be a Jesuit 'way of doing things',[2] and student life was so organized that, to an extent, individuals were encouraged to keep an eye on each other's social conduct.[3] For the Jesuit fathers themselves the Constitutions of the Society were meant to be beyond criticism. And yet the discipline had its rationalist element. Sermons and the daily Mass linked the religious tone of school discipline to a rationalized dogma, and teachers maintained their close watch over student lives partly through informal talks with individual pupils.[4] As we have argued before, it is when student society is left entirely to its own devices that those devices are most liable to become fetishes and unexplained conventions. Youthful society is primitive society.[5]

A final rationalist influence upon extracurricular life was the literary Academy, originally formed by the *Ratio Studiorum* as the academic *élite* of a larger, religious organization, the students' Sodality. During at least the first two centuries,[6] membership in the Academy carried high prestige, since academicians were supposed to be selected on both scholastic attainment and character. The work-schedule itself represented discipline; it included the presenting and cross-questioning of papers by students; and since the sessions were held under a Jesuit moderator the Academy presumably provided the authorities with a means of informal

[1] A demand carried by restriction of social freedom—E. B. Castle, *Moral Education in Christian Times*, 83, 85.

[2] Barrett, 86–87. The emotional element in Jesuit training was perhaps most pronounced when (and if) the student became a Novice. As Barrett describes his own experience in the late nineteenth century, the techniques used in the Novitiate produced a 'chaos of feeling' and nervous tension (ibid., 69–70, 309–10). Barrett later left the Society and became its passionate critic, but others have pointed out a similarity between Jesuit training and Chinese thought-reform—Robert Lifton, *Thought Reform and the Psychology of Totalism*, 455.

[3] See p. 224, note 1.

[4] E. B. Castle, *Moral Education in Christian Times*, 82. Castle points out that Jesuit teachers were of very high calibre, both in learning and in human understanding. This may have applied less in the third century when Boehmer says Jesuit schools were in decline. Boehmer, op. cit., 187.

[5] In a school designed to produce leaders, the best solution is to give senior boys power of administration and even punishment, but to facilitate maximum contact in *differing* situations between teachers and pupils, particularly senior pupils, the taste-setters.

[6] Later on, many schools' Academies split up into smaller clubs, debating, classical, literary, scientific, and so on.

influence over leading students.[1] One might also suppose that the Academy's prestige, added to the ceremony with which scholastic prizes were awarded, tended to channel student energies and thought into academic matters and away from criticism of the school *status quo*. But these last are mere suppositions, awaiting further research.

In general the Jesuit school did implant the notion that learning and reasoning were highly relevant to faith. Formally, the kind of reasoning involved was dominated by Aristotelian logic, and this logic is not without inadequacies.[2] But at least the Aristotelian and Thomist tradition fostered respect for the mind in general and for science in particular. As a result rationalist and scientific attacks on orthodox Christian views of the universe sparked an intellectual response from Jesuit scholars.[3] Although their premises and motives were theological rather than purely scientific, they did try to *prove* Galileo and Kepler wrong.[4] Their search for proof led them to empirical investigation; and in areas where theological assumptions seemed less relevant, the Society produced some notable scientists and mathematicians.[5] Above all—from the standpoint of political leadership—they produced men who could apply science to practical human problems. During the Portuguese attack on the Paraguay Republic, the invaders found a Jesuit-Indian fortress so well made that they suspected the two fathers commanding it of being disguised engineer officers. The intellectual outlook nourished by Jesuit education refutes completely the Victorian gentleman's assumption that classical humanism and technology must always dwell in

[1] The Sodality itself exerted social pressure for religious correctness. cf. Boehmer, op. cit., 112. cf. Barrett, op. cit., 305.
  The same applied to classes, which were often divided into smaller groups, debating teams, called *decuriae*, whose leaders, the *decurions*, were supposed to report minor misconduct—Castle, *Moral Education in Christian Times*, 84.
[2] For a clear criticism of both Aristotelian logic itself and its tendency to breed acceptance of unquestioned premises (useful to the preservation of 'academic schizophrenia' perhaps) see Russell, op. cit., 195-9.
[3] Descartes, Diderot, and Voltaire, opponents of the Jesuit position, had all been educated at Jesuit schools. Voltaire always expressed great respect for his teachers and their humanity.
[4] Including theory of probability.
[5] E.g., the geometrician Gregoire de Saint-Vincent, Francesco Grimaldi (refraction of light), and Roger Boscovitch ('repellent forces'). cf. Fülöp-Miller, op. cit., 403-4, 427. Nineteenth-century evolutionary theory prompted the biological research of Father Wassman who found 'divine' mathematical harmonies (the 'golden section') common to the proportions of many plants and insects.

alien worlds. The achievement of Jesuit education also suggests to us that under certain conditions a totalitarian system can produce imaginative leadership, *both* political and technological.

Can Communist education, as it develops in Russia and China[1] during the next decades, do the same? This book lacks the space, and I lack the qualifications, to consider the question with any thoroughness. The few points I do make concern the relationship between ideology and innovation, and the comparison in this respect between Roman Catholic dogma and Marxism-Leninism. From the standpoint of combining moral ideology with flexible thinking, the Jesuits enjoyed a great advantage over the Communists: the former's ideology was primarily other-wordly, whereas the latter's is inherently of society. The moral—and allegedly, scientific—prescriptions of Communist ideology invade questions of social policy and the social sciences to a greater extent than did the requirements of the Jesuit's dogma. This statement must obviously be qualified: it is true, for instance, that St Ignatius applied Thomist notions of cosmic hierarchy to social organization. We have also seen that, although scientific experimentation by Jesuits increased over time, their theology tended to hamper the physical scientist, certainly in building theories. By comparison, Communist ideology has granted the physical sciences relative freedom of inquiry; in these fields it might be said that a certain 'academic schizophrenia' has indeed been displayed.[2]

With regard to political policy-making and the social sciences, however, the matter is altogether different. Jesuit leaders clearly felt that they could select a variety of strategies and policies without eroding ideology—as long as their long-run *intent* was loyal to the faith. As social scientists, likewise, they could penetrate the spirit of alien cultures, acquire great understanding of other

---

[1] The discussion that follows refers primarily to scholarship and education in the Soviet Union; the outcome may be different in China. I talk about the Jesuits in the past tense, since our survey of their intellectual achievement only covers the Society's first three centuries.

[2] At times Communism may be said to have restricted scientific inquiry by imposing too narrow a control from on top, by giving central authority and its favoured experts the right to decree what lines were worth pursuing. This, however, is not quite the same thing as restraint by ideology *per se*. Certain theories have been outlawed as 'bourgeois', but in other conflicts between dogma and free inquiry the latter has seemed to be the winner. cf. Robert Campbell, *Soviet Economic Power*, 172-3.

religions, and yet preserve the core of their own spiritual message.

For Soviet policy-makers, on the other hand, ideology always threatens to become a blinker. We know that, in fact, considerable changes in policy *are* made, but many of them have to be carefully squared with ideology. Sometimes ideological requirements affect the policy itself; sometimes the effect is verbal; sometimes it is a bit of both, with a convenient phrase disguising what might otherwise be thought unorthodox. When, for example, Soviet economic planners needed a yardstick to determine how they should allocate cost-saving capital, they were unable to use the capitalist device of the interest-rate, the rate of return on capital deployed. So instead, they used the notion of the capital 'pay off period' which, as Robert Campbell points out, is 'essentially the rate of interest turned upside down'.[1]

More restricted, probably, than Soviet policy-making are the social sciences. It must be remembered, however, that over the long-term the two are related, that the social science education of today affects the leaders of tomorrow. Here again, changes of course have been facilitated by various, largely verbal stratagems, including the one of giving old ideological concepts new meanings.[2] But all too often, a change merely results in the establishment of another orthodoxy, restricting research and theory to a confined area. Within that area good research may indeed be done, but outside the area political considerations and the prevailing interpretation of the ideology limit speculation.[3] The ideological invasion of scholarship is even more pronounced in the schools, where history is taught with a strong Leninist and patriotic emphasis.[4] (The syllabus deals with modern Russia, but no mention is made of Stalin.) In general, Soviet education does not encourage social criticism.[5]

[1] Both the rate of interest and the pay-off period describe the return expected from capital over a given period. Thus, if capital invested in a certain project will pay itself off—in reduced costs—in five years, that is the same as saying that it will earn 20 per cent. interest a year. See Campbell, op. cit., 101-4.

[2] For examples of this in psychology (e.g., changing implications of man's plasticity) see Raymond Bauer, *The New Man in Soviet Psychology*, 142-3.

[3] Liberal society, too, has its fettering orthodoxies, but these seem to confine to much less an extent. cf. Bauer, ibid., 131, 176-7.

[4] Bereday, 200.

[5] Nicholas DeWitt, 'The Soviet Student: Profile and Prediction', *Teachers College Record*, Columbia, November 1962.

The dependence of Jesuit and Communist loyalty-indoctrination on a grand ideology is, of course, far from the methods employed by the public school. The Burkian conservatism of the latter abhorred rationalized dogma as it abhorred any comprehensive abstract theory. From the standpoint of producing imaginative leaders, the Communists' use of dogma to implant Party loyalty has both advantages and disadvantages. Unlike public school methods, it does probably instil respect for rationalization. for large-scale planning and, since the ideology is an ideology of social change, for the stimulus of theory in looking ahead. The disadvantage of ideological loyalty, especially when the ideology enters into every question of social life, is that it may produce an over-simplified and distorted view of reality. Ironically, the urge of the intellectual to synthesise—to find categories and a unified theory which explains life's complexities—will become unrealistic and therefore unintelligent if pressed too far. Hence the meaning of the word 'synthetic'—and the distrust in which men of action frequently hold theoreticians.

In the case of the Jesuits, a successful balance was struck between theory and practice, between ideology and rationalized planning,[1] on the one hand, and the flexibility of common sense, on the other. Whether Russia, and China, can find a similar, enduring balance remains to be seen. Certainly—to take an example from economics—Soviet socialist planning permits more flexibility, more local decision-making, more bargaining between different levels, than Westerners usually give it credit for.[2] Moreover, the attention which Russian schools give to practical, on-the-job training, quite in addition to academic subjects,[3] will surely help prevent the Russians from becomming a nation of ideologues who see human problems in mainly abstract terms. This does not alter the fact, however, that Russian children are receiving moral indoctrination whose tenets are exaggeratedly labelled 'scientific'.[4] To the extent that the products of such a system are unable to

---

[1] This is not to suggest that in the Jesuit case the impulse for large-scale planning came solely from the possession of a comprehensive ideology.

[2] Campbell, op. cit., 83–113.

[3] DeWitt, op cit., 95–97.

[4] Bereday, op. cit., 408.

distinguish between reason and faith, their power to make rational judgments is in jeopardy.[1]

Our comparative survey of totalitarian education may seem to confirm the Western liberal's trust in social freedom as the wellspring of intelligent public leadership. We have shown that, when totalitarian education tries to produce imaginative men, the pitfalls and difficulties it faces are immense.[2] Even when it succeeds in creating a sphere of free thought, it lacks the advantage of a more liberal system which can permit cross-feeding of criticism between completely different spheres, between social life and the classroom, or, within the classroom, between the social sciences and the physical sciences. To exercise the mind and yet maintain unquestioned its social fetters, the totalitarian school must divide thought into compartments—and even in our own society we know that such compartments can be stultifying.

Yet the issue is not resolved simply by saying that liberal schools can more easily produce imagination than can totalitarian schools. The question is how *much* more easily, *and do they in fact do it*. Social freedom provides the best environment, but how many liberal schools take advantage of that environment? Creative thought, like any other thought, needs energy and application as well as opportunity.

In terms of producing intelligent public leaders, Soviet education may still secure the advantage. Even if liberal democracy produces a greater aggregate of imaginative people, it will not necessarily send enough of those people into public service. On this point totalitarian education holds a valuable card: through propaganda and indoctrination it can at least make sure that public office enjoys high prestige and a correspondingly high

[1] The theology of the Jesuits, by contrast, clearly awarded a place to faith, for all its trust in reason.
[2] Many of the problems totalitarian education faces are the same as those faced by military training systems which must instil strong conviction and loyalty—and yet must produce leaders of resource and initiative. The dilemma is heightened in an age when irregular warfare, political persuasion, and technology loom large in the field commander's concern. David Boroff states these problems very well in an article on the U.S. Military Academy—'West Point: Ancient Incubator for a New Breed', *Harpers*, N.Y., December 1962.

standard of recruitment (relative to the intake of non-governmental professions). Nor is it a question of directing purely *intelligent* people to government service. Especially in the case of democracy, in systems where popularity is exalted as a political asset, rational leadership can only be given by men who are brave as well as intelligent, men ready to take an unpopular step when they think public interest demands it.[1] Democracy has still not solved the problem, 'Who shall govern?'

[1] John F. Kennedy, *Profiles in Courage.*

Bibliography

Amery, L. S., *My Political Life*, Vols. I and II, Hutchinson, London, 1953.

Arnold, Matthew, *Higher Schools and Universities in Germany*, Macmillan, London, 1882

Ashby, Eric, *Technology and the Academics*, Macmillan, London, 1958

Bagehot, Walter, *The English Constitution*, Oxford University Press (World's Classics), London, 1958.

Baldwin, Stanley, *On England (And Other Addresses)*, Hodder and Stoughton, London, 1938.

Bamford, T. W., 'Public Schools and Social Class, 1801-1850', *British Journal of Sociology*, September 1961, London.

Barnard, H. C., *A Short History of English Education*, London U.P., 1947.

Barrett, E. Boyd, *The Jesuit Enigma*, Boni and Leveright, New York, 1927.

Bauer, Raymond, *The New Man in Soviet Psychology*, Harvard U.P., Cambridge, Mass., and Oxford University Press, London, 1952.

Bendix, Reinhard, *Max Weber*, Doubleday, New York, 1960.

Benedict, Ruth, *The Chrysanthemum and the Sword*, Houghton Mifflin, Boston, 1946, and Secker and Warburg, London, 1947.

Bereday, George, et al, *The Changing Soviet School*, Constable, London, 1960.

Boehmer, H., *The Jesuits*, Castle, Philadelphia, 1928.

Bradby, G. F., *The Lanchester Tradition*, Richards Press, London, 1954.

Briggs, Asa, *Victorian People*, Odhams Press, London, 1954, Chicago U.P., 1955.

Bruner, Jerome, *The Process of Education*, Harvard, Cambridge, 1960.

Buck, Pearl, *The Good Earth*, Methuen, London, 1931.

Burke, Edmund, *Reflections on the Revolution in France*, Liberal Arts Ed., New York, 1955.

Campbell, Robert, *Soviet Economic Power*, Houghton Mifflin, Boston, 1960.

Carter, B. E., *The Office of Prime Minister*, Faber and Faber, London, 1956.

Castle, E. B., *Ancient Education and Today*, Penguin Books, Harmondsworth, 1961.

Castle, E. B., *Moral Education in Christian Times*, Allen and Unwin, London, 1958.

Chen, Theodore, 'Elementary Education in China', *China Quarterly*, London, April-June, 1962.

Clark, Gerald, *Impatient Giant: Red China Today*, McKay, New York, 1959.

Clark, G. Kitson, *The Making of Victorian England*, Methuen, London, 1962.

Connolly, Cyril, *Enemies of Promise* (rev. ed.), Macmillan, New York, 1948.

Corbin, John, *Schoolboy Life in England*, Harper, New York, 1898.

Crawley, James, 'Japanese Army Factionalism in the Early 1930s', *Journal of Asian Studies* May, 1962, Ann Arbor, Mich.

Creel, Lorraine, *Concept of Social Order in Early Confucianism*, Ph.D. thesis, Chicago, 1943.

Cronin, Vincent, *The Wise Man from the West*, Hart Davis, London, 1955.

D'Arcy, M. C., *St. Thomas Aquinas*, Clonmore and Reynolds, London, 1953.

DeWitt, Nicholas, 'The Soviet Student: Profile and Predictions', *Teachers College Record*, November 1962, New York.

Dale, H. E. *The Higher Civil Service*, Clarendon Press, Oxford, 1941.

Darwin, Bernard, *The English Public School*, Longmans, London, 1929.

Dawson, Christopher, 'Tradition of a Christian Monarchy', *The Month*, May 1953, London.

Dichter, Ernest, *The Strategy of Desire*, Boardman, London, 1960.

Disraeli, Benjamin, *Sybil*, Oxford University Press (World's Classics), London, 1950.

Donham, Paul, 'Is Management a Profession?', *Harvard Business Review*, Boston, October 1962.

Dornbusch, Sanford and Hickman, Laurern 'Other-Directedness in Consumer-Goods Advertising; a Test of Riesman's Historical Theory'. *Social Forces*, December 1959, Chapel Hill, N. Carolina.

Dostoevsky, Fyodor, *Brothers Karamazov*, Modern Library Ed., New York, 1950.

Drever, James, *Greek Education*, Cambridge University Press, London, 1912.

Durkheim, Emile, *Education and Sociology*, Free Press, Glencoe, 1956.

Escott, T. H., *England: Her People, Polity and Pursuits*, Chapman and Hall, London, 1885.

Fairbank, J. K., *Chinese Thought and Institutions*, Chicago U.P., 1957.

Fairbank, J. K., and Reischauer, Edwin, *East Asia: the Great Tradition*, Houghton Mifflin, Boston, 1960.

Farrell, Allan, *The Jesuit Code of Liberal Education*, Bruce, Milwaukee, 1938.

Fei, Hsiao-tung, *China's Gentry*, Chicago U.P., 1953.

Fei, Hsiao-tung, 'Peasantry & Gentry', *American Journal Of Sociology*, Chicago, Vol. III, No. 1, 1946.

Feiling, Keith, *Life of Neville Chamberlain*, Macmillan, London, and St Martins Press, New York, 1946.

Finer, Herman, *The British Civil Service*, London U.P., 1927.

Floud, Jean, *The Social Class and Educational Opportunity*, Heinemann, London, 1956.

Fromm, Erich, *The Fear of Freedom*, Routledge, London, 1960.

Fuller, J. F. C., *The Army in My Time*, Rich & Cowan, London, 1935.

Fülöp-Miller, Rene, *The Power and Secret of the Jesuits*, Braziller, New York, 1950.

Fu-sheng, Mu, *The Wilting of the Hundred Flowers*, Heinemann, London, 1962.

Galbraith, J. K., *The Affluent Society*, Hamish Hamilton, London, 1958.

Gernet, Jacques, *Daily Life in China on the Eve of the Mongol Invasion, 1250-1276*, Allen & Unwin, London, 1962.

Giles, H. A., *Civilization of China*, Holt, New York, 1911.

Green, S. W., *Education as a National Unifying Agency in China*, M.A. thesis, University of California, Berkeley, 1929.

Greene, Felix, *Awakened China*, Doubleday, New York, 1961.

Greene, Felix, 'China: Tomorrow's Giant', *Observer*, 22 October 1961, London.

Guttsman, W. L., 'Aristocracy and the Middle Class in the British Political Elite, 1886-1916', *British Journal of Sociology*, March 1954, London.

Guttsman, W. L., 'The Changing Social Structure of the British Political Elite, 1886-1935', *British Journal of Sociology*, June 1951, London.

Gutwillig, Robert, 'The Select Seventeen', *Esquire*, November 1960, New York.

Hale, Lionel, *A Fleece of Lambs*, Cape, London, 1961.

Halévy, Elie, *History of the English People in the Nineteenth Century*, Vol. IV—*The Victorian Years, 1841-1895*, E. Benn, London, 1950, and Barnes and Noble, New York, 1960.

Hart, B. H. Liddell, *The War in Outline*, Faber and Faber, London, 1936.

Hu, C. T., 'Communist Education: Theory and Practice', *China Quarterly*, April-June 1962, London.

Jacobsen, Jerome, *Educational Foundations of the Jesuits in Sixteenth-Century New Spain*, University of California, Berkeley, 1938.

Jennings, Ivor, *Cabinet Government*, Cambridge University Press, London, 1951.

Keenleyside, Hugh and Thomas, A. F., *History of Japanese Education and Present Educational System*, Hokuseido, Tokyo, 1937.

Keir, John, *A Soldier's Eye View of Our Armies*, Murray, London, 1919.

Kennedy, John F., *Profiles in Courage*, Pocket Books, New York, 1956.

Kennedy, John F., *Why England Slept*, Hutchinson, 1940, and May Fair, London, 1962.

Kennedy, J. H., *Jesuit and Savage in New France*, Yale, New Haven, 1950.

Keynes, J. M., *Essays in Biography*, Hart Davies, London, 1951.

Kipling, Rudyard, *Stalky & Co.*, Macmillan, London, 1899.

Kingsley, J. D., *Representative Bureaucracy*, Antioch Press, Yellow Springs, Ohio, 1944.

Kitto, H. D. F., *The Greeks*, Penguin Books, Harmondsworth, 1958.

Kracke, E. A., *Civil Service in Early Sung China*, Harvard, Cambridge, Mass., 1953.

Kuo, Ping Wen, *Chinese System of Public Education*, Teachers College, New York, 1915.

Lamb, G. F., *The Happiest Days*, Michael Joseph, London, 1959.

Land, Edwin, 'Patents and New Enterprises', *Harvard Business Review*, September-October 1959, Boston.

Latourette, Kenneth, *The Chinese—Their History and Culture*, Macmillan, New York, 1946.

Lewis, Roy, and Maude, Angus, *The English Middle Classes*, Phoenix House, London, and Knopf, New York, 1950.

Lewis, Roy and Maude, Angus, *Professional People*, Phoenix House, London, 1952.

Lifton, Robert Jay, *Thought Reform and the Psychology of Totalism*, Norton, New York, and Victor Gollancz, Ltd., London, 1961.

Lowell, A. Lawrence, *Colonial Civil Service: The East India College at Haileybury*, Macmillan, New York, 1946.

McCabe, Joseph, *A Candid History of the Jesuits*, Putnam, New York, 1913.

McCloskey, H., 'Conservatism and Personality', *American Political Science Review*, March 1958, Columbus.

Mack, Edward, *Public Schools and British Opinion Since 1860*, Columbia U.P., New York, 1941.

Mair, Lucy, *Primitive Government*, Penguin Books, Harmondsworth, 1962.

Malim, Frederick, *Almae Matres*, Cambridge University Press, London, 1948.

Marsh, Robert, *The Mandarins: the Circulation of Elites in China*, Free Press, Glencoe, 1961.

Massingham, Hugh, 'Our Man in Threadneedle Street,' *Queen*, 6 February 1962, London.

Maurois, André, *King Edward and His Times*, Cassell (Pocket Library), London, 1949.

Mayer, Martin, *Madison Avenue, U.S.A.*, The Bodley Head, London, 1958; Penguin Books, Harmondsworth, 1961.

Minchin, J. G. C., *Our Public Schools: Their Influence on British History*, Sonnenschein, London, 1901.

Morrison of Lambeth, Lord, *Government and Parliament*, Oxford University Press, London and New York, 1959.

Newsome, David, *Godliness and Good Learning*, Murray, London, 1961.

Niebuhr, Reinhold, *Moral and Immoral Society*, Scribners, New York, 1932.

Nivison, S., and Wright, A. F., *Confucianism in Action*, Stanford U.P., and Oxford University Press, London, 1959.

Ogilvie, Vivian, *The English Public School*, Batsford, London, 1957.

Pascoe, C. E., *Everday Life in Our Public Schools*, Griffiths and Farran, London, 1881. (Includes essays by former senior prefects.)

Pear, T. H., *English Social Differences*, Allen and Unwin, London, 1955.

Perham, Margery, *The Colonial Reckoning*, Collins, London, 1961.

Perham, Margery, *Lugard*, Vols. I and II, Collins, London, 1956.

Pitcairn, E. H., *Unwritten Laws and Ideals of Active Careers*, Smith, Elder, London. 1899.

Pringle, John, 'The British Commune', *Encounter*, February 1961, London.

Public Schools from Within: A Collection of Essays Mostly by Schoolmasters, Sampson Low, Marston, London, 1906.

Radin, Paul, *The World of Primitive Man*, Schuman, New York, 1953.

Raven, Simon, *The English Gentleman*, Blond, London, 1961.

Raven, Simon, 'Perish by the Sword', *Encounter*, May 1959, London.

Raymond, John *The Age of Baldwin*, Eyre and Spottiswoode, London, 1960.

Riesman, David, *Constraint and Variety in American Education*, Double-day, New York, 1958.

Riesman, David, with Glazer, Nathan, and Denny, Reuel, *The Lonely Crowd*, Yale U.P., New Haven, Conn., 1960.

Reischauer, Edwin, *Japan Past and Present*, Duckworth, London, 1947, and Knopf, New York, 1958.

Robinson, Ronald, *Africa and the Victorians*, Macmillan, London, 1961.

Robson, W. A., *The Civil Servant in Britain and France*, Chatto and Windus, London, and Hogarth, New York, 1956.

Russell, Bertrand, *A History of Western Philosophy*, Allen and Unwin, London, 1941. Simon and Schuster, New York, 1945.

Salter, Arthur, *Memoirs of a Public Servant*, Faber and Faber, London, 1961.

Sampson, Anthony, *Anatomy of Britain*, Hodder and Stoughton, London, 1962.

Sansom, George, *The Western World and Japan*, Cresset Press, London, 1950, and New York, 1950.

Schumpeter Elizabeth (principal author and editor), *The Industrialization of Japan and Manchukuo, 1930-1940*, Macmillan, New York, 1940.

Schumpeter, Joseph, *Capitalism, Socialism, and Democracy*, Harper, New York, 1950.

Snow, C. P., *The Two Cultures and the Scientific Revolution*, Cambridge University Press, London, and New York, 1959.

Steele, John (transl.), *I-Li or Book of Etiquette and Ceremonial*, Probsthain, London, 1917.

Stevens, Frances, *The Living Tradition*, Hutchinson, London, 1960.

Stout, H. M., *Public Service in Great Britain*, University of North Carolina, Chapel Hill, 38.

Strachey, G. L., *Eminent Victorians*, Chatto and Windus, London, 1948.

Tawney, R. H., *Equality*, Allen and Unwin, London, 1952.

Thomas, Hugh, *The Establishment*, Blond, London, 1959.

Thompson, David, *England in the Nineteenth Century*, Penguin Books, Harmondsworth, 1959.

Thring, Edward, *The Theory and Practice of Teaching*, Cambridge University Press, London, 1883.

Tocqueville, Alexis de, *Democracy in America*, Vols. *I and II*, Knopf, New York, 1959.

(From) Veblen Thorstein, *The Portable Veblen*, Viking, New York, 1948.

Watkins, Frederick, *The Political Tradition of the West*, Harvard U.P. Cambridge, Mass., 1957.

Weber, Max, *Essays in Sociology*, Oxford University Press Inc., New York, 1946.

Webster, F. A. M., *Our Great Public Schools: Their Traditions, Customs and Games*, Ward Lock, London, 1937.

Whitfield, George, 'The Grammar School through Half a Century', *British Journal of Educational Studies*, May 1957, London.

Whyte, William, *The Organization Man*, Cape, London, 1957.

Wiebe, Gerhard, 'Creativity', *Public Opinion Quarterly*, Fall, 1962, Princeton.

Wingfield-Stratford, E., *The Squire and His Relations*, Cassell, London, 1956.

Woodruff, Philip, *The Men Who Ruled India*, Vol. II: *The Guardians*, Cape, London, 1953.

Worsley, T. C., *Barbarians and Philistines*, Hale, London, 1940.

Worsthorne, Peregrine, 'British Class and Diplomacy', *Foreign Affairs*, April 1959, New York.

Yang, C. K., *The Chinese Family in the Communist Revolution*, Technology Press, Cambridge, Mass., 1959.

Young, G. M., *Victorian England: Portrait of an Age*, Oxford University Press, London, 1960.

Yutang, Lin, *Famous Chinese Short Stories*, Pocket Library, New York, 1954.

Index

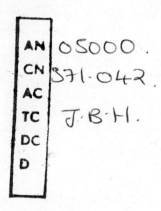